# Rookie on Tour

## THE EDUCATION OF A PGA GOLFER

# Rookie on Tour

THE EDUCATION OF A PGA GOLFER

*Carl Paulson and
Louis Janda*

G. P. PUTNAM'S SONS

NEW YORK

G. P. Putnam's Sons
*Publishers Since 1838*
a member of
Penguin Putnam Inc.
200 Madison Avenue
New York, NY 10016

Library of Congress Cataloging-in-Publication Data

Paulson, Carl.
Rookie on tour: the education of a PGA golfer / by Carl Paulson and
Louis Janda.
p.     cm.
ISBN 0-399-14378-5
1. Paulson, Carl.   2. Golfers—United States—Biography.   3. PGA
Tour (Association).   I. Janda, Louis H.   II. Title.
GV964.P37A3   1997
796.352′092—dc21                    97-13408   CIP
[B]

Printed in the United States of America

1   3   5   7   9   10   8   6   4   2

This book is printed on acid-free paper. ∞
Book design by Ellen Cipriano

*For my parents, who taught me about life,*
*and for Butch, who taught me about golf*

.................

# Preface

The fulfillment of a dream is probably the most satisfying experience of one's life. The book you are about to read represents the beginning of that journey for Carl Paulson.

For thirty years, I have had the opportunity to teach golfers from a wide range of ability levels. These include both PGA and LPGA Tour players, as well as a number of golfers who aspired to reach the highest levels of competition. My greatest satisfaction has come from working with junior players, and I am proud to have instructed more than forty juniors who went on to earn college scholarships. One unforgettable junior player I was privileged to instruct was, of course, Carl Paulson.

Carl came to me when he was fourteen, and from the moment I saw him lace up his shoes for the first time, I knew he was something special. Gifted athletes have a certain look about them. It is as if they could stare a hole right through you. Carl had that look. He had an intensity so compelling that you could feel it when you were around him. Along with these personal qualities, Carl had a natural golf swing and athletic grace. Over the past twelve years, Carl has refined his swing, and he has lost none of his intensity.

Through Carl's experiences, you will learn about a side of the Tour you have not seen before. You will learn about sponsorships, travel arrangements, endorsement pools, and priority rankings—facets of Tour life that all relatively anonymous rookies must master if they are to succeed. Most of what we see on television and read in golf magazines presents the Tour from the perspective of the stars, but Carl's story is far more common. And in that sense, it is more real.

You will especially enjoy the human side of Carl's story. You will share his triumphs, his failures, his highs and his lows. You will come to understand how Carl could feel on top of the world at one point, and profoundly discouraged a few months later. And I believe you will come to admire Carl as much as I do. He is a young man chasing his dream, and he is willing to put in the hard work that it takes to succeed.

As you will see as you read the following pages, Carl has had his share of disappointments. I believe it is his reaction to these disappointments that ensures his eventual success. He never allows his frustrations to get the best of him; they only inspire him to work harder. He also has an uncanny ability to leave his work at the office. No matter how rough his day on the course has been, once he takes his spikes off, he has put it behind him. He is one of the very few people I've known who can shoot 78 in the morning and be a delightful dinner companion in the evening. I believe this quality, which many of us could benefit from emulating, will serve Carl well throughout his career.

I would be remiss if I did not mention a critical element of

Carl's success—his family. His father, Ned, and his mother, Susan, have created an extremely strong foundation that provided Carl with the inner strength so necessary for success. The Paulson clan, including aunts, uncles, grandparents, grandchildren, brothers and sisters, is the strongest family I have ever encountered. All of the members of this family are ready to give of themselves to help, protect, and encourage any family member in need. Carl is indeed fortunate to have the love and support of such a wonderful family.

The following pages represent only the beginning of Carl's story. He has a swing that won't break down, and he has a burning desire to be the best. He is a "can't miss" prospect for a long and successful career on the PGA Tour. Remember Carl's name. You will be reading a lot about him in the future.

*C. A. "Butch" Liebler*

# Prologue

Jack Nicklaus had finished the tournament ten under par. I was at ten under too, but I had one chance left. I had a fifteen-foot putt for birdie on the eighteenth green, the seventy-second hole of the tournament. If I could knock this one in, I would win my first major, the Masters. That green jacket would look great on me.

I lined up my putt carefully. It had a slight right-to-left break. I stood dead still over the ball, confident that I could knock it in the hole. My stroke was silky smooth, and the ball started several inches to the right of the hole. Finally, it took the gentle break to the left and fell directly into the middle of the cup. I had won the Masters. The crowd went wild. I smiled slightly and touched the bill of my cap in acknowledgment. . . .

Actually, Jack Nicklaus wasn't really there. And to be honest, there was no crowd cheering me on. And actually,

I wasn't really on the eighteenth green at Augusta. I was on the putting green of my home course waiting to tee off with two of my friends.

I was twelve years old, and like everyone else who has played golf, I had dreams of sinking a birdie putt on the eighteenth green to beat Nicklaus, or Watson, or maybe even both of them, to win the Masters or the U.S. Open.

Back then I had dreams of playing on the PGA Tour, but I don't know how serious I was. All of my friends had the same fantasies, but none of us was so good that such thoughts could be called more than pleasant diversions. I did win the Virginia State High School championship my senior year, but there were plenty of players in the state who could, and did, beat me on any given day. While I hoped that I would continue to improve so my thoughts of playing professionally would be more than idle dreams, I was realistic enough to know that the odds of that happening were long, very long.

There are a handful of junior golfers who achieve a "can't miss" label. Johnny Miller won the National Junior Championship and qualified to play in the U.S. Open before he started college. Curtis Strange won the NCAA championship while still a freshman at Wake Forest University. Phil Mickelson won a PGA event, the Tucson Open, while he was a junior at Arizona State. And of course, there was Jack Nicklaus, who almost won the U.S. Open before he was old enough to vote. But I wasn't in their league. I was good enough to earn a full scholarship at the University of South Carolina, a major golf school, but there were hundreds of junior golfers around the country who were as good as I was. I knew all of us would not make it to the Tour.

But there was good reason to be optimistic. On my best days I was capable of playing as well as anyone I knew, and there were lots of guys who did not reach their full potential until they were a little older. Paul Azinger and Jeff Sluman, for instance, could not even earn a starting place on their college golf teams, yet they both went on to win the PGA, one of the four major tournaments. Maybe I was not a "can't miss" prospect, but I was good enough to justify my hopes that I would reach the top level, the level at which I could tee it up with anybody in the world and know that I had a chance to win.

Back in the days when I won junior tournaments often enough to keep my dreams alive of beating Nicklaus, I did not realize how hard it is to make a living on the Tour. Most people see the same handful of names at the top of the money list year after year and assume that Couples, Norman, Pavin, and the like are simply more skilled than the guys who are struggling to make it into the top 125. So it would seem that if one practices hard enough and finds the groove, success is inevitable. But I have learned that it doesn't work that way. Granted, the guys who are consistently near the top of the money-winning list have something the others do not, but it is not obvious what that something is.

If I could take someone who had been playing on the minitours for years, put him up against Pavin or any one of the other big names, and disguise the two of them, I would defy anyone to distinguish between the big star and the struggling professional-in-the-making. The unknown can hit the ball just as far and as straight off the tee as the star, he can hit his irons just as crisply, and he can chip and putt with the best of them. And the star will hit an occasional duck hook into the woods, he will come off an iron a couple times a round and leave it in the trap to the right, and he will miss a two-foot putt more often than you might expect. Indeed, the unknown may even beat the star four times out of ten in a casual match. But yet one of these men earns several million dollars a year while the other may spend his later years handing out balls at a driving range.

Sitting around the locker room listening to the guys talk, I have heard it said that there are five hundred players around the country who strike the ball well enough to play on tour, and I believe it. So what is the difference between the guys who finish in the top ten year after year and the guys who never earn their card?

The elusive "something" that separates the winners from the strugglers is a mental toughness. It is mental toughness that makes it possible to get up and down from deep rough when a match is on the line. It is deep-seated desire to win that gives one the courage to hit approach shots close to the pin during the closing holes of a tournament. It is a complete absence of fear when faced with three-foot side-hillers during the critical round. It is a refusal to give up when having an off day. And it is a combination of all of these qualities.

Crucial to the development of any promising golfer is learning to take these qualities to the next level of competition. What makes this learning process so arduous is that there will be more times to suggest he does not have what it takes than those occasions that tell him he does. After all, in any given year on tour, the player of the year will lose twenty to twenty-five tournaments and may win three or four times. The best golfer in the world will lose five or six times as often as he wins. While I won enough college tournaments to give me reason to believe that I had what it takes, there are always the painful memories of hooked tee shots, of mishit irons, of putts lipping out of the cup, of letting a tournament slip away, that haunted me at the most inopportune times.

For me, one of the most painful memories was my loss in the Virginia State Amateur in 1992 in the semifinal round when I was four up with four holes to play. I had the match won, but somehow I managed to let it get away. Was I an all-American golfer or an all-American choke? Did I have what it took to hit pure shots over the last nine holes in a professional tournament? I did not know for sure. All I could do was to continue to strive to reach the next level.

Mental toughness can be elusive, but I know it has been important in my own development. The most vivid evidence I can remember comes from my experience during my senior year at the University of South Carolina. During the early part of the season, I could not seem to score. I was hitting the ball pretty well, but I came up a little short during tournaments.

One late afternoon I was alone on the range, hitting balls into the setting sun, when my coach, Steve Liebler, called to me from the top of the rise. "Carl, come on up here. I want to have a talk with you."

I could tell from his expression that it was not going to be a talk I would enjoy. But what could I do? He was the coach, so I trudged up the hill. "What is it, Coach?" I asked. He didn't respond. He simply pointed to his truck and said, "Get in."

We drove a half-mile in silence to a small storage shed. He stopped his truck, pointed at the door, and said, "Let's talk in there." I was getting both a little nervous and a little pissed. Maybe I wasn't playing as well as I had at the end of my junior year, but I was still his number-one man. What did he think all these dramatics would accomplish?

But I did as I was told and walked into the shed. It seemed even smaller on the inside; it couldn't have been more than eight by ten, and it was cluttered with equipment. My annoyance faded into anxiety when Steve turned his back to me and locked the door. I was worried that he had gone over the deep end. Given his temper, it was not beyond the realm of possibility.

He started out slowly, but he picked up steam real fast. I cannot remember all he said, because it took him two full hours to tell me what a bad attitude I had. I do remember his saying at one point—shouting, to be more precise—"You think you're going out on tour and beat guys like Norman and Couples? You haven't got the balls to do that." After that, he got downright nasty. The gist of his harangue was that with my attitude I was letting myself down, him down, my teammates down, and the university down. Hell, I was probably letting the whole state of South Carolina down, but I don't remember if he went quite that far.

Once he was finished and I could be confident my life wasn't in danger, I got mad, really mad. I could feel my face burning, and it wouldn't have surprised me if steam was coming out of my ears. He had no cause to talk to me like that. I was practicing hard and I was trying my best. What else could I do?

But the funny thing is, I started to play better. I won back-to-back tournaments that year and finished near the top in several others. I won the Ping Intercollegiate and the Billy Hitchcock Championships and was named SEC Player of the Year. He was right—I didn't have the right attitude. His tongue-lashing helped me make the necessary adjustment, because I went on a tear that season. Somehow, Steve knew what I needed to hear.

In my defense, I do believe my attitude needed only a slight adjustment. Basically, I think I have the approach it takes to win. I suspect losing the State Amateur in the way that I did, for instance, could have been a death knell for some golfers. It would have ruined their confidence.

I am probably fortunate in that I have never been obsessed with making it to the very top. I have always focused on making the transition to the next level, and I continue to take that approach. So while I did have my share of daydreams of beating Nicklaus and Watson while I was a junior golfer, I never intimidated myself with doubts about whether I could compete with the best golfers in the world. I have never thought about whether I am good enough to beat Greg Norman or Fred Couples, despite Coach Liebler's challenge. Instead, I have focused on whether I could compete at the next level. After I proved myself as a high-school golfer, I aimed at winning at the college level. It was not until my junior year at South Carolina, when I had achieved some success, that I began to think seriously about turning professional. And until I earned my card in December 1994 I never worried about whether I could compete with the guys on the Tour. Once I did earn it, however, I knew I would have to move my game up another notch if I was going to make it.

With the exception of a handful of the top names, I believe this struggle to maintain what it takes is never-ending. There are countless stories of golfers who tasted success and then were never heard from again, but perhaps the most poignant example is Mike Donald. At the end of seventy-two holes of the 1990 U.S. Open, Mike was tied for first and would have won had Hale Irwin not sunk a fifty-foot putt on the eighteenth hole. Mike had a three-stroke lead with three holes remaining in the playoff round, then lost to Irwin's birdie on the nineteenth hole. Two years later, Mike lost his card and could not get it back at Q-School. The level of competition on tour is simply unbelievable.

The following pages are the story of my effort to reach the next level—each time I faced it. There are, of course, the big questions. Do I really belong on the Tour? Do I have what it takes to win? Am I capable of becoming a golfer who consistently finishes in the top ten?

But I must find answers to the less obvious, but equally critical questions. Can I tolerate the life of a golfing nomad, moving from motel to motel, not seeing my wife nearly as often as I would like? Do I have what it takes to endure the inevitable string of poor rounds, when even the strongest begin to wonder why they are wasting the best years of their lives? Do I want success on tour badly enough that I can put off establishing the roots and stability my friends enjoy?

I do not have the answers, and I doubt if I will until long after this book is written. But even though I have survived my share of low points, the high points are so exhilarating that I'm determined to continue trying until I succeed. Let me share my experiences with you. And let me begin my story by recounting one of the most exciting days I had during my rookie year—a day that convinced me that I will make it to the next level.

# CHAPTER I

## October 1995

I was worried. My tee time for the first round of the Disney Classic in October 1995 in Lake Buena Vista, Florida, was less than forty-five minutes away, and I had hit yet another eight-iron ten yards left of my target. Every time I tried to cut the ball, I would come over the top and pull it left. I needed that soft cut shot if I was going to have any chance of having a good week. I turned to my caddy, Al Walker, and gave him a look that said, *What the hell is going on?*

As always, Al was encouraging. "Nothing to worry about. You're swinging good, you'll find it."

Al is not your typical Tour caddy. In his early fifties and a retired high school math teacher, his keen blue eyes, gray hair, and neatly trimmed beard suggest that he would be more at home behind a college lectern than toting a sixty-pound bag around eighteen holes. I hooked up with Al in July, and it was not a coincidence that I had been playing well since then. Besides, I liked being around Al. He looked so intelligent that I had to look better by association.

I didn't want to quit on a bad shot, so I hit one more eight-iron. The swing felt smooth, and this time the ball at least looked as if it wanted to move to the right. It came down three or four yards left of the stick and actually took a small hop to the right. Not great, but the best I had that day. I will never understand how you can play so well one day and then wake up pulling the ball the next. I guess that is why golf never gets boring—and why it can be maddening.

I felt good coming into the tournament. I had made a lot of cuts over the previous three months and I had finished strong the week before at the Buick Classic at Calloway Gardens. I was five under after the final round to finish in fortieth place and earn a respectable check. It was especially gratifying since my parents and fiancée had come down for the weekend to watch me play. Nothing can put a chill on a family get-together like a pair of 74s, so I was happy that I had played well and everyone had enjoyed the visit.

Disney was a tournament I looked forward to, because I liked the courses. My first round was on the Palm course, which has the kind of layout that suited my game. It was long, over 7,000 yards, but with lots of trouble off the tee. I had been driving the ball so well for several months that I was confident that I'd avoid any big numbers and have lots of opportunities for birdies. And I would need lots of birdies to make the cut, since par always took a beating at Disney. With everything set for a good week, I had to wake up with this tendency to pull my iron shots.

I was worried. I had been playing well and scoring well, but there just is not any room for mistakes in a tournament where everyone is putting up red numbers. As we walked to the practice green, I said to Al, "We'll have to bandage it up for the round and look for something on the range later."

"You're driving the ball and putting as well as anybody out here. That's what it takes to score on this course. We'll do fine."

Al was like every other caddy on tour in one respect. When the red numbers were going up on the board it was "*We're* really playing well." But should a tee shot find water, it was "Boy, *you* really yanked that one."

I putted for about fifteen minutes before moving on to the first tee to meet my amateur partners. The Disney is a pro-am event where each pro plays with three amateurs for the first three days, with each round on a different course. The cut comes after the first three days, and the surviving pros play the last round on the Magnolia course.

My partners seemed like good guys. Evan was clearly the serious golfer of the group. He was a good six feet three, and middle age had not caught up with his waistline. He didn't have much to say when we introduced ourselves, but he handled his driver the way low handicappers do. He could help our team.

Russ, an accountant from the Tampa area, hadn't been as successful in the battle of the bulge, and I could tell from his practice swings that we would spend some time searching for his tee shots. But his easy smile assured me that he would be a pleasant addition to our group.

John, whose wife and two teenaged daughters were there to see us off the first tee, was going to be the one to keep us loose. His first joke of the day came a split second after the introductions were completed—and it was funny. He did have to tell it in a low voice, though, so his family couldn't hear it. Sometimes amateur partners try so hard to be entertaining that they become overbearing, but John was not like that. His extroverted nature came through clearly, but he was too polite to allow himself to get on anyone's nerves.

My partners looked as though they had more in common

with Al than with me. As to be expected, all three were successful businessmen in their late forties to early fifties. You have to be successful if you're going to pay $6,500 to play three rounds of golf. They were a loose group, and I could tell I would enjoy their company. I was lucky not to have any of those tense Wall Street types who take the game so seriously, they won't allow themselves to have any fun. Contrary to what a lot of the pros think, I've found that pro-ams can be fun as long as you get good partners. Maybe I've been luckier than most, but I have had very few pro-am days that I didn't enjoy.

The first hole at the Palm is an ideal starting hole for me: a medium-length, straightaway par five; a definite birdie hole. I hit a good drive, about 280 yards down the left side of the fairway. After my partners hit their drives from the forward tees, they all had a joke they wanted to tell as we walked down the fairway—funny jokes at that. The sun was shining, I got off the first tee well, and my partners were enjoying themselves.

When I reached my tee shot, I had a little letdown. I had about 220 yards to the green with the wind at my back, which would make it difficult to stop the ball. The pin was tucked behind a bunker on the right side of the green, a position that called for a soft fade—precisely the shot I had been having trouble with. It was no time to try anything stupid that would get the day off to a bad start. I hit a conservative shot, a three-iron to the middle of the green. It came off the clubface just as I wanted it to, but the ball took a big hop once it hit the green and ended up on the back fringe. A good lag putt and a tap-in gave me a birdie for the first hole. My partners were so excited, you would have thought I had just won the Open. But I liked their enthusiasm, and I felt good walking to the second tee.

The second hole was uneventful. A solid drive down the right side went a little farther than I thought it would and ended up in a bunker. But there had been a lot of rain and the sand was firm, so it was an easy eight-iron to the green. Two putts from thirty feet gave me a par.

The third, a short par three, would have been a birdie hole on any other day. But the pin was on the far right side of the green, which demanded that dreaded cut shot. It was only an eight-iron, so I didn't think I could go too far wrong, but I hit an absolutely terrible shot. I came over the top with the clubface closed and ended up on the far left side of the green, at least fifty feet from the flag. I was not happy as Al and I walked to the green. "Dammit," I said, "how could I hit such a bad shot?" Al did not have a response this time. I reminded myself that I was one under after two holes and calmed down some. "We'll have to find a way to bandage it up if we're going to make it through the day."

"Two putts and we're on to the next hole," Al reassured me.

There was nothing tricky about the fifty-footer. It looked straight and flat, and as long as I could get it on line, I should be able to get it close enough for a tap-in par. I hit the putt well, it held its line, and the damn thing hit the back of the cup for a birdie two. My partners started running around the green giving me high fives. Their enthusiasm was contagious, and I felt good, really good. I was two under after three holes, even though I didn't have my A game.

The fourth hole brought me back to reality. A good drive left me with a seven-iron to yet another pin tucked on the right side of the green. I didn't pull it quite as badly this time, so I was only thirty-five feet left of the hole. I hit the first putt too aggressively, and missed the five-footer coming back. I was pissed. You can't make mistakes like that when you are trying to deal with a swing problem. Not when it will take a healthy red number to make the cut. No one had a joke for me while we were waiting to hit our tee shots on five.

I got some confidence back on the fifth. A good drive left me 165 yards to the pin. This time my seven-iron was right on line, but it pulled up about ten feet short of the hole. I hit a solid putt that was dead center, but it stopped inches from the cup.

The mood of our foursome picked up on this hole as well. Russ, the 15 handicapper, had hit two good shots, but his approach plugged in the fringe on the left side of the green. I watched him looking at his ball warily, and after a minute or so he asked, "Pro, do I have to play this from here?"

"No, you get a drop." I explained the procedure for getting relief, and damned if Russ didn't chip it in the hole for a net eagle. My partners went wild. I hadn't been keeping track of our team score, but with my two birdies and Russ's net eagle, we had to be at least four under par. Their high spirits helped me to relax. I reminded myself that I was still one under par and I had just hit a solid seven-iron without coming over the top. Everything was still good.

The sixth was a tough hole. It was a long par four with water down the left side of the fairway. I hit a three-wood off the tee, because it was extremely narrow in the area where my driver would stop. I hit it right down the middle, but I was faced with another pin tucked behind a bunker on the right. Whoever set the course up didn't have much imagination. I concentrated really hard on my nine-iron, trying to make sure I got the ball moving left to right. I hit it good, perhaps the best shot I had hit all day. It was fading right into the pin, but it came up five yards short. I was over the bunker, but the ball nestled in the rough just short of the green.

Even though I missed the green, I was feeling good walking down the fairway. I had hit the shot the way I wanted to, and while it was a little short, it would leave me with an easy chip. But I was in for a very unpleasant surprise when I reached my ball. The rough was stringy Bermuda, at least six inches deep. I couldn't believe it. I said to Al, "How could the rough be this deep so close to the green? I don't know how to hit this shot, I've only got fifteen feet to the pin. There's no way to get it out of here and keep the ball anywhere close to the hole." Al must have been concerned. He couldn't even manage a "you can handle it."

I took my pitching wedge and tried to pop the ball out of the thick grass. It came out hot, but it hit the flagstick squarely and stopped a foot from the hole. I tapped it in, relieved to get my par. I was feeling good again. That is the kind of break you get when things are going your way.

The seventh was a par five with a sharp dogleg right. To have a chance for birdie, you had to hit a high draw over some palm trees on the right. If you could pull the shot off, it was an easy birdie, but the slightest mis-hit could result in bogey or worse. Driving had been the strongest part of my game, so there was no reason not to go for it. And I absolutely killed it. It took off just to the right of the palm trees and then drew back into the middle of the fairway. I was left with 210 to the pin against a slight breeze. The pin was—where else?—on the right side of the green, a position that demanded another cut shot. I told Al, "Maybe I should play it safe, just knock it on the middle of the green." Al knows I don't expect him to give me advice, but that I like to talk out loud to myself when he is close by. That way my muttering doesn't seem so strange to anyone else.

I thought about it for another minute. "You know, maybe I should try to hit the cut. There's not much trouble around the green, so even if I don't pull it off, I should be able to get it up and down for birdie."

"Makes sense to me," said Al.

I usually do not like to try anything new in a round, because you never know what might happen. It is safer to estimate how you are likely to mis-hit your shots and allow for it. But this was a good place to try something different, to make a slight adjustment. I closed up my stance a little, which would make it easier for me to make a full turn. It worked, and I hit my three-iron perfectly. The ball seemed to hang forever against the blue sky, then it floated ever so gently toward the right and directly toward the flag. The ball took one good hop forward before settling only fifteen feet from the stick. I knew the putt had to go in after such a great shot, and it did, dead center. My partners went crazy. They were screaming and yelling and telling me what a great golfer I was. Just your typical pro-am, and boy, was it fun.

A solid five-iron and two putts from twenty-five feet got me a par on the 200-yard eighth hole. As is often the case in pro-ams, we had quite a wait on the ninth tee, so I looked back toward the eighth green to watch Fred Funk and his partners play the hole. The scene bordered on the weird. There was no gallery following our group, nor was anyone following Fred's group. It was late in the afternoon, but you would think there would be at least a girlfriend or a wife somewhere to be seen. The atmosphere was more like that surrounding a member-guest at the local country club than a PGA Tour event.

Fred looked up at me and smiled after knocking his fifty-footer in for birdie. I extended my arms as if to say, "What the hell was that?" Fred just shook his head and turned to help his amateur partners line up their putts.

After his group putted out, Fred came up to me and asked, "How're you playing?"

"Not bad," I said. "I'm three under. How are you doing?"

"Good. I'm three under too." He paused for a few seconds before adding, "But I've had to sink three fifty-footers to get there." We both laughed, and then he said, "I saw your eagle back there.

You're hitting the ball real good, keep it up." It made me feel good that an established player would offer me encouragement.

The group ahead of us was approaching the green, so it was time to turn my attention to the ninth hole. It was a short par four with water about 240 yards from the tee. I laid up with a three-iron, which left me 145 yards into a wind that was stiffening. I knocked down a seven-iron to keep it under the wind, and it was dead on line. It stopped a foot short of the hole for a tap-in birdie. I was feeling really good after shooting four under on the front, and my partners were not shy about expressing their enthusiasm about being eight under as a team.

We had another long wait on the tenth tee, and for some reason the heat and humidity seemed to close in on me. Two weeks earlier we had had frost delays in Illinois, and it felt strange to be so hot in October. My teammates had more jokes to tell during the wait, and I passed the time by juggling my ball on my sand wedge. It always impresses the amateurs that we can do this indefinitely, but you don't make it on Tour unless you have pretty good hand-eye coordination.

The tenth was a tough par four, but I crushed my drive and it ended in the middle of the fairway. I had 145 yards to the pin with the wind blowing to the right; an eight-iron would be enough to get me there. After pulling out the eight, I turned to Al. "You know, maybe we ought to hit the same shot we did on the last hole."

"Sounds good," said Al.

I exchanged the eight- for the seven-iron, and the shot was a carbon copy of my shot on nine. It left me with another tap-in for birdie. My confidence was really building. Getting it to five under after ten holes will do that for you.

The eleventh was a long par five that could only be reached in two with two perfect shots. My drive put me in position where it was possible, and I started to feel excited. Another birdie would mean that I could do something really, really good. I had about 250 yards to the pin, and a perfect three-wood might reach the front of the green, but it would leave me with a difficult two-putt. I decided to go with the driver; it was the only chance I had to get the ball back to the hole. I came off the shot a little and left the ball well to the right, in deep rough. I managed a respectable chip shot, but my twelve-footer for birdie lipped out of the cup.

I was disappointed as we walked to the twelfth tee. I couldn't help but feel that I had left a stroke back there. "But," I reminded myself, "you took a chance and it didn't work out. Sometimes it does. And, after all, you're still five under."

The twelfth was a tough par three, about 210 yards long. The pin was at the very back of the green, and I knew I would need a three-iron to get the ball to the hole. But I thought about how I had paid the price on the previous hole for being too greedy, so I decided to play it safe and hit the four-iron. There was too much trouble to deal with if I was to miss the green. The four-iron would get me to within twenty-five feet and a safe par. I hit the four just as I wanted to. The ball shot off the clubface and turned over directly toward the pin. It ended up four feet from the hole.

For the first time, I began to feel nervous as I walked toward the green. It was the prospect of going six under. I rushed the putt and pushed it to the right. A great chance wasted. The pit of my stomach seemed to sink a good six inches. I felt as though I had wasted chances on two holes in a row, and I needed to give myself a pep talk. "Things are still good. Don't forget, you are five under par."

A good drive on the thirteenth left me with ninety-three yards to the pin. My sand wedge hit a foot short of the hole and almost went in on the first bounce. It then backed up, and almost went in again. Another tap-in for birdie. Six under par!

I do not like to think about anything but executing shots during a round, but after going six under, I could not help but think that this might be my week to make a big move on the money list. I was 220th coming into the tournament, and I needed to get into the top 125 to be exempt for 1996. My year had gotten off to a slow start: I had not made a single cut during the first four months. But I had been playing solidly for quite a while and I had missed only two cuts during the past three months. It took only one extraordinary tournament to retain your card, and I wondered if this might be my week to do it.

I breathed deeply before hitting my tee shot on fourteen. It was a reachable par five, but there was water down the right side of the fairway. I hit a solid, conservative shot, leaving me with 260 yards to the pin. I was tempted to go for it with my driver, but I remembered what happened the previous time I tried that. I took out my three-wood and absolutely killed it. The ball ended up on the front of the green, seventy feet short of the pin. My first putt wasn't bad, but it wouldn't stop until it was four feet past the hole. I was really nervous while I was lining up my second putt. The only thought I had was, "If you knock this in, you'll be seven under par." I tried to push those thoughts out of my mind by concentrating on taking a smooth stroke. The ball hit the back of the cup for birdie four. Seven under! My partners went wild.

A drive and a nine-iron left me with an eight-foot downhiller for birdie on the fifteenth. Even though it was short, it was a tough putt because that green was very grainy; it would push the ball to the right. I decided to hit the ball firm, right at the hole. I was putting well enough that I was confident I could make the four-footer coming back if I missed. I started the ball on line and, as I expected, the grain pushed the ball to the right. But it caught the lip of the hole and dropped in for birdie. Eight under par! I was getting very excited. And I was swinging with so much confidence, I didn't think it was unrealistic to birdie the last three holes.

A hard eight-iron on the 170-yard, par-three sixteenth left me with another eight-foot downhiller. This time the grain was with the putt and I knew it would be straight and lightning fast coming down the slope. As I was lining up the putt, I noticed a good-size spike mark directly on my line. My spirits sank. It probably wasn't more than a quarter-inch high, but it might as well have been a sequoia. There was no way I could make the putt. If I started it on line, it would surely be knocked away by the tuft of grass.

I decided to hit the putt just to the right of the mark and hope for the best. At worst, I wanted to leave myself a tap-in for par. I hit the ball where I intended, and once it passed the spike mark it bounced ever so slightly to the left, just enough to catch the right lip and drop in. Nine under par! This was one of those rare instances that I was thankful for slightly bumpy greens.

Of course, my partners went completely berserk, and I was feeling pretty good myself. I had never been nine under par before. I had been eight under three times, twice in competition, but nine under was a personal record. My nervousness was replaced by what I can only describe as a calm sense of confidence. I was swinging so well, I wasn't thinking about protecting my score. I was thinking about getting another birdie or two. A 61 might break the course record, or the tournament record. There had to be some record a 61 would break.

The seventeenth was a short par four, a good birdie opportunity. A solid drive left me with the perfect distance for my pitching wedge, and I knew I was going to hit it close. I did, and I knocked in the three-footer to go ten under.

This time my partners were whooping and yelling so loudly that a couple of the guys from Fred's group drove up to the green to find out what was going on. When Russ told them I was ten under, they couldn't believe it. I'm not sure I could either, but I was determined to go for eleven under on the last hole.

I was not pleased to discover that we had a wait on the eighteenth tee. I felt confident, but I wanted to get on with it. I didn't want to lose my momentum. When the group ahead of us finally cleared the fairway, I hit my best drive of the day. I smashed it, and it had to be at least 300 yards, dead center in the fairway. When I first looked up at my eight-iron soaring directly toward the pin, I thought it was my best shot of the day. But it hit about five feet short and backed up another seven or eight feet. My twelve-footer was an easy putt, slightly uphill, with a gentle left-to-right break. I was completely calm as I stood over the ball. I did not think about my score, setting a course record, or the money list. I thought only about knocking that sucker into the hole. There was no doubt in my mind. I hit the putt well, but it died right on the lip of the cup. I "settled" for a 62, ten under par! Later, some of the guys in the locker room gave me a hard time about leaving my putt for a 61 short. "Lagging up to protect your 62?" they asked.

But I was happy, very happy. And my partners were happy too. As a team we finished seventeen under par, which was the low team score for the course. My partners would get some nice prizes and I would earn some "unofficial" money that would come in handy nonetheless.

As excited as I was, the whole scene was not quite what I expected it to be the first time I was leading a tournament. It was getting dark, and other than my playing partners, there was nobody, and I mean nobody, around to cheer my performance. We were, in fact, congratulating each other when a Tour official invited me into the press tent. Because the tournament was being held over three courses, there were no television cameras and only a handful of reporters around. But I enjoyed the thirty minutes it took to describe my round to the ten or twelve reporters who were present. It was the first time I had been invited to meet with the press as the tournament leader, and it was an experience I could easily get used to.

As soon as the interview was finished, I went to the locker room to call my biggest fan, my dad. He was excited—and relieved—to hear my score. He keeps track of me through one of the golf Websites on the Internet and he saw the 62, but he did not want to let himself believe it until he heard it from me. Once before, in the Memphis tournament, he read that I shot eight under but the scoring officials had mixed up my score with that of Dennis Paulson. It is too bad they had not confused us when they sent out the checks.

I wish my best day as a rookie pro had some dramatic ending, but life on the Tour can be surprisingly routine, and this day was no exception. I caught up with Scott McCarron, my roommate for the week, and for dinner we went to Perkins, a family-style restaurant that has good food at reasonable prices. Scott had not played very well (he was to have his magical tournament the following week), and I didn't want to make him feel worse by talking about my round. He asked me a few questions about it, which I was happy to answer, but I tried to get him to talk about his wife, Jennifer. She had been traveling with him throughout the year, but went back home a few weeks earlier because their baby was about to be born. Scott missed her a lot.

We got back to our condo about nine-thirty, I looked at the paper for a few minutes, and I was in bed before ten. I had to be up at six the next day for an early tee time, and I wanted to get a full night's rest. I fell asleep within minutes with no thoughts of making a big jump on the money list, of keeping my card for 1996, or of winning the tournament.

Those thoughts would come on Friday.

CHAPTER 2

## Developing a Game

I've always enjoyed stories of how several of the legends of golf got started with the game. Tales of men like Snead, Nelson, and Hogan, who saved the nickels and dimes they earned caddying to buy a couple of well-worn clubs, are enough to inspire anyone. But mine is a 1980s, middle-class kind of story. My initial interest in golf resulted from the opportunity to drive a golf cart.

The year was 1981. I was ten and my family was living in Irvine, California, where my father, a marine pilot, was stationed. He worked the long hours of a military officer, which did not leave him much time for two of the three things he loved most—his family and golf. His third love was piloting high-performance planes, but most days my brother and I knew we came first. There were, of course, those rare occasions when we would not want to speculate on how he would rank his priorities.

My dad wanted to play golf with his pilot friends on weekends, but he also wanted to spend time with me. The natural solution was to take me along to the golf course. And to keep an active ten-year-old content for five hours, Dad let me drive the cart. I loved those Saturday mornings. Not only did I get to spend them with my dad, but driving the cart was about the most fun thing I could imagine doing.

We had been going out to the course at El Toro Air Station for a month or so when one Saturday morning there was quite a backup on a long par three. We weren't going anywhere for at least fifteen minutes, so my dad asked me if I wanted to hit a shot. I was a little concerned that someone might take my place in the driver's seat of the cart, but despite my misgivings I said, "Sure." I put all of my eighty pounds into it and smacked the ball 110 yards down the middle of the fairway. He was amazed at how natural my swing was and threw down a half-dozen more balls for me to hit. I didn't make solid contact with all of them, but I hit several right on the sweet spot.

My dad is the sort of person who believes wholeheartedly in achievement and the work ethic. He saw in me a natural ability, and he was not about to let it remain undeveloped. That afternoon he went home and cut down an old five-iron for me. He told me that if I wanted to go with him the following Saturday, I would have to take 150 practice swings in the backyard every evening. I sure wasn't going to miss the chance to drive the cart, so I swung that five-iron enough to fill our backyard with divots.

Over the next three or four weeks, my dad invited me to hit a couple of balls whenever the opportunity presented itself. Finally, he decided I was ready to play for real. In his typical type A style, he thought that I should learn the proper technique before I went any further. He arranged a series of lessons for me with the head pro at El Toro, Wally Bradley. Wally was a big, laconic man in his early forties who had a gentle way with children. He was the perfect teacher for a kid just getting started. He taught me enough those first few weeks that I could make solid contact with the ball with some consistency. I fell in love with the game immediately.

Wally didn't always have the most conventional teaching techniques. One day I went for my scheduled lesson and told him, "I'm popping my driver up a lot. Can you help me?"

"I think we can do something about that," Wally said. "Follow me." He was walking in the direction of the putting green.

"But I'm having trouble with my driver, not my putter," I protested.

"I heard what you said. We're going to hit some tee shots from here, and you'd better not make any divots in my nice, pretty green."

I didn't pop up many tee shots after that.

I played only a couple of times a week during that first year because I was very involved with soccer, baseball, and basketball, but I did enter every tournament I could. None of my friends played golf, so I relished the opportunity to compete against kids my own age.

I wasn't an instant success the way many of the PGA players were. My first tournament, which I still remember clearly, was in the Pee Wee division of the Junior World at San Diego. It was held on an executive-type course, only about 5,000 yards long, and it was encircled by a chain-link fence. Parents were not allowed on the course, so there was always a group of adults, faces pressed to the fence behind the first tee to watch their potential champions tee off. I remember looking back just before I hit my first tee shot and seeing the large grin on my dad's face. I wanted to hit a shot that both of us could be proud of. I probably felt as much pressure standing on that first tee as I ever have. I did manage to make solid contact with the ball, and it flew 120 yards down the fairway. I turned to see my dad give me the thumbs-up sign. I gave him a small smile and started down the first fairway with all the insouciance a ten-year-old who wasn't much bigger than his bag could manage. I played well that day, but I missed the cut by one stroke.

A month later, I entered my first tournament played on a regulation eighteen-hole course, and again I played well. I shot 119. No, I wasn't one of those junior golfers who seem destined for great things right from the start.

Even though my scores were nothing to shout about, I learned an important lesson about how to approach tournament play. I was playing in a local junior tournament, one in which parents could follow their children, and disaster struck on the third green. My third shot on the par four was forty feet above the hole, and I hit my first putt much too hard. It ended up a good ten feet past the hole. I hit the second putt so it would hold the line, but I knocked it four feet past the cup. Now I was left with a slick downhiller with four to five inches of break. It slid by the cup and didn't stop for another two feet. I was hot. I hit my fourth putt carelessly and, of course, it lipped out. I batted the ball past the hole a couple of times more, to prove to myself that I didn't care, before knocking it in.

As I walked off the green I turned to my dad and said, "I'm just going to have fun now. I don't care what I score."

"Okay. Let's go home, then," he said.

"What do you mean? I want to finish the round."

"Look, Carl, I always want you to have fun. But if you're not going to try to do your best, there is no point to entering these tournaments. You always do your best, no matter what."

I was embarrassed. I knew my dad was right, and I did try as hard as I could on every shot for the rest of the day. And I can honestly say that I've never given up in tournament play since that day. Yes, there are days when I cannot seem to get off the bogey train and it is difficult to sustain my enthusiasm. But if I have to birdie the last hole to shoot 78, I tell myself that 78 is better than 79.

Over the next two years I played golf two or three times per week, and during the summer my dad would drop me off at the course in the morning and pick me up on his way home a couple of times each week. My scores were improving steadily, but my dad's insistence that I work hard at learning the game was a constant. He continued his requirement that I take 150 practice swings in the backyard before he would take me to the course. To my mom's relief, I learned to skim the grass with my swing, so the divots were slowly beginning to fill in.

Despite my rapid improvement, I wasn't setting the world on fire with my play in junior tournaments. I finished near the top in my age bracket, but there were a number of kids who could beat me—and beat me soundly. Like every other golfer, junior or adult, I wanted to play my best at these tournaments, but I was not concerned that I did not win anything. I loved the game, I loved the competition, and I was having fun.

I remember passing two milestones within a year of taking up the game. My dad always looked for ways to encourage me, and one method I liked was our record keeping of my best composite score at El Toro. In those days pars were hard to come by, because my best drives were only 140 or 150 yards. So it was always a special occasion when I could come home and tell my dad to mark down a par for yet another hole. We really whooped it up the day when I marked down a par for the final hole, a long par four. He made me feel as though I had really accomplished something. My dad has always been good at that.

The second milestone that initial year was the first time I broke 90. I had just turned twelve, and my paternal grandfather was visiting us. I learned later that most people found him to be an extremely intimidating figure—he was a captain in the navy—but I knew him only as a kindhearted man whose visits I anticipated eagerly. I looked forward to his visit that summer, especially because it meant I would have someone to play golf with during the week.

The first time we played together, I kept my driver in the fairway and my putter was on fire. I came to the eighteenth hole needing only a bogey for an 89. My excitement of showing my grandfather what an accomplished golfer I was got the best of me, however, and I tripled the final hole. My disappointment was obvious to my grandfather, and he put his arm around me as we walked off the eighteenth green. He assured me that it would not be long before I broke 90. I took his words more literally than he expected and talked him into playing again the next day. I shot 88 and was on top of the world.

A third milestone occurred about two years after I began playing. My dad and I continued to play together on most weekends. Usually I would have to hit two solid shots to reach his drive. He took his golf very seriously, which was reflected in his six handicap. But I had grown several inches and put on nearly forty pounds during those two years, and the gap between our tee shots and our scores was narrowing. Finally, on a cool, overcast Saturday morning in May, it happened. I shot 77 to his 78. He did not say anything as we putted out on the eighteenth green, and although I was filled with pride that I beat him, I was also a little worried that he might be upset. I knew how much it bothered him when he lost to his friends. As we walked through the parking lot to the car, I turned to him and asked, "How do you feel?"

For the first time since about the eighth hole, he smiled. "I feel great. I knew it was only a matter of time until this day came. I'm just so proud of you and happy that it came so soon." He gave me a hug, we tossed our shoes and clubs into the trunk, then we drove off to McDonald's to celebrate.

During the middle of the eighth grade, my dad was transferred to Norfolk, Virginia, for what he thought would be a temporary assignment. Since my parents expected to be there for only a few months, they rented an apartment close to the base and enrolled me in a Catholic school in Norfolk. I was pleased with their decision, because eighth-graders in the parochial schools could play on the high-school golf team. I made the team easily, but I was by no means a standout. I won my share of matches against older kids who were much bigger and stronger than I was, but there were still lots of players who could grind me into the dust. My game was, however, developing to the point where I knew I was good. I had the sense that with just a little more size and a little more practice, I could reach the point where I could beat anyone in the city. I was serious enough about my game that I gave up baseball and basketball. I wasn't quite ready, though, to give up soccer, a sport I loved almost as much as golf.

That summer, my dad received permanent orders for Norfolk, so my parents bought a house in Virginia Beach and I enrolled in First Colonial, a public high school. That was also the summer that I met my second—and current—teacher, Butch Liebler. Butch was the head pro at Cavalier Country Club, where my grandfather—my mom's dad—was a member. Butch had taught a number of outstanding golfers, including his brother Steve, who played on the Tour for five years. My dad, who liked to believe his two sons could accomplish anything, wanted the best teacher for me, and Butch's reputation was second to none in the Tidewater area. I had my first lesson with him within a week of our move to Virginia Beach.

I liked Butch the moment I met him. In many ways he was a lot like Wally Bradley, my first teacher. Butch was in his early forties, and at five-feet-nine, a little shorter than Wally, but he had the same low-key, gentle manner about him. He must have liked me as well, because when I went for my second lesson and handed him his fee, he said, "You don't have to pay me for lessons anymore. We're going to work together as a team, and we're going to accomplish something special."

His words were a real boost to my confidence. He was telling me that he had so much confidence in my ability that he could enhance his reputation as a teacher by working with me. Maybe I really was as good as I liked to think.

That first year in Virginia Beach was one of the roughest of my childhood years. I was a freshman at a large high school, and on the first day of class I didn't know a soul. I was never the most serious student in the world, but that year I had even less interest than usual in my schoolwork. It did not help that the kids who seemed to accept me the quickest had a reputation as a rather rough group. I wanted to fit in, and to my new friends, golf was for nerds. Gradually I spent less and less time at Cavalier.

My dad was on me constantly during this time, and in retrospect I'm surprised his tirades didn't have more of an effect. He was the quintessential marine colonel, and no one could deliver a lecture with more enthusiasm and vigor than he could. His number one rule for both my brother and me was that we had to have a B average to participate in sports. One grading period, my brother George earned only a C in history, which meant he couldn't play tennis for at least six weeks, something he couldn't accept. He went to his teacher and said simply, "I have to have a B."

His teacher, understandably taken aback, replied, "What do you mean? You earned a C."

"You don't understand," George said. "My dad will kill me if I get a C."

"Surely you're exaggerating."

"Have you read *The Great Santini?*" George asked.

George's teacher, who met our father at a back-to-school night, found the comparison realistic enough that he gave George a B.

George and I respected our dad enormously. We were careful to avoid arousing his ire, but on the other hand, we were never frightened of him. He was full of bluster, but he never once touched either of us in anger. And he touched us with affection often.

But it was Butch who helped me get out of my ninth-grade, acting-stupid mode. I knew something was coming, because he called my parents the night before a scheduled lesson and asked one of them to accompany me the next day, something he had never done before. When I got there with my mom, he asked me to start hitting balls. He didn't say anything for about ten minutes, and then he asked, "Why aren't you playing better?"

I didn't have an answer for him, so I said simply, "I don't know."

"Why aren't you practicing more?" he asked.

Again, I could only respond with "I don't know."

His questions seemed endless. "Why aren't you doing well in school? Why are you running around with kids your parents don't approve of? Why are you hurting your mother?"

I could only respond with more "I don't know"s.

I tried to keep my composure. Macho ninth-grade boys aren't supposed to be bothered by a little hassling, but tears were stinging my eyes.

Butch let me hit balls in silence for another ten minutes before starting in again. This time he did not have any questions, but he had plenty he wanted to say to me. "You don't deserve to have so much talent if you're going to throw it away. You can be a bum if you want to, but you're not going to take me down with you. If you can't shape up and take golf—and your life—seriously, we're through. I don't want to have anything more to do with you."

The tears were streaming down my face, and there was nothing I could say. I had messed up. I had let my parents down and I had let Butch down. I resolved to work harder, to take both golf and school more seriously, but I could not get the words out. I could only express my shame and frustration by pounding balls in a furious silence.

Mercifully, the "lesson" ended after an hour when Butch hugged me and told me he loved me. He said that would not change no matter what I decided, but that I should not come back until I was sure about what I wanted to do.

My practice regimen and my study habits improved dramatically after that, and I began to blossom as a player. During my sophomore year I finished second in four tournaments, one of them a statewide event. I did not win anything, but people were talking about me as one of the top junior players in the state. My relationship with Butch grew during this period as well. He could see the change in my attitude, and he was willing to work as hard on my game as I was. I began to think of him as a friend as well as a teacher.

One special day is etched in my memory, one that reflects my development as a golfer, and it was in the spring of my sophomore year. As usual, I went to Cavalier after school to play, and Erick Mellott, the assistant pro, joined me. I had a solid front nine—34, one under par. My grandfather joined us for the back nine, and I started knocking down the pins with my irons and sinking everything on the greens. It took me only 30 strokes to make it around the back nine, and my 64 set a new course record. That day meant so much to me because my grandfather was there to see it. He played an important role in my continued interest in golf, and he was the one who made it possible for me to play and practice at Cavalier. I doubt that I would have developed to the point I am now without his help and support.

At the end of my sophomore year, Butch called me into his office. He told me, "The time has come for us to make a decision. You've got a very good swing, a swing that you can win with at the high school level, and probably at the college level. But I don't think you can reach your full potential unless we make a few fundamental changes. If we make these changes, you're going to lose ground for a while. You'll play worse for six months, maybe a year, but these are changes you have to make if you want to have a shot at being an exceptional player. What do you want to do?"

"What kind of changes are we talking about?" I asked.

"First, we have to develop a swing that relies more on the large muscles of your body. Right now, you rely too much on your hands. Secondly, you have to learn to work the ball. You can't be a great player unless you can hit a draw when the situation calls for it, and then on the very next hole, hit the fade."

"Sounds good to me. Let's do it," I said without hesitation.

"Not so fast," Butch said. "If we start this, you're going to have to hit thousands of balls every week to feel comfortable with your new swing. And then, when you play, you have to hit the shot the hole calls for even when you don't have confidence in it. One time you'll try a draw and leave it in the trap to the right. The next time you try the shot, it will hook too much and you'll end up in the trap to the left. It will take time and a lot of hard work before you will develop the confidence that the ball will draw precisely the five yards you want it to."

"You know I'll do the work," I answered. "When do we get started?" If Butch thought I should make the changes, then I had to try. My confidence in his judgment was total.

I worked very hard that spring and summer. As Butch asked, I hit several thousand balls each week, and every time I played I tried to hit the shot the hole demanded, even when I doubted that I could pull it off. By the time golf season started in the fall of my junior year, I was beginning to feel more comfortable, but I still hadn't mastered the changes. I played about the same as I had my sophomore year, but I had the strong feeling that I had much better shots in me, shots that would come with consistency in the very near future.

Although my play my junior year wasn't as good as I hoped, it was good enough to place me in the top five or six junior golfers in the state. I was pleased with that, because I looked forward to being named to the Virginia team that competed against North and South Carolina in the Virginia–Carolina matches. The match is similar to the Ryder Cup, with a mixture of team and individual competition. Eight players are selected for each team, and it was an honor I knew I deserved.

When the team was named late that fall, my name was conspicuous only by its absence. At first I was stunned. After a few days, I became angry about it. The State Junior Champion is an automatic pick, but there is no formal procedure for picking the rest of the team. Maybe my record didn't justify my number-two ranking in the state—which my dad conferred upon me; maybe I wasn't even fourth or fifth—where I saw myself. But how could anyone leave me out of the top eight? I couldn't believe it, and I was nearly as indignant about the slight as my dad.

I see myself as an intensely competitive person, but it does seem to be true that there are times when I need to have a tongue-lashing, as Butch and later his brother Steve could so effectively deliver, or some slight like being left off the Virginia team to motivate me to move to the next level. About a week after the team was announced, I made an announcement to Butch and my dad:

"Next year I'm going to win everything in sight so there will be no possible way they can exclude me from the team."

I never worked as hard on my game as I did that winter and spring. Every day, I went to the course straight from school and stayed until dark. The course was rather short, barely 6,000 yards, and quite compact, so I could play it in two hours. Then I would hit, chip, and putt until it was too dark to see where my shots were going. When it was raining or snowing, Butch would set up a net in the cart barn and I would hit balls for hours under his watchful eye. I was getting very close to mastering the changes Butch and I had made a year earlier, and I couldn't wait until my senior year.

It did not take long for my hard work to pay off. I won the State Junior Championship by nine strokes that summer, and later in the fall, I won the State High School Championship. I did play in the Virginia–Carolina matches the following summer.

Since there could be no doubt that I was the top junior player from Virginia, I asked to be matched against Jason Weidner, the top player from the Carolinas. Jason had done well in several national tournaments and had quite a reputation, much stronger than mine. Almost every college that had a shot at winning the national championship was trying to recruit him. We did play, and it was an exciting, close match. Unfortunately, I lost to Jason, one-down.

Because I did not play in any national tournaments, the colleges that were interested in me were limited to Virginia schools and a couple of others in the Southeast. The offer that interested me the most was from South Carolina, because Steve Liebler, Butch's younger brother, was their coach. My relationship with Butch had grown so close that I imagined that I would develop a similar relationship with his brother.

Butch tried to tell me that I might be disappointed. One

afternoon when I was discussing my options with him, he said, "Steve is a completely different person than I am. He's much more intense and he's a strict disciplinarian. You might not like his style."

"How different can he be?" I asked.

"Let me tell you about an incident that happened just last year. South Carolina was playing a tournament on a course that wasn't too long, but extremely tight. Steve wanted his team to play it conservatively, so he ordered them to hit irons off the tee on a number of the holes. During a practice round, one of the guys, Rick Williams, decided it would be worth the gamble to hit driver on a par five. What he didn't know was that Steve was about seventy-five yards away watching them. When Steve saw that driver he ran to the tee, grabbed it out of Rick's hands, and broke it over his knee. He told him, 'I guess you won't be hitting that club again.' "

"What happened next?" I asked incredulously.

"Well, Rick didn't know what to do. He just stood there, shifting his weight from foot to foot. Steve was completely exasperated, and he shouted, 'Don't you have anything to say for yourself?'

"Rick finally said, 'Coach, that was your driver.' "

We laughed together before Butch went on. "On the other hand, there are things Steve can give you that I can't. I can teach you how to hit all the shots you'll ever need, but I can't teach you anything about playing on the Tour, if you decide that's something you want to try. Steve was there for five years, and he knows how to turn talented college players into Tour professionals."

"I think I want to try it. Don't forget," I reminded Butch, "I grew up with a Marine colonel. How much tougher can a golf coach be?"

"I have no doubt you'll find out. And you might not like the answer. But you can be sure that you will learn a lot if you go there."

"That's it, then. I'm going to South Carolina."

"Okay, but don't come home crying to me if you don't like it."

The fall of 1989, I enrolled as a freshman at the University of South Carolina and earned the number-five spot on their golf team.

Butch was right about my reaction to Steve's style. His temper and his yelling did not bother me much. I had a father who prepared me for that. And as blustery as my dad could be, he always allowed me to express my opinion, so confrontations did not bother me. When Steve got on me about something, I would let him know my point of view and he would respect it, even if he did not like it. The guys who did not stand up to him had a much harder time than I did.

I did have trouble adjusting to the discipline that Steve demanded. We had to be at practice at 6:00 A.M. Monday, Wednesday, and Friday. For someone who has always enjoyed sleeping, this was tough on me.

I also had trouble adjusting to the competition. I spent my high school years being thought of as one of the top players in the state, but at the college level, everyone was one of the top players in his state. No one was moving aside for me just because I was the Virginia Junior Champion.

All in all, it was a tough year for me. I was away from home for the first time and none of my friends came with me to South Carolina. I had a coach who did not appreciate my ability and was always on my back. And I did not seem to be able to move up to the next level, the level at which I could compete successfully with the best college golfers in the country. By the end of the year I was sick of golf. And I was not certain I wanted to return to South Carolina.

My dad had been transferred back to California the previous summer, so I went back home and spent the summer surfing in the Pacific Ocean. I hardly touched a club. Every few days my dad would ask, "Shouldn't you be practicing?"

"Dad, I had a really tough year playing golf. I need a break," I would answer.

"How tough can playing golf be?" His disapproval was obvious, but he seemed to know this was something I had to work out for myself.

That summer, I did not think too much about what I would do in the fall, and I was not sure what would happen. The thought of returning to South Carolina was not a pleasant one, and transferring to a school in California seemed like an attractive prospect.

In the end, I decided to return to South Carolina. I had not made any plans to do anything else, and I did not like the idea of quitting. I had never run away from anything, and I did not want to set a precedent that would make quitting easier in the future.

A summer of surfing had predictable effects on my game that fall, effects that were painfully obvious to both Steve and to me. Steve got my attention immediately when he left me off the team that traveled to a tournament in New Mexico. It was one of those messages that got through loud and clear, and I responded to it. I began immediately to work harder, hitting balls by the hour. Gradually, my game improved.

The day before the team left we had a practice round, and it was one of those days when everything fell into place. I was six strokes better than anyone who was going to the tournament. The only thing Steve said to me was, "I should have known you'd make me look like an ass."

His response only strengthened my resolve to move my game up to a level where he would never again think of leaving me off the team. I knew I had made it when I won my first college tournament, the Metro Conference Championship, late that fall.

My junior year was a good one. I moved up to the number-two spot on the team and I had five top-ten finishes that year. I finished the year with a flourish when I won the LSU Invitational.

I suppose playing on the PGA Tour had been in the back of my mind for a number of years, but I never spent much time thinking about a career as a professional golfer. After all, the odds of making it to the Tour are smaller than making it to the NBA, the NFL, or the major leagues in baseball. There are five hundred guys on major league teams, but only 156 golfers can play in a given PGA tournament. But during my junior year, my play had progressed to the degree that I thought a future in professional golf might be more than an adolescent fantasy. I had known for several years that I had the shots to play on the Tour. I could blow my drives forty to fifty yards past most of my competitors', and I never had much of a problem hitting my long irons dead straight. My short game still had a long way to go, but I had made a lot of progress over the previous couple of years. It was not until my junior year, however, that I was convinced that I also had what it takes mentally to make it at the very highest level of competition.

I did have a setback that summer in the Virginia State Amateur tournament held at the Golden Horseshoe in Williamsburg. I looked forward to it, because I knew that if I played my game there was no one who could beat me. I breezed through the opening rounds and I was cruising through my semifinal match against Jerry Wood, a good friend I had met playing junior golf in Virginia.

I birdied the fourteenth hole to go dormie, four up with four to play. This golf, what an easy game. At times, anyway.

The fifteenth hole was a medium-length par five, a hole I expected to birdie six times out of ten. Well, my tee shot caught a bunker, I had trouble in the rough around the green, and I ended up with a bogey. I was disappointed that I could not close out the match on a hole made for my length, but everything was still fine. I was three up with three to play.

After our tee shots on the par-three sixteenth, it looked as if the match was over. Jerry was thirty feet from the pin, while I had a ten-footer, straight uphill, for a birdie. You guessed it. Jerry knocked his putt in the hole, while mine lipped out. I still did not see how I could lose, but my stomach tightened up a notch or two as we walked to the seventeenth tee.

Bad drives on the seventeenth and eighteenth holes resulted in two bogeys, and in a flash, the match that I could not lose forty-five minutes earlier was even.

I did not have a chance in the playoff. I did manage a good drive on the first sudden-death hole, but I did not finish the swing on my pitching-wedge second shot and dumped the ball in the bunker to the right. I blasted out fairly well, but I missed my eight-footer and Jerry's two-putt par beat me.

An all-American choke by an all-American golfer. If I could let a match like that slip away, how could I possibly have the mental toughness to beat the best golfers in the world out on tour?

I did not think about those questions immediately; I was too angry at myself. I made the forty-mile drive back home to Virginia Beach in about thirty minutes, and by the time I arrived home, I had regained most of my sanity. My friends were having a Fourth of July party, and I was not going to let golf spoil a good time.

By the next day I realized that the match could provide a

valuable lesson. It is a cliché to say you have to lose in order to win, but it has become a cliché because it contains a large grain of truth. I told myself I had learned something important, something that would keep me from giving away a tournament in the future.

If only it were that easy. I would discover over the next few years that I had much more "learning" to do.


When I returned to South Carolina for my senior year, I became more serious about practice than I had ever been. I was confident in my ability, but I also knew that I was not yet at the point where I could compete consistently with the best two hundred players in the country. I worked hard and, except for the brief lull that I described earlier when Steve locked me in the equipment shed for a tongue-lashing, I played well. I won back-to-back tournaments the spring of 1993 and I was voted Southeastern Conference Player of the Year, an honor that meant a great deal to me. One of my victories came in the Ping Intercollegiate, a tournament that attracted all the best players in the country. Justin Leonard, who was playing in the Masters that week, was the only player of any note missing from the field, and I was sorry he was not there. Had he been entered, I really would have beat everyone in the country. I felt ready to try the next level.

As pleased as I was with my play, I was realistic enough to know that making it to the Tour was still a long shot. I was not a Phil Mickelson or a Justin Leonard, both of whom had won the National Amateur and the NCAA Championship. Unlike them, I did not have the experience of being one of the best junior golfers in the country. They had the opportunity to develop a confidence in their games that I was years away from achieving.

On the other hand, there was no doubt in my mind that I had the shots, tee to green, to beat either of them. If I could develop a short game that was even average by Tour standards, there was no one against whom I could not win my share of matches.

But taking one's game on tour is a formidable task. There are at least five hundred guys, maybe more, who could be stars on tour if they could play as well during tournaments as they do in their practice rounds. It is easy enough to swing freely and with confidence when you are playing a nassau with your friends, even if the bet is a bit too large to feel comfortable. If you lose, it is not that big a deal. You cut back on your expenses for a week or two and there is no harm done. But on tour, every shot could mean the difference between making the cut and missing it. And every time you miss a cut, you are one step closer to having nowhere to go the following year.

Mickelson and Leonard have the advantage of a decade's worth of experience being the very best. It is one thing to believe in yourself, to know you have the game to compete with anyone. It is a very different thing to feel that confidence when you are standing on the tee of a long par four with out-of-bounds on the left and water on the right.

I believed I could get there. After all, I had busted 300-yard drives down the center on such holes dozens of times in college tournaments. But then again, I was realistic enough to understand that no one could know for certain how they would react to the pressure of playing on tour until they got there. I had to make a transition to a higher level if I was to succeed, and I wanted to give it a shot.

I was ready to turn pro.

# CHAPTER 3

# *Turning Pro*

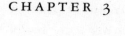

It was a Wednesday afternoon, and I was still numb. I am not the sort of person who lets bad play get me down, but this was different, this was too important. I had been pointing toward this for four years, and now it was over and I would never have another chance.

I, along with everyone else on the South Carolina team, had played poorly during the NCAA regionals in the spring of 1993 and we failed to qualify for the national tournament. My own mediocre play meant that I would not be going as an individual, either. If this all-American wanted to see the most important of all college tournaments, the 1993 NCAA National Championship, he would have to watch it on television.

When the phone rang, it only annoyed me. I thought about ignoring it since I could not think of anyone I wanted to talk to, but that was just plain dumb. "Get over it," I reminded myself, "golf isn't important enough to put the rest of your life on hold."

"Hello," I said, trying to sound more upbeat than I felt.

"Hey, Carl. It's Michael." It was Michael Christie, one of my best friends. He was an ex-teammate who had been playing the minitours since his graduation the previous year.

"Hi, Michael. How're you doing?" I thought he had called to commiserate over our poor showing at the regionals.

"Not bad. Say, what would you think about turning pro next week?" Michael was known for getting right to the point.

"Turn pro? What are you talking about?"

"There is a Carolinas Tour event in Pinehurst next week. Do you want to play?" he asked.

"Jeez, I don't know. This is the last thing I expected you to be calling about. Let me think about it for a while." I had intended to turn pro sometime after the NCAA national tournament, but when we didn't qualify I was left without a game plan. I had not yet recovered sufficiently from the disappointment to be able to think about my next step.

"What is there to think about? You're going to be a professional golfer. What's the point in putting it off?"

He was right about that. "Well, why not? Sure, I'll play."

"Good," Michael said. "I'll give them a call this afternoon and let them know we're coming."

The Carolinas Tour was one of perhaps a dozen minitours around the country. It later became the Hurricane Tour and is currently called the Power-Bilt Tour, but like all the minitours it gave people like Michael and me an opportunity to sharpen our games and find out just how good we were. With only a handful of exceptions—men like Phil Mickelson, Justin Leonard, and Tiger Woods—no matter how well you play in college tournaments, you cannot know for certain if you have what it takes to make it at the next level of competition until you are there.

The minitours are especially good because they give guys like Michael and me a chance to play a different course every week, something that is not that easy to do well. I once read that Lee Trevino advised anyone who was thinking of turning pro to take a two-week trip and play a different course every day. He said you did not have to shoot lights out, but if you could consistently shoot par or better on new courses, then you might have reason to believe you're good enough to make it. There are dozens of good golfers around, many of whom can consistently burn up their home courses. But for some reason they cannot post low scores until they have played a course a dozen times or so and feel completely comfortable. I do not understand what it is that makes these people different from the pros who can shoot 68 on a course they have never seen before. I am not sure anyone really does. But it is something everyone has to find out for himself, and the minitours are the place to start.

I had a curious blend of feelings on the drive from Columbia to Pinehurst. There was definitely a sense of excitement. Although I never articulated my desire to make it on tour until my junior year at South Carolina, I think it had been somewhere in the back of my mind for a long time. I could not acknowledge it to myself, much less anyone else, until I was confident that my game was strong enough so it would not seem like a foolish fantasy when I announced my plans. Entering this event represented my commitment to becoming a professional golfer, and I was exhilarated about it.

But I felt a twinge of nervousness too, and I was not sure what that was all about. Maybe it was fear of the unknown. I had never talked much to Michael about his experiences on the minitour, so

I did not know what to expect. I believed, though, that the nervousness was a good sign. If you do not feel the emotion, if you cannot feel the adrenaline coursing through your body when you compete, then you probably will not be very successful at it. You have to have that fire if you are going to make it, and I knew I had it.

It was one of those perfect June days when we arrived at the course on a Sunday afternoon. It was in the low eighties, with just a few high clouds, and the oppressive humidity that you learn to live with when you grow up in the South was still a couple of weeks away. I could not wait to get on the course.

We went into the pro shop to register for the tournament and pay our entry fee. The assistant pro was coordinating the event, so I handed him my check, signed my name on the roster, and checked the box under "Professional." That was it. I had turned pro.

Most of the tournaments on the Carolina Tour were two-day events, held on Mondays and Tuesdays, but a few were three-day events. The entry fee for the two-day events was $250 and for the three-day tournaments it was $325. As I would learn, the number of people who were entered varied greatly from tournament to tournament. Sometimes there were as few as thirty players, other times as many as 150. The purse was taken from the entry fees, which were divided among the top one-third finishers. So winning a tournament could mean anywhere from a few hundred to several thousand dollars. No one has ever gotten rich playing the minitours. In fact, I am not sure anyone has broken even.

The starter informed us there were three groups of tourists from Ohio ahead of us, so we had about a twenty-minute wait before we could tee off for our practice round. Anyone paying greens fees had priority over two professional golfers no one ever heard of, but that was okay. It gave us time to hit a few balls on the range and roll a few on the putting green.

I tried to play the round the same way I would play any practice round on an unfamiliar course before a college tournament. It is critical to learn where not to hit the ball. Anytime I teed it up I knew I would get my share of birdies. My length meant that I could reach most par fives in two, so I would expect birdies on at least a couple of those holes. And I could reasonably expect to hit it close enough on a couple of other holes to get birdies there. So playing well meant avoiding bogeys, and every course has places that guarantee bogey or worse. To focus our attention, Michael and I agreed to our usual bet of five dollars per hole.

We both played well that day, although I lost ten bucks to Michael. But the course suited my game. It was slightly more than 7,000 yards long, so I thought I had a realistic chance to do well in the tournament.

I had an 8:10 tee time for Monday morning, so after our practice round, we had some dinner and went back to the motel to relax. Not that we had any choice. Pinehurst has to be one of the quietest towns in the entire country. I felt calm when we turned out the lights around ten. The following day would be my first round as a professional golfer, and I was ready for it.

I shot 72-74 for the tournament, finished about tenth, and cashed a check for $450. Not a bad start for my career as a pro.

I headed directly back to Virginia Beach from the tournament. I had not seen my family for several months, and I wanted to talk to Butch about my plans. It was after ten o'clock Tuesday evening when I arrived at my parents' house, and my dad wanted to hear a blow-by-blow description of my first professional tournament. I do not think I could ever provide him with too much detail about my play.

It was close to midnight when I described my one-putt par on the final hole, and I was ready for bed. But my dad was not finished talking. "I've got everything set up with your sponsors," he told me.

We had talked several months earlier about my playing the minitour, and it was just too expensive for us to do it alone. We knew it could be a long time before I would be able to support myself playing golf, and the only way I would ever get to that point was if I could play regularly. Between the entry fees and travel expenses, I would be lucky to play in one tournament a month if I had to pay for it myself, even with my family's help.

Over the years, several people at Cavalier told my dad they would be interested in sponsoring me when the time came. So over the previous few months my dad had been talking with them and had put together a syndicate for me.

"Tell me about it," I said.

"There are ten shares, and for the remainder of this year, everyone is putting in $2,000. If there is a profit at the end of the year, you get twenty percent and the investors get eighty percent. For 1994, everyone kicks in $3,500, with the same deal for the profits. After that, the amount the investors put in depends on where you're playing. If you make it to the Nike Tour in '95, they'll put in $5,000; if you make it to the PGA Tour, it will be $6,000. So you have at least two and a half years where you won't have to worry about the money. It will give you a good chance to develop your game. If you're making progress and it looks like you're on your way to making it, I have no doubt they would be willing to extend it for another couple of years."

"What if I don't need the money?" I didn't want to sound cocky, but who knew what might happen.

"You have the option of terminating the arrangement at the

end of any year. All you have to do is tell them you want to go it alone."

"Sounds good. Thanks a lot, Dad."

He stood up, gave me a hug, and said, "This is the start of something big. I just know it, Carl."

"I hope you're right, Dad." There was a chance he could be right, but I also knew that he had a blind confidence in my ability. It was something I had to come to feel myself if I was to succeed.

The next morning I was eager to get to Cavalier to talk over my plans with Butch. He was standing behind the counter in the pro shop when I arrived, and as soon as he saw me he shouted across the room, "Hey, pro. I hear you're a big winner." My dad had already told him about my tenth-place finish.

We went into Butch's office, and after pouring me a cup of coffee, he said, "Well, so you're starting all over again."

"I'm not sure what you mean."

"Every time you move up to a new level, it's like starting all over again. When you went from beating your friends on Saturday afternoons to the high-school golf team, you had to improve before you could win. The same thing was true, as you well know, when you went to South Carolina. Nobody moved over for you there, and you had to elevate your game to the next level before you could start winning.

"Well, nobody is going to move over for you on the minitour, either. There are a whole lot of conference champions and all-Americans out there, and they're all convinced that they're better than you are and they can't wait to prove it."

"I know. I know I have to get better, but I'm sure I can do it. You know how much better my short game is now compared to when I started college. And I know I have still-better shots in me. I'm not finished improving, not by a long shot."

"I know you're not," Butch said. "But I'm not talking about your game. I'm talking about your head. I'm trying to tell you that you have got to be patient. You have as much talent as anyone I've ever known, but talent isn't enough. And it's not enough to know you're good. You've got to believe, and I mean really believe, that you can beat anyone in the world. If you have any doubts as to whether you're one of the very best, you won't be able to trust your swing when it counts, and you won't make it.

"Let me tell you something else," Butch said. "Playing a tournament every week in a different city is unlike anything you've ever done. You'll be alone. You won't have your coach and your teammates to give you encouragement. You'll have to do everything all by yourself, and it's not easy. There have been thousands of guys over the years who had the game to make it, but they didn't have what it takes up here," Butch said as he tapped his temple with his index finger.

"I guess I have a lot to learn." I knew he was right, but I was a little annoyed. I wanted him to be more upbeat.

"You've got a whole lot to learn, Carl. But I know you can do it. I've watched you develop these past ten years and I know you've got what it takes, both physically and mentally. But you have to give yourself time. You can't get discouraged if you go out there this summer and don't play worth a damn. It will all be new to you, and it may take a while for you to adjust."

"I'm not expecting much this summer, I'm just looking forward to getting the experience."

"That's good." Butch walked across the room and filled his coffee cup before continuing. "What's your thinking regarding the next several years?"

"I don't know, I haven't thought about it much. Just to get the experience and to get better."

"That's good," Butch said. "I'm glad to hear you aren't being unrealistic about all this. Let me tell you what I believe you should be thinking."

"Sure," I said.

"I think you have to give yourself at least five years. It took you almost three years to blossom as a college player, and this will be even tougher. The guys you will be competing against now were the best players in college. The mediocre players are selling insurance. So it seems to me that playing on the Tour in five years is a realistic goal."

"Five years? I hadn't thought about it in specific terms, but isn't five years a long time?"

"Not for what you're trying to do. Remember, you're aiming to be among the best 150 best golfers in the country, and you have a long way to go. Also, keep in mind that most golfers reach their peak around their early to mid-thirties, so you've got at least ten or twelve years before you will be playing your best golf."

"I guess it all makes sense."

"Take my word for it, it does. I don't want you to expect too much of yourself the first couple of years. You've got the ability. You've just got to give yourself the time you need to develop it. You've got to try as hard as you can, but at the same time, you can't put any pressure on yourself—if that makes any sense," he said with a soft chuckle.

"Carl," Butch continued, "there are never any guarantees, but in my heart I know you'll make it. Now, let's go out and hit a few balls and see how our new pro is swinging the club."

I took a week off to recover from the spring semester and to work with Butch. He knows my game so well that he only has to see me hit a half-dozen balls to know if I have developed any bad habits.

He saw a few things he did not like—my left-hand grip had become a little weak and my backswing had become a hair shorter than usual. We made a few minor adjustments, and within an hour I was hitting the ball as well as I had all year. I was ready for my first summer as a professional golfer.

I met my friends Michael Christie, Jerry Wood, and Chris Anderson in Myrtle Beach for a Hooters Tour event. The Hooters Tour, now called the Jordan Hooters Tour, is one step down from the Nike Tour and is an ideal place to learn what it is like to be a pro. The tournaments are all four-day events, from Thursday through Sunday, with a cut after the first thirty-six holes. They have officials who travel with the tour, and unlike the minitour, carts are not allowed. The only real difference between the Hooters and PGA Tours is that you can carry your own bag in the Hooters events.

It is not inexpensive to play on the tour. The entry fee is $500 per event, so that, taken along with travel expenses, seven nights in a motel, eating every meal out, and another $100 if you find a caddy you like, means you're lucky to get through a week for less than $1,100 or $1,200. The upside is that the purse for each tournament is $100,000, with $15,000 going to the winner.

When I played the Hooters Tour in 1993 and 1994, anyone with $500 could enter an event. Nonetheless, the level of competition was intense. There were, to be sure, a handful of players out there who were wasting their time and money, but 95 percent of the guys had enough game to justify their hopes of making it to the PGA Tour. The Hooters Tour has become more popular over the past couple of years, and I understand that currently the demand for spots has exceeded supply. Now there is a qualifying tournament to determine eligibility to play in their events. It only gets tougher to break in with each passing year.

My second start as a pro was not quite as satisfying as my first. I shot 76-72, to miss the cut by two shots.

Over the weekend, I spent the mornings practicing with Jerry, who also missed the cut. During the afternoons we followed Michael and Chris around the course. Chris faded on Sunday, but Michael finished strong with a 68 and cashed a check for $1,800.

The first few weeks of the summer were pure excitement, but it did not take long for me to understand what Butch had been trying to tell me. The travel quickly became tedious. I never enjoyed long car trips, and the reality of taking one every Sunday evening was not a lot of fun. Laundry was another activity that never had much appeal for me, but it was even worse when you had to search for a place to do it in an unfamiliar town. Also, it was that summer that I developed a love-hate relationship with Shoney's. There was something distasteful about going to the same restaurant so often, but it seemed like every town had one and you could not beat their breakfast bar. But I was young and I could adapt to anything if it meant I had the chance to play in a tournament every week.

Although I was disappointed in my play that summer of 1993, I was getting used to the schedule and I was beginning to feel like a professional golfer.

Despite the drudgery of being constantly on the road, in most ways that summer was like one long vacation that I was able to spend with my best friends. Michael, Chris, Jerry, and I traveled together and we had a great time. We practiced hard, we played hard, and we also took time out to relax and have a little fun. It became our habit to go out every Friday night. At least one of us, and on rare occasions all four of us, would make the cut, so we would have reason to celebrate. And if we did not make the cut, we had to go out and have a few beers to be able to properly bemoan our bad luck.

Our Friday nights out usually began with a nice dinner—which, on our budget, was something like Applebee's or

Ruby Tuesday's, anything that was a step up from Shoney's. Next, we would find a bar with a pool table. We all loved to play pool and we were all pretty good at it. My experience has been that professional golfers are usually first-rate pool players. It must be a similar type of eye-hand coordination required.

One night in West Palm Beach was especially memorable. All four of us missed the cut, so we had more than our usual reason to go out for some serious commiseration. We found a bar that was packed but nonetheless had one free table. Eight ball was our usual game, and Michael and I teamed up against Jerry and Chris. After a couple of games, two guys at the bar asked if they could play the winners. Michael and I took them on for a beer, and we won handily. The moment Michael knocked in the eight ball, two other guys claimed the right to play us. Well, we beat them too, and before you knew it we had four beers on the table. This continued for another two hours—Michael and I were both knocking in everything in sight—and we were accumulating beers much faster than we could drink them. By the time we had thirty or forty bottles, we started giving them away to anyone who walked by our table. Needless to say, we attracted quite a crowd. We were the most popular guys in West Palm Beach that night.

It was so much fun that I almost forgot the sting of shooting 75 earlier in the day.

I had my ups and downs that summer. I played in seven events and made four cuts, but I never really played worth a damn. I am intense enough that I would get angry with myself when I did not play well, but on the other hand, it was encouraging to make the cut more than half the time when, by my standards, I was playing poorly. I knew I was capable of hitting much better shots and putting up much better numbers.

I was sorry to see the summer end, but I had to return to Columbia at the end of August to finish my degree in marketing.

Playing Division I golf meant a great deal of travel, so it was nearly impossible to take a full schedule of classes and maintain respectable grades. South Carolina was good about it. They recognized that few golfers could be expected to finish their degree requirements in four years, so all golf scholarships covered five years of course work.

That fall I arranged my schedule so I could play minitour events on Mondays and Tuesdays, leaving the rest of the week for classes. I also practiced with the golf team, working especially hard on my short game. From tee to green, I could hit the ball as well as anyone, and although my short game had improved dramatically while I was at South Carolina, it still was not where it had to be if I was to be competitive at the professional level.

Late in September 1993, I decided to send in my application to the PGA Tour to play in their National Qualifying Tournament, known affectionately as Q-School. To be accepted, I had to furnish two letters, one from a PGA professional stating that I could play well enough to be competitive on the Tour, and another attesting to my character. Steve and Butch wrote the letters for me.

I had mixed feelings about entering. I didn't really think I was ready for the Tour, and I had to take two more classes in the spring semester to graduate, something that was very important to me. But I had begun to play better over the previous few weeks, and when it comes to golf, anything can happen. Perhaps I did not want to admit to myself that I thought I had a shot at making it, so I decided to enter with the rationalization that it would be good experience. Certainly, there was something to be learned from it. This, by the way, was not a trivial decision. The entry fee was $3,000. I would have to learn a hell of a lot to justify that much tuition.

Q-School consists of three stages. The first stage is held during late October at twelve to fifteen sites with about seventy entrants at each site. Approximately the top third finishers at each site qualify for the second stage. These players are joined by a number of others who were exempt from the first stage—mostly pros who played on the PGA and Nike Tours that year but did not earn enough money to qualify for the following year. There are about eight sites for the second stage, and again each site has about seventy to eighty entrants. Approximately the top third from each site make it to the finals, and they join a handful of others who were exempt from both the first and second stages. The first and second stages are four-day tournaments, while the final stage consists of six rounds, with a cut to the low ninety players after the fourth round. The low forty earn their card to play on the PGA Tour for the following year, with the next seventy earning full playing privileges for the Nike Tour.

I had to indicate on the application which site I wanted to play at, and I chose the Country Club of Indiana, a Nicklaus course near Indianapolis. I had never played there, but I heard from several guys that it was a very long, demanding course. Par was a good score there, which meant it was the kind of course that offered me the best chance of qualifying for the second stage. My short game was not at the point where I could successfully compete on a course where everyone was hitting short irons to the green and putting for birdie every hole. I do not have much of an advantage when I have a wedge to the green while most of the field is hitting an eight-iron. But if they are hitting three-woods while I'm hitting four-irons, I'll do okay.

None of my friends had ever played in a Q-School tournament, so I did not know what to expect. And while I am not the sort of person who tries to anticipate the unknown, I was taken aback when I arrived at the course. Everyone was riding around in a cart! The atmosphere was indistinguishable from a minitour event, with one important exception—tension permeated the air.

Even though I didn't know anyone there, I could feel the

anxiety and pressure. It was a stark contrast to my experience on the minitour and the Hooters Tours, where guys seemed to be almost as intent on enjoying themselves as playing well. There is usually a lot of joking and kidding on the practice tee, but at Q-School you rarely saw a smile, and you never heard a joke. Mostly what you heard were guys wishing their friends a somber "Good luck."

I had convinced myself I was there only for the experience, so while I was nervous when I teed off on the first hole of the tournament, I was not feeling especially tense. I busted my drive 300 yards down the center, and as I walked down the fairway I said to myself, "Who knows what might happen this week."

The course was as tough as everyone had said. I played well that first round, but I still ended with a 75, three over par. I felt more relaxed the second round, and when I finished the day one under for the round, and only two over for the tournament, I began to feel some of the tension that was so apparent on the faces of the other players. I hit the ball even better during the third round than I had the first two days, but the putts would not drop. Still, I shot even par for the day, which put me two over for the tournament and well within the cut line. It looked as if five over would earn a trip to the second stage, so all I had to do was match my worst round of the week to make it. It took a little longer than usual to fall asleep that night.

My game just never came together for me during the fourth round. I was nervous, but no more so than I had been many times during college tournaments. I do not know what happened. Perhaps I was swinging a little more quickly than usual, or maybe my anxiety was making it difficult for me to concentrate. Whatever it was, I bogeyed two of the first three holes before settling down. I played the next twelve holes passably, adding three more bogeys against a single birdie.

I arrived at the sixteenth tee six over par for the tournament, so I knew I still had a chance. Two pars and a birdie would get me to the second stage for sure, and there was a chance that three pars would do it. The odds were good that the pressure was getting to the other guys too. I hit my drive on the sixteenth hole solid, but I pushed it slightly and it ended up a couple yards off the fairway in light rough. The pin was tucked behind a trap on the right side of the green, but since I had only an eight-iron left, it seemed like a good opportunity for the birdie I needed. I pushed the shot again. This time the ball bounded off the cart path and splashed into a pond guarding the right side of the green. I could see the ripples gently washing against the bank, and all I could do was watch until the surface of the pond was smooth again. I was in a state of shock. Had the ball landed a foot to the left, it would have left me an easy chip to save my par. But I guess it was not meant to be. The double bogey put me out of the tournament, and I limped home with a 79.

Even though I went into the tournament telling myself I was playing for the experience and that it was not realistic to expect to make it through Q-School that fall, I was very unhappy. I had played well for three rounds, I was almost a lock to make it to the second stage, and I let it slip away.

I am not even sure what I learned from the experience. I suppose there was something valuable about having the opportunity to play in such a pressure-packed situation, but I do not know to this day if I choked or not. I realize that it looks that way to an outsider—what else can you say about a 79 when all I needed was a 75? But the truth of the matter is that I have had my share of high scores when playing with my friends when there was no more pressure than the annoyance of having to hand over twenty or thirty bucks at the end of the day. Sure, I felt tight during that final round, but I had felt more tension during college tournaments and still managed to get more birdies than bogeys.

I think there must be a subtle distinction between nervousness and fear, even though they feel similar. I can play well when I am nervous, maybe because I do not expect it to throw any glitches in my swing. But if any thoughts slip into my head about what might happen if I take a bad swing, it becomes that much harder to swing at the ball the way I should. I think the secret to golf is to take each swing the same way you did when you were twelve years old playing an imaginary match against Jack Nicklaus. It was so easy in those days to approach each shot confident that it would be the best of your life.

Perhaps I approached that last round guarding against bad shots and trying to avoid a high score. Maybe I was afraid of taking a bad swing rather than concentrating on making the best swing I could. I do not remember having those thoughts, but they might have been tucked away somewhere in the back of my mind.

But maybe it was something as simple as an off day. Everyone who plays golf feels a need to explain both good and bad rounds, and perhaps the answer is as simple as that—it was just one of those bad rounds. Sometimes your good rounds come at times that make you look like a real pressure player; sometimes your bad rounds come at times that make you look like you need someone to give you the Heimlich maneuver.

I do not know.

I do know that confidence is critical. Regardless of why I shot that final-round 79, if I was to make it through Q-School in the future I would have to find a way to approach those crucial rounds secure in the knowledge that I could hit the shots I had to. I promised myself that I would be ready the next time.


Anyone who plays golf competitively has to learn to get over disappointments quickly. The reality of the game is that there will be a lot more days when you lose than when you win. I had always been able to do this. When I blew the semifinal match in the Virginia State Amateur, I was a basket case for a couple of hours, but I was still able to have a good time at a party later that evening. But this time, I had trouble shaking it. Immediately after the tournament, I returned to Columbia to finish the semester, but I was having trouble getting back into the groove. I did everything I always did—I spent a lot of time with my girlfriend Heather, I went to my classes, studied for tests, I even practiced with the golf team. But I wasn't enjoying it as much as I usually did. The image of that ball bouncing off the cart path by the sixteenth green crept into my mind more often than I would have liked.

Christmas break was the final cure. I returned to Virginia Beach to spend the vacation with my family and with my friends from high school. It was a clear reminder of what was really important in life, and I was finally able to put the 79 in its proper perspective. It really did not make a bit of difference in the overall scheme of things.

Butch and I had a lot of time to talk over the recent discouragements, and I was surprised by his reaction. The first thing he said to me was "I'm really proud of how you did up there."

"But, Butch," I protested, "I blew it during the last round."

"You can look at it that way if you like," Butch said, "but I like to think that the first three rounds proved you can be competitive at the very highest level. Don't forget, everyone has to lose before they can learn to win. Tom Watson had the reputation of being a choker the first couple of years he was out on tour, and look at him now. Everyone considers him to be one of the greatest of the modern players. You'll lose a lot more before you start winning, so be grateful for every chance you have to get yourself in that position. Those experiences will make you a better player."

Butch's words made everything fall into place. The guys who

had reason to be discouraged were the ones who went into the final round with no chance to qualify. They had reason to wonder if they were good enough to make it. My first three rounds proved I had the ability. All I needed was a little more experience.

I returned to Columbia eager for spring to arrive. I needed only two more classes to graduate, so I had plenty of time to practice. I would be prepared the next time an opportunity presented itself.

The Carolina Tour schedule began in March, and I played in about seven or eight events during the spring of 1994. I planned my classes so I would have Mondays and Tuesdays free, so I could spend the first half of the week as a professional golfer and the second half as a student. I always looked forward to the weeks when I had a tournament scheduled. With each event I was gaining experience as a pro, and it was just plain fun. One of the most rewarding aspects of golf is all the people you meet and all the friendships that develop. And most of the guys who played in the events had a lot in common. We were about the same age, we tended to be sports nuts, we liked to relax after the round over a few beers, and we all had aspirations of making it to the Tour. It was an easy place to make new friends.

I started out slow that spring, but my play improved steadily and I actually came out ahead for the last two or three events— something that is not easy to do. Some people have observed that the minitours are nothing more than legalized gambling, and it would be hard to argue with that view. The purse comes from the entry fees, and every tournament provides several more opportunities for players, in effect, to bet on themselves. For $10 per day, you can play skins—which means an eagle, and on rare occasions a birdie, could be worth several hundred dollars. Most events had a one-day tournament for the final round. So if you did not play well during the first round, you could put up another $75 and have a chance to win something the second day. Another option, for another $75, was a back-half, one-day tournament. This tournament within a tournament was open only to those players in the bottom half of the field after the first day's play. So, if you played poorly in the first round, it gave you an opportunity to compete against other guys who had not played well. Everyone hoped to shoot a low enough number during the second round to win the back-half tournament and cash a check in the regular tournament.

I usually entered every competition I could — not in the spirit of recouping any losses, but because I believed I was good enough to win at any time. I appreciated that there were enough good players to make winning a long shot, but I would bet on myself before I would bet on anyone else. Mostly, though, I wanted the chance to play regularly so I could improve my game. I never entered a tournament with the thought that I had to win enough to cover my expenses. And I was grateful to my sponsors for providing me with that luxury.

The spring flew by, and before I knew it I was set for graduation. My family, including all the aunts and uncles, came down to Columbia for the week, and as usual we had a great time together. It was a double-barreled celebration in a way. I had completed my degree in marketing, and that meant that I had become a full-time professional golfer. Somehow, it seemed different to me. It was one thing to play golf while I was still in school, but now that I had finished, the golf took on a new seriousness. I was no longer a college kid dabbling at golf, I was a professional who was serious about developing his game to the highest possible level. It did not matter if it took the full five years Butch thought it would, I was willing to work at it until I made it.

By the end of May I was ready to join my friends on the Hooters Tour. My game was peaking, and I was hitting the ball great. I got off to a fast start, making the cut at the first three events I played in. I actually had a small profit to show for my efforts.

The following week the tournament was in El Paso, Illinois, perhaps the smallest town to ever host a Tour event of any kind. This town was so small it didn't even have a Shoney's. After our practice round on Tuesday, I decided it would have been a good week to take off. Not only did I lose $50 to Michael and Chris, I learned it was not the kind of course on which I would ever score well. It was rather short, not even 6,700 yards, and the greens had so many contours they would have fit right in at any miniature Wacky Golf course. Tricked-up greens may be fun for the every-day golfer when the stimpmeter reads seven or eight, but we don't get to play them under those conditions. We played them when they were hard and fast, when there were lots of places where it was impossible to keep a six-foot putt within ten feet of the hole. It seemed to me that such conditions made luck more important than skill.

Despite my misgivings about the course, I shot 71-70 for the first two rounds. Not only did I make the cut handily, I was only five strokes off the lead. I played solidly on Saturday, but those critical four-foot downhillers killed me and I ended the day with a three-over-par 75. The round dropped me back in the crowd, seven strokes behind the leader.

Sunday, I teed off about ninety minutes ahead of the leaders, but it was a great feeling to be within shouting distance of the lead. Although I had been making cuts, I had not been making them by much, so I had pretty early tee times for the weekends. It was nice to be able to sleep until nine and still have time to linger over the morning paper during a leisurely breakfast before heading for the course. It was a feeling I hoped I would have reason to get used to.

When I arrived on the first tee, I was surprised to see a crowd of spectators. Granted, it was a small crowd, but there were definitely enough people there to qualify as a crowd. There was never much of a gallery for Hooters events, but there must have been a couple of hundred people milling around the first tee—a good ten percent of the town's population.

I hit the ball well that day, and in contrast to Saturday's round, my putter was working well. I birdied two of the first three holes, then added another birdie at eight to finish the front nine at three under par. A bogey on ten worried me; I did not want to lose all the ground I had made up on the front nine. It turned out to be just a momentary slip, though. I added three more birdies on the twelfth, fifteenth, and sixteenth holes. My final-round 67 wasn't enough to get me to a position to win, but it was enough to make a serious move on the leader board. I climbed from a tie for nineteenth to a tie for third, and my check for nearly $5,000 was by far my largest payday as a professional golfer. I was excited. I had not missed a cut in a month, and I was making a nice profit for my sponsors. Life was great.

Golf is a funny game—if you have a warped sense of humor, that is. I had been hitting the ball crisply for a couple of months; I am not sure if I had ever played better. But just like that, it left me. I struggled throughout July and August, and missed four cuts in a row.

I can appreciate how frustrating golf can be for everyone, regardless of their handicap, but I cannot help believing that it is especially frustrating for those of us who are trying to earn a living at it. The difference between playing well and playing poorly is so subtle. We do not go from hitting the ball great to slicing it out of bounds. If we did something like that, we would know how to fix it. For me, the difference between playing well and playing poorly might mean hitting the ball a groove or two low on the clubface a half-dozen times per round. Sometimes you can get away with it, but more often than not it means hitting it five yards short of your target and burying the ball in a bunker. Sometimes I am a hair too quick on the downswing and the clubface is closed a fraction of an inch when it contacts the ball. So the shot drifts to the left instead of flying toward the pin.

Also, when you're playing 7,000-yard courses instead of the 6,000-yard courses that most weekend golfers play, these minor imperfections make a bigger difference. When you have 130 yards to the pin, you can still catch the corner of the green with a clubface that is a quarter-inch off from being square. But when you are 190 yards out, that quarter-inch can make the difference between birdie and bogey. All this taken together may mean a difference of only two or three strokes per round, but that difference is enough to separate the stars from the wanna-bes.

The frustration professional golfers experience lies in trying to fix that quarter-inch problem. It is almost impossible to watch someone and see what might be causing such a minute difference, and it is nearly as difficult to feel it yourself. All you can do is beat balls on the range while concentrating on the fundamentals and hope that the magic returns—the magic of having everything come together so when you're faced with a shot that requires 160 yards to clear a pond with 170 yards to the bunker behind the green, you know that a cut seven-iron will give you precisely the 165 yards you need.

Even though I was not playing well during the later part of the summer, I continued to have a great time. Michael, Chris, Jerry, and I were still traveling together, and I was getting to know a lot of the other guys. Since I was missing a lot of cuts, Tuesday became one of my favorite days of the week. Unless we were invited to play in the pro-am, it was the only day we had a chance to see the course, and by midsummer there were about a dozen of us who were having our own little tournament. We would pair off in teams of two, and each team would play all the other teams for $5 per hole. As the round progressed, there were always a number of presses, along with a few more creative side bets thrown in, so it was not unusual for several hundred dollars to change hands at the end of the day.

One Tuesday was especially wild. Twelve of us showed up for our one-o'clock tee time, and Michael Christie and I were teamed up against the other guys. It was one of those days when neither Michael nor I could play worth a damn, but we were hitting the ball well enough to justify our belief that as long as we kept pressing, we would eventually break even. We both shot in the mid-seventies, and I think there were only a couple of holes on which we did not have the same score—the kiss of death in best ball. We set a new record that day, losing almost $400.

We had no choice but to call for an emergency nine. The informal rule was that anyone who lost money had the right to call for an emergency nine, and the winners did not have the option of declining. We both played great on the final nine. Michael had three birdies, and I had two to go along with an eagle three. And unlike the first eighteen, we ham-and-egged it almost perfectly, having the same score on only one hole. We set a second record for the day, and our winnings on the emergency nine helped us finish the day less than $100 in the hole.

Playing on the Hooters Tour was almost like summer vacations during junior high school. I was able to do precisely what I liked best—spend my days on the golf course with my friends. In some ways, it was even better. Unlike junior high, when I had to be in the house by sunset, we were able to go out and raise a little hell during the evenings. I wondered if professional golf would always be so much fun.

It was about this time that I sent in my application to play in the Q-School tournament again. I would have felt better about sending in the check for $3,000 had my play been sharper, but I had a couple of months to turn things around. And sure enough, within weeks, I seemed to be coming out of my slump. I was swinging at the ball with confidence again, I was hitting a high percentage of crisp shots, and best of all, I was putting red numbers on the scoreboard. I made the cut in the final two tournaments before returning to South Carolina for the first stage of Q-School. My game was peaking at exactly the right time.

This year would be different.

# CHAPTER 4

# The Fall Classic

"Hey, Dad. Would you go to the car and get me a sleeve of balls?"

I was warming up for the first round of Q-School in late October 1994, and I did not want to take a chance on damaging my titanium driver by hitting the rock-hard range balls with it. The first and, as I would learn later, the second stages of Q-School were big events only in the eyes of the contestants. The Titleist reps, with their unlimited supply of new balls for the range and the players, didn't make an appearance until the finals.

"You mean you're going to hit eight bucks' worth of balls out there?" my dad asked, incredulous at the prospect.

"I need them, Dad." He turned away and headed toward the car.

I wanted the balls, but I also wanted to give him something to do. He was caddying for me, and while I was nervous, he made me seem like a picture of tranquillity by comparison. His fidgeting was distracting me.

Although I was hitting the ball pure, I could not get rid of the nervousness as I warmed up. I had been playing well the previous month, although my scores did not always reflect it, so I had reason to feel good about my chances. All I needed were a few putts to drop.

The pressure was more intense than it had been the year before. In '93, I planned to return to Columbia to finish my degree if I did not make it. This year I was a full-time professional golfer, so I wasn't sure what I would do if something good didn't happen. I reminded myself of what Butch had told me about being patient; I was only starting the second year of my five-year plan to make it to the Tour. But the truth was, I wanted to do well. I wanted it badly.

I do not know if anyone except those of us trying to make it to the Tour can appreciate how much pressure there is in Q-School. I felt it even though this was my first serious attempt. It was much worse for a lot of the other guys. A number of them had the game to play on tour but hadn't been able to make it through Q-School—some in as many as ten tries. Others had been on tour for a year or two, lost their card, and were trying to get it back. And a handful had been out there for a number of years, even won a time or two, but after a couple of bad seasons had to go through the ordeal of Q-School all over again. If those guys did not make it, they would be forced to think about giving it up. At least I could tell myself that I was just getting started and had lots of time ahead of me.

I was giving myself five years to learn if I was good enough to make it, but I could understand how five years could easily turn into fifteen or twenty. There were a number of guys who were still trying to get to the Tour although they were in their thirties and, in a few cases, their forties. The difference in the games of those who can make a good living year after year and those who cannot quite get there is so slight that it makes it nearly impossible for anyone to give up on the dream. It might be as little as one stroke a round; at most, two, two and a half. And at Q-School, the difference between getting to the Tour and having nowhere to go for a year might come down to a single stroke over fourteen rounds. Such was the nature of the Fall Classic, as the guys sardonically referred to it.

My dad returned with the sleeve of balls. After finishing my warm-up routine with three tee shots, I hopped into the cart and my dad drove me to the putting green. He was not such a dedicated caddy that he was willing to carry my bag for the four days. I liked to walk, but he pleaded a bad back, so he would follow me down the fairway in the cart.

I selected the Country Club of South Carolina in Florence for the first stage. It was not as tough as the course in Indianapolis from the year before, but I had played it several times during college and I felt comfortable there. My choice was justified by a first-round 68 on a windy, chilly day. I was only one stroke off the lead, and in the top third by four shots. It was no reason to get overly confident, but I could not help but love my position.

It was especially important to me to do well, because I was planning to attend a high-school friend's wedding on Saturday, and I knew it would be more fun to see my old friends if I could tell them I had qualified for the second stage.

The next morning, we were running a little late. I was sharing a room with Jerry Wood, since I had learned long before that I would never get a good night's sleep with my dad's snoring. Because I wanted to have plenty of time to warm up, I suggested we stop by McDonald's for a sausage biscuit to go. But my dad insisted on having a regular breakfast at Shoney's. We had eaten there the previous morning and he wasn't about to do anything different after my 68. He is a rational man in most respects, but I have never seen anyone more superstitious when it comes to golf. He has been known to wear the same shirt throughout a tournament when I had four good rounds. Once, he woke up at four A.M. on a day when I shot 69, so the following morning he set his clock for four A.M. So I was happy to eat at Shoney's even if it meant a few minutes less on the range. It sure beat his wearing a dirty shirt.

The second round went well for seventeen holes, but I was irritated as I walked off the eighteenth green. I hit the ball great all day, and was three under par going into the last hole. I busted my drive down the center of the fairway and hit a four-iron to the fringe on the back of the green. My chip almost went in the hole, but it slipped two feet past the cup. And then I missed the damn two-footer. It always hurts to end a round like that. But by the time I checked over my scorecard and signed it, I was feeling good again. I was six under for the tournament, and in the top third by seven shots. I could not see how I could miss going on to the second stage.

Jerry woke up before I did on the morning of the third round. He looked out the window and said, "We won't be playing today."

I jumped out of bed for a look. It was a hard rain, the kind that looks as if it will never end. I called the course, and they confirmed that play had been canceled for the day. I was not happy.

It is never fun to have a tournament round washed out, but this was especially bad timing. I was playing terrifically, I was on a roll, and now I would have nothing to do all day but think about what could happen over the next two rounds. It also meant that with the tournament extended by a day, I would have to miss my friend's wedding.

We did the best we could to make the time pass. But after a

movie, lunch, and countless hands of gin, it was only four o'clock in the afternoon. Another movie got us to dinner, and I finished off the evening staring vacantly at the television. Finally, it was time to turn out the lights.

It was cold and windy the following morning, and the drizzle was just hard enough to call for the rain gear. It was a miserable day for golf, but playing under such conditions was better than spending another day in the motel room.

The first hole was a short, dogleg-left par four. I hooked my tee shot badly, but I got lucky and it bounced off a tree to the edge of the fairway. I didn't have a shot to the green, so I laid up about forty yards short. A great pitch left me with four feet for par. The rain had slowed the greens dramatically, so I told myself to hit the putt solidly. I still left it six inches short. I went up to tap it in, but hit it so hard that the damn thing bounced out of the hole. Double bogey. What a way to start.

I played the next eight holes well. Birdies on the two par fives got me to even as I made the turn. My confidence was back.

On the tenth tee, I flat-out topped my driver, something I do maybe once a year. I hit a three-wood to where my drive should have been, and an eight-iron and two putts got my bogey. I put a good swing on my tee shot at eleven, a par three, but three putts later, I was two over for the day. I felt shaky.

I scraped by with pars on the next four holes and felt better by the time I reached the sixteenth tee, a long, downhill par three. I hit my three-iron great, but it was a yard short and plugged under the lip of the front bunker. I could not get it out, and I was lucky to escape with a bogey.

I thought I could get a shot back at the seventeenth, a par five that was easily reachable in two. But I topped my driver again. The nerves hit me all at once, and I could feel my heart pound and my hands tremble. A three-wood and eight-iron got me to within twenty feet, and I knocked that sucker right in the center of the hole for a birdie four. I was so happy and so proud of myself for not letting the hole get away from me.

The eighteenth hole was extremely difficult—a par four, 450 yards uphill—so I told myself I could salvage the round with a solid par. I immediately duck-hooked my tee shot into the water on the left. The adrenaline kicked back in, and all I could think was "double bogey." My drop left me 350 yards to the green, and I played it safe with a five-iron to the middle of the fairway. A nice seven-iron to eight feet gave me a chance for bogey, and somehow I managed to get the ball in the hole. My 75 put me well within the cut line, but I knew another poor final round would eliminate me.

Lying in bed that night, I could not help but think about 1993. I went into the last round there with several strokes to spare, and I blew it. I knew all too well the same thing could happen again.

I tried to change my perspective. I reminded myself that I had three good rounds the year before and there was no reason why I could not have three good rounds again. The only difference would be that my bad round would be on the third day this year. I told myself that a solid, conservative round would get me to the second stage easily. I fell asleep while trying to visualize myself hitting to the center of the greens.

I do not know why, but some days you wake up filled with confidence. You have the sense that hitting good golf shots is the easiest thing in the world. Other days, you wake up with the feeling that you will be lucky to keep the ball in play. Thankfully, that Saturday morning was one of the good days, a confidence day.

I stuck to my game plan and played conservatively, hitting more three-woods and irons off tees than drivers. When I reached the seventeenth tee, I was only one over for the round and one under for the tournament. It looked as though two over would make it, and I was tempted—for just a moment—to hit my eight-iron the rest of the way in.

There was not much trouble off the par-five seventeenth tee, so I took my driver out and absolutely crushed it. A four-iron would get me to the green, but there was water to the left, so I pulled out an eight-iron to lay up. As I was standing over the ball I thought about how well I'd been hitting it all day. I didn't see how I could hit my four-iron badly enough to get me into trouble. I went back to the cart to get the four, and I hit it on the sweet spot, right to the middle of the green. Two putts later I was back to even par for the day.

I hit another great drive on the eighteenth hole that left me with a five-iron to the green. As my dad handed me the club, he said, "Middle of the green and we're going to second stage."

"Right. Middle of the green."

I pushed the shot slightly, but the pin was back right, so the ball ended up ten feet from the hole. I gave my dad such an enthusiastic high five that it must have been heard in the clubhouse. I lagged to within inches of the cup, got my par, and gave my dad another high five. I was as happy as I had ever been about golf. I shot even par on a critical day. It was a clear sign that I had what it takes.

After turning in my card, I gave Heather a big hug. She had come to watch the final round. I said, "Why don't we jump in the car and head to Virginia Beach. If we don't stop, we can still make Chris's reception. That's the best part of a wedding anyway." It was a five-hour drive, but we made it shortly after the party began. It was great to see Chris and meet his bride, and it was great to celebrate with all my friends.

The second stage was at Queen Harbor in Jacksonville, Florida, in the third week of November. It was another course I had played in college and I liked it a lot, probably because I had played well there. I knew the competition would be a notch higher, but I felt ready for it. I was playing solid golf, and after my even-par final round at first stage, my confidence was good. Jerry didn't make it through the first stage, so I roomed with Scott Medlin, a friend I met playing the minitours. My caddy shared the room next door with my mom, who had come to watch me play.

Scott and I both played great the first round, and our 67s led the tournament. We were on top of the world, and my dad took us to the Outback for dinner to celebrate.

I hit the ball just as well during the second round, but the putts wouldn't drop. My even-par round left me five under for the tournament and tied for fifth place.

I got off to a great start the third round, going three under through the first five holes. My tee shot on six, a short par four, was down the middle. As I reached the ball, I saw my brother and sister-in-law standing nearby. I knew they would be arriving sometime during the round to watch the rest of the tournament. I walked over to say hello, and I was amazed at how big my sister-in-law was—she was eight months pregnant. She is a small woman, and it was the first time I had seen her since she announced she was expecting. As I was standing over my ball, all I could think about was how big her stomach was. I could not focus on the shot. Like a dummy, I swung at it anyway and hit an absolutely awful shot, coming within a hair of shanking it.

I salvaged a bogey, but all four wheels had come off. I hit a poor chip on eight for another bogey, and then on eleven, I blocked my tee shot to the right and it ended up next to a tree. I had no choice but to take an unplayable lie, and I finished the hole with a double. I could not believe it. I was throwing strokes out the window right and left.

I played okay the rest of the nine, but missed a five-footer for par on the last hole to finish with a 74. My score dropped me all the way from fifth to twenty-eighth. Only twenty-four players were going to the final stage, so I was outside the cut line. Man, what was it about those third rounds?

That night in bed, I had a very serious talk with myself. I knew I would have to shoot at least two under to make it, but I could not dwell on that. All I could do was go out there, concentrate, have some fun, and play the way I knew I was capable of playing. I had a solid fourth round on a much tougher course at the first stage, and there was no reason I could not do it again.

I got a break for the fourth round. Morris Hatalsky, a nineteen-year veteran who had won nearly two million dollars on tour, was paired with me. It was the first time I had played with a veteran, and I was so excited about it that it helped me forget some of my nervousness.

We both got off to a good start. Morris had four solid pars, and I knocked in a birdie on three to go one under. On the fifth green, Morris had to move his coin since it was in my line, and when he went to tap in his two-footer, he forgot to move it back. "Hey, Morris. Did you move your coin back?" I reminded him. It would have been a two-stroke penalty had he not done so.

"Oh, man. I forgot." He moved his mark over the width of a putter head, and knocked the ball into the back of the cup.

As we walked to the next tee, he said, "I've done a lot of stupid things over the years I've been on tour, but that's one thing I've never done. Thanks a lot, kid. Those two strokes look mighty big right now."

For the next few holes, Morris told me about life on the Tour. I remember his saying, "You'll love it out there, kid. Not only is it like one long vacation, you'll make some of the best friends you'll ever have. You travel with the same people year after year, so it becomes your family. And it's a close-knit family. We have to take care of each other out there."

When we made the turn, I was one under and Morris was even for the round. We were still outside the cut line. I said to him, "We both have to play well this nine if we're going to make it."

"Kid, you are absolutely right. Let's go do it."

And we did. I was having so much fun playing with him that I almost forgot how much pressure I was under. Morris got birdies on twelve, thirteen, and fourteen, then added another at sixteen. I birdied the two par fives, so we arrived at the eighteenth tee fairly sure that pars would get us to the final stage. We both hit good drives; Morris was down the right side and I was in the left-center of the fairway. He put his five-iron within ten feet, and I gave him the thumbs-up sign.

I had 155 yards to the green, the perfect distance for an eight-iron. The pin was on the left side of the green, tucked behind a bunker, with a pond to the left of the green. I turned to my dad and said, "Center of the green, and I think we're going to the final stage."

"Center of the green, and let's get out of here," he answered.

As I stood behind my ball, picking my target, I had a surge of confidence. I knew I could hit it close, and it might be important for me to do so. I began the day believing that two under for the day would get me inside the cut line, but the conditions were nearly perfect. The cut might be a stroke lower. I stepped back again and looked at the pin. All the trouble was on that side of the green, and a bogey would ensure that I would not make the cut. On the other hand, I had played great all day and I had the perfect distance for the eight-iron. I would be kicking myself for an entire year if it turned out that I needed a birdie and I had played it safe. I had to go for it.

I swung with confidence and the ball felt solid coming off the club. I knew it was going to be close, but my dad apparently was not as confident. "Go, go," he yelled at the ball. It came down pin high, a couple of feet to the right of the hole, and took one small hop back. It was within five feet.

Morris laughed, and yelled across the fairway, "It's good to see a young guy with some cajones these days."

We both knocked in our birdie putts. We were both going to the final stage.

Morris and I, of course, had quite different reactions to making the cut. He expected to do it. He had already been there, and had he not made it, it would have been a major disappointment for him. He was more relieved than happy.

In some ways there is more pressure at the second stage than the finals. If you make it to the finals, at worst you are assured of being able to play in at least a few Nike tournaments. If you do not make it past the second stage, it is either the minitours, which are too expensive for most guys to play regularly, or the foreign tours. I do not think Morris would have been interested in playing on the Asian tour after playing with the best golfers under the best conditions in the world for nineteen years.

I, on the other hand, was on cloud nine. I entered Q-School thinking that if I made it to second stage, it would show progress from the year before. And while I had enough confidence in my ability to believe I could make it to the final stage if I played well, it was not something I was counting on. I was so excited that I found a phone and spent the next half hour calling all my friends. It was one hell of a great day.

I headed back to Columbia late that afternoon, and when I arrived I saw the huge banner Heather had draped across the front of our apartment, which read, "Congratulations, Carl." She had invited a bunch of my friends over, and we all went out to our favorite bar to celebrate. It was a perfect end to a perfect day.

I had ten days before the final-stage tournament began, and I used the first three days to relax and recover from the tension of the second stage. The combination of the pressure and the excitement had left me feeling drained. On Tuesday I headed for Atlanta to meet my family at my older brother's house. George went to Georgia Tech on a tennis scholarship, and it had become a family tradition to attend the Georgia–Georgia Tech game on Thanksgiving. I had planned to spend several hours each day practicing but the weather was awful. It rained every day, and I did not get a chance to hit a single ball. I left for Orlando on Sunday.

The finals were being held at Greenlefe in Haynes City, just south of Orlando. I had not played there before, but after my practice round on Monday, I felt good about what could happen. It was a long, tough course — the kind of course where par would be a very good score. After Tuesday's practice round on the secondary course, I was not as confident. It was much shorter and much tighter than the primary course. It did not play to my strengths, and I did not like it at all.

The finals are always held at a facility with two courses. There are 180 guys playing, and with the short December days, it would be impossible for them to finish the round if everyone played on a single course. The tension is so great that even guys who normally play quickly take their time to study every putt. As I was about to learn, you could expect to be out on the course for six hours.

The atmosphere at the final stage is similar to that of the first and second stages, only ratcheted up several notches. At the first stage, there are always several guys who cannot break 80 for four straight rounds, so you have the feeling you only have to beat about half the field to finish in the top third. Everyone at the second stage can play, but again there are a handful of guys you can count on to self-destruct. These guys are usually first-rate players, but for one reason or another they have developed a mental block that keeps them from getting to the finals. There are a few all-Americans in this category, guys who were beating everybody else in college. But they can't seem to deal with the pressure of knowing their future depends on four rounds of solid golf. I had the feeling that I had to beat about 60 percent of the guys to make it past the second stage.

No one makes it to the finals, however, without being able to flat-out play golf, and play it under pressure. Every year there are a number of former Tour winners entered, sometimes as many as twenty. Probably another twenty or thirty guys have several years of Tour experience. All 180 guys have been working their entire lives to get to the Tour, and they all know they are good enough to do it. And since only forty players out of the 180 entrants will get their card, you know the odds are against you. The pressure is simply unbelievable.

There are a lot of stories, of both tragedies and triumphs, that circulate the locker room. Some of them are undoubtedly apocryphal, but they all have enough of the ring of truth to allow everyone to identify with them. The one I heard most often that fall was about the player who, the year before, arrived at the seventeenth tee of the sixth round needing only to play the final two holes three over par to get his card. He finished with two doubles and missed qualifying, for the fifth time, by a single stroke. Later, in the locker room, he announced that he would never play golf again, and no one had heard from him since.

On the more positive side, I heard several guys mention Curtis Strange, who had bogeyed his final three holes to miss his card by a stroke in his first attempt at Q-School. Curtis, of course, made it through the following Q-School and went on to win two consecutive U.S. Opens. There were a number of established players who had squeaked through Q-School by a stroke or two, four or five times before they made it big.

Both kinds of stories were exchanged in reverential tones between shots on the range and on the practice green. The few guys who tried to break the tension with a joke or some ribbing did it in a forced way that rarely elicited so much as a smile. This was business. And very serious business at that.

My first round was on the long course, and I played solidly. I walked off the seventeenth green two under par, and since eighteen was a long par five, I thought I had a shot at finishing with a 69, certainly no worse than a 70. I hit a good drive, long and down the right side of the fairway. My best three-wood would only get me to the bunker in front of the green, so I played it safe with a five-iron. I did not finish the swing, and the ball drifted into the trees on the right. It ended up within inches of the base of a tree, between two roots, so I had no choice but to take an unplayable. I managed to punch the ball to the back of the green, and then promptly three-putted for a double bogey. I was not happy about the finish, but I knew even par would not hurt me. All in all, it was not a bad start.

The second day I played on the short, tight course, and my game plan was to play defensively. I hit mostly irons and three-woods off the tee, but my iron play was off slightly. I was not hitting the ball badly, but it seemed as if I missed half the greens. Thankfully, my short game was on, and I finished the day even par again. The entire day had felt like such a struggle that I felt relieved about the result.

After the first two rounds, the players are reshuffled according to their scores, and I was right at fortieth place. It meant I would have to play the short course again, but I was happy to get it out of the way. I told myself I just had to get by that third round, which had been giving me trouble, and my length would give me an advantage on the longer course over the final three rounds.

It always amazes me how differently you can play from day to day, and the third round was one of those days when golf seemed like the easiest game in the world. I was splitting the fairways with my tee shots and my irons were knocking down the pins. Had I putted just a little bit better, I could have had a real low score, but as it was, I was four under par with four holes to play. I turned to my dad and said, "It will be nice to have a cushion going into tomorrow." The field was cut to the low ninety players after the fourth round, and I did not want to put too much pressure on myself.

The fifteenth hole was a short par four, and a three-wood left me with a hard wedge to the green. I hit it flush and I was thinking birdie as the ball soared directly at the flag. It was a foot short, however, and plugged in the front lip of the bunker. I was lucky to get it out and escape with a bogey.

My seven-iron on the par-three sixteenth was solid. It left me with a twelve-footer for birdie. As I walked onto the green, my heart rate increased by several beats per minute. My ball was directly above the hole, and I knew it was going to be unbelievably fast. It was downhill, downgrain, downwind, downsun, down-everything. I tapped the ball to get it rolling, and it didn't stop trickling down the slope until it was five feet past the cup. "Damn, here come my third-round jitters," I said under my breath. I did not have a chance of making that putt, and when it missed on the right edge, I was so mad I could not see straight. I could feel my face turn beet red, and I would not have been surprised if my playing partners could see smoke coming out of my ears. I was finished for the day. I limped home with two more bogeys and turned a great round into an infuriating 72. I left the course without speaking a word to anyone.

When I got back to the motel, I remembered that my college roommate, "Shep" Shepard, had come down that morning to watch me play. I was so self-absorbed with my own frustration that I did not even speak to him after the round. I did not know where he was staying, so I could not call him to apologize. I felt like a real jerk.

Shep called me later that evening, and I was able to explain what was going on with me. He knew me well enough to understand that my fit of temper would be short-lived, and I was glad he was willing to make allowances for it. We agreed to have lunch after my round the following day, and I felt better after I hung up the phone.

My brother, George, my mom, and Heather came down for the final three rounds, so we all went to a movie that evening. I liked having their company. They kept me light on my feet and made it difficult for me to obsess about the golf. I felt relaxed, and even pleased, about my play by the time I turned out the lights that evening. I made it by the dreaded third round with even par, and after three days I was still tied for fortieth place. It was a much better position than I had hoped for, and a solid round would get me past the cut.

The fourth round began in much the same way as the third one had. I was playing great, and I walked off the seventeenth green four under par. I was certain to make the cut, and I had put myself in great position for the final two rounds.

Perhaps I was thinking too much about the remaining two rounds, but I hooked my tee shot on eighteen into the left rough. I was blocked out by the trees, and all I could do was punch it down the fairway about seventy-five yards. My approach shot hit the fringe and kicked to the right, but it left me with an easy chip, so I still had a good shot at a par. I hit the chip and it ran ten feet past the hole. I should have learned my lesson from the tee shot, but all I could think about while I was standing over that putt was that if I made it, I would be four-under going into the fifth round. I would be in absolutely great shape. I hit it three feet past the hole, and of course, I missed it coming back. Another damn double bogey. Why the hell couldn't I finish off my good rounds?

I made the cut with a couple of strokes to spare. That was important, because it ensured that, at worst, I would be able to play full-time on the Nike Tour. The top forty guys get their PGA Tour card, the next seventy get full playing privileges on the Nike Tour, and the others can enter Nike events as space permits.

The fifth round was solid, if unspectacular: two bogeys, two birdies, for another 72. It was a boring round, but it put me in a position I liked. I was still tied for fortieth place going into the final round. I had a realistic chance of getting my card.

My uncles, Bill and Lou, arrived Sunday morning for the final two rounds, so dinner at Bennigan's that evening was like a family reunion. It was a great time, but I could not keep thoughts of what could happen the following day out of my mind. I was distracted, and as soon as I finished my dinner, I excused myself. I wanted to get back to my room and try to get a good night's rest.

My dad followed me out of the restaurant. He put his hands on my shoulders and said, "Son, no matter what happens tomorrow, I want you to know I'm proud of you."

"It's not over yet, Dad. We've got a lot of work to do tomorrow," I said.

"I know we do. We'll go get 'em tomorrow."

Shortly after ten that evening, I heard rain beating against my window. I opened the front door, and my heart sank. It was a downpour, and if it lasted long, the sixth round would be postponed. I sure as hell did not want to have to face the final round twice.

The morning finally arrived, and the sun was shining brightly. It was one of those perfect days for golf. There was not a breath of wind, the course was soft, and the tees were up. I knew the course would play easy under those conditions, so I thought I had to be under par if I was going to make it. I was ready. I could do it.

Although I felt good on the first tee, I pulled my drive into the woods on the left. From there I was able to put it in the bunker guarding the right side of the green. The wet sand caused me to misjudge my bunker shot, and I left it ten feet short. I stroked the putt well, but it spun out after catching the right lip. A bad start. I needed to be under par for the day and I opened with a bogey.

We had a ten-minute wait before we could tee off on two, and I tried to collect my thoughts and my emotions. I was in a position that I would not have believed possible a year earlier. I had a chance to get my card going into the final round of Q-School, and I was not about to let it slip away. I had to grind. I had to concentrate. I could still do it.

It turned around for me on the second hole. I hit a six-iron to within twenty feet and knocked it in for birdie, and I was back to even for the day.

I got two more birdies over the next nine holes, so I was two under for the day and four under for the tournament going into twelve. The twelfth hole was a short par four, just a three-iron and wedge. I got too quick on the tee shot and hooked it badly. It stayed in bounds by two feet, but I had no shot to the green. It was behind a bush, and the smart thing to do was chip it back to the fairway and take my medicine. After studying the shot for a few minutes, I decided there was a good chance I could get the ball up quickly enough to clear the bush. It was risky, but I was on the bubble and a bogey might be fatal. I began to take practice swings, and my club hit the bush on the follow-through.

"What are you doing?" my dad asked with panic in his voice.

"Don't worry, I'm going to chip it out."

"Good" was his only response.

He took the cart back to the fairway to wait for my chip. I decided to go for it. I put a mighty swing on the ball with my wedge, and cleared the bush by inches. The ball made it to the front of the green.

When I got back to the cart, my dad had his head in his hands. "Carl, don't ever scare me like that again," he said.

I two-putted for my par and went on to get a solid par on the thirteenth. The fourteenth was the toughest hole on the course. It was a long, dogleg left, with out-of-bounds close to the right side of the fairway. If I could get past that hole with a par, I was golden. I pushed my drive slightly, but the soft course saved me. I was not more than twenty feet from the OB stakes. I pushed my four-iron again, but I hit it pin high, just off the right side of the green. My chip shot was good, but it stopped six feet short. My par putt died on the lip. A bogey. I was back to one under for the day.

As I waited to hit my drive on fifteen, I told myself, "This is it. This is what it is all about. Suck it up, and hit some solid shots." I thought four pars would probably make it, but three pars and a birdie would make it for sure.

A good drive and a seven-iron left me with thirty-five feet for birdie. I hit the best putt ever that did not go in the hole. It melted over the left lip. "A par is good," I said to my dad as I handed him my putter.

The sixteenth was a four-iron par three, and I hit a great shot. It was fading gently into the pin, but the soft green would not let it release, so I had a twelve-footer for birdie. This time I burned the right lip, but once again I had to settle for par. Although I wanted a birdie badly, I was feeling good. I was swinging great and my stroke on the greens was smooth. Surely, I would get a birdie on one of the last two holes.

A great drive and a solid nine-iron left me with eight feet for birdie on seventeen. But once again, I hit a good putt that just would not drop.

The eighteenth hole was a difficult, three-shot par five. The only way I could bogey was by missing the fairway, so I used my three-wood off the tee, even though I had been hitting my driver great all day. Big mistake. It was one of those decisions that, in retrospect, you wonder what the hell you could have been thinking. I let the tee shot get away from me on the right. It cleared the first stand of trees and was headed for Oscar Brown country. Time seemed to stand still, and I think my heart stopped beating. After what seemed like an eternity, the marshal signaled that the ball was in bounds. My heart began to pound so hard, it made my shirt flutter.

When I got to my ball, I saw that I had a small opening through the trees to the fairway. The safe play, however, was to punch it out to the left, but that would leave me a long iron to the small, well-guarded green. I looked over toward my dad, and he was so white he looked like a ghost. "Are you all right?" I asked.

He didn't say a word, but he did manage to nod up and down.

I did not like the idea of hitting a long iron into that green, and the opening to the fairway was large enough that a well-struck shot would make it through easily. If I deserved my card, I should be able to hit a solid shot under pressure. I had to go for it.

I put a good swing on the ball with my one-iron, but I pulled the shot slightly. Nonetheless, it caught the left side of the fairway, 150 yards from the green. When I got back to the cart, my dad gave me a forced smile, but he was still white as a sheet and still uncharacteristically silent. "Center of the green, and we'll make it," I said.

He responded with a goofy smile and a nod.

The approach shot was as easy as it gets. The pin was on the left side of the green, with a gentle right-to-left breeze. All I had to do was hit it at the center of the green and let it drift toward the pin.

I took a good swing at it, but the ball squirted off my nine-iron toward the right. It caught the right edge of the green but took a small hop to the right. It ended up between the fringe and the bunker.

My heart was pounding. If I did not get it up-and-down, there was no chance I would get my card. I used the L wedge, and the instant the club met the ball, I thought I hit it too hard. But the ball hit the green softly and trickled a foot past the hole. I was golden. I could not miss a one-footer. I had my card. At least, I was pretty sure I had my card.

I walked over to the edge of the green to wait while my playing partners putted out. They were near the cut line too, so they were taking plenty of time with their putts. As the minutes dragged by, my confidence about the one-footer began to wane. "Just hit it firm and you can't miss it," I told myself at least a dozen times. When it was finally my turn to putt, I lined the one-footer up carefully. I did not see any break, but I still wanted to hit it firm so the grain couldn't throw it off line. My hands were shaking like leaves on a tree in West Texas as I stood over the ball. I was not thinking clearly, but I could still hear the voice in the back of my mind: *Hit it firm. Hit it firm.*

I hit it so hard the ball jumped up when it hit the back of the cup, but it did fall in. I had made it. I had earned my card. I was ecstatic, but at the same time my body felt like lead. I had used up all my available energy for the day.

My dad and I hurried over to the scoreboard. We believed we were in, but if a few guys who teed off before me had low numbers, there was still a chance I would come up a stroke short.

Given my anxiety, there was simply too much information to digest. My dad finally asked, "What's it going to take?"

"Three under," the official answered without turning around.

Finally, I could relax. I could savor the sense of exhilaration that engulfed my body.

I was dissecting my round with some of the other guys when an official approached me. "Carl, you're one of ten guys who tied for thirty-seventh place. We have to have a playoff."

I panicked. "You mean it's not over?"

"No, no. The low forty plus ties make it. You've got your card. We just have to establish the rankings."

I still did not understand what he was talking about, but as long as I did not have to worry about my card, I did not mind the playoff. We teed off in two threesomes and a foursome. Mike Smith and I birdied the hole, seven guys got pars, and John Adams, a veteran player, made bogey. He did not seem concerned, and his casual attitude about being the first person eliminated convinced me that the playoff was a mere formality. It would be another month before I learned how wrong I was.

Mike and I played two more holes. We both parred the first one, but my par on the second beat his bogey, so I had the thirty-seventh ranking and he had number thirty-eight.

I had to stay in Haynes City for the three-day business school for all the first-time qualifiers, but that evening Heather and I drove to Disney World to celebrate. I had never been in such a celebratory mood. We went to the Outback for dinner and drank a good deal of Australian beer. We did not talk much that evening. There did not seem to be much left to say, and I felt too tired to try to put my thoughts into words. We mostly grinned at each other.

The three days of the business school passed quickly, maybe because I was still in a daze. We were given suggestions about financial planning, dealing with the press, and adjusting to life on the road. The best part of the experience was that it gave me a chance to get to know the other guys. Joe Acosta and I spent some time together, perhaps because we were the two youngest guys there, and we decided to room together come January.

During lunch one day, we were trading stories about the tournament and one of the guys told me about something odd that happened during the final round. Tom Scherrer, a University of North Carolina grad who had been runner up to Justin Leonard in the 1992 U.S. Amateur, called a penalty stroke on himself. His dad, who was caddying for him, got careless on one hole. As he was looking for a yardage marker, he accidentally kicked Tom's ball and moved it a few inches. No one but Tom and his dad noticed it, but Tom called the penalty on himself. His dad was on the verge of tears, because he knew how big that stroke might turn out to be.

What Tom did was far from unusual. You hear stories all the time about guys on the Tour who call penalties on themselves when no one else noticed the infraction. I have done it myself in college tournaments. It points out, I think, how different golf is from other sports, and how different golfers are from other athletes. Can you imagine a major league baseball player who was called safe on a close play at first telling the umpire, "No, I'm out. I heard the ball hit his glove before my foot hit the bag." It has never happened, and it will never happen.

It is a common occurrence to ask officials for a ruling during a tournament, and much of the time the ruling will not be as favorable as the player thinks it should be. But I have never seen a player scream at an official and make nasty comments about his heritage the way athletes in other sports do every day. I would not go so far to say that golfers have more integrity and more class than other professional athletes, but the way golfers conduct themselves does make me proud to be part of the game.

I still had not recovered from the tension when I returned to Columbia. I felt good, but I felt very tired. I did not want to do anything but sleep and drink a lot of beer. And that's what I did for an entire week.

I could not wait for January.

## CHAPTER 5

## *A Slow Start*

Although I had had only about four hours sleep the previous night, the adrenaline was pumping and I was wide awake and alert. I was somewhere over the Pacific Ocean on my way to Hawaii for my first PGA event of the 1995 season, the United Airlines Hawaiian Open. As I stared vacantly through the window at the clouds, several images raced through my mind. I smiled as I remembered my imaginary matches with Jack Nicklaus and Tom Watson. Here I was, ten years later, on my way to play those guys for real. There were brief moments when I thought I had to be dreaming. It was too exciting to be true.

If I was to make it out there, however, I could not be starstruck. "You earned your way to the Tour," I reminded myself. "You proved you've got the game to compete with anyone." I forced myself to review my accomplishments: the college tournaments I won, the former Tour winners

I beat at Q-School. Within seconds, though, the pure excitement of my adventure would reassert itself and I would be reduced once again to thinking, like a little kid on the night before Christmas, "You're on your way to a PGA event. You're about to tee it up with guys you've been watching on television your whole life. You're one of them, one of the best golfers in the world." It was an exquisite feeling.

At that moment, Brett Pendergast, my seat mate and one of my best friends from college, began to stir. He had been one of the top junior golfers in Virginia, and he was coming to Hawaii to caddy for me. The send-off party my family and friends had had the night before had taken its toll on Brett, and he did not have any trouble sleeping on the plane.

"Are we almost there?" he asked while he stretched, trying to get the kinks out of his back.

"About another half hour."

"Do you want to take a look at the course when we get there?" he asked.

"No, I think we should get settled in tonight. I'm beat, I just want a good night's sleep. We can check out the course tomorrow." We were staying with an old Marine friend of Brett's dad.

We talked for a few more minutes, each of us pretending to be more casual and matter-of-fact about the upcoming week than we felt. I was glad Brett wanted to come along with me. It would be great to have a friend along to share my excitement.

Forty-five minutes later, I learned a not-so-exciting aspect of Tour life. My luggage, including my clubs, was lost. I tried to stay cool, but the agent could hear the panic in my voice and promised to let me know as soon as he learned anything. There was nothing to do except try to get a good night's rest — if I could stop worrying about my clubs.

The airline called early Saturday morning. They had located

my luggage, but it would not arrive until late Saturday evening. I had hoped to practice some that morning, but not having my clubs made that impossible. Although I was antsy to hit some balls, I did not mind too much. It gave Brett and me an excuse to spend the day at the beach, surfing. The waves were lousy on the East Coast, and I had given up the sport shortly after moving away from California.

On Sunday, I spent four hours on the range. December in Virginia Beach had been bitterly cold. I didn't get to practice much, and I needed the work. There are some guys who claim they do not need to hit balls between tournaments, but I have trouble believing it. I can tell when I go three days without practicing. It is not much of a difference, but a single stroke over two days is all that separates the guys who make the cut from those who do not. I knew I had to be at the top of my game if I was to have any chance of playing over the weekend in my first tournament.

I made it to the course by nine o'clock Monday morning to register for the tournament. My check for the $100 entry fee was in hand as I approached the woman at the registration table. "Hi, I'm here for the tournament. Paulson, Carl Paulson."

"Good morning. Welcome to Hawaii." She checked her papers for several minutes before looking up. "I'm sorry, but I have you listed as the sixth alternate. Do you have a commitment number?"

The blood rushed from my head and I suddenly felt a little dizzy. I did not know what she was talking about. "I'm not sure what you mean. I called the Tour office Friday morning and they said I was in."

"Did they give you a commitment number?"

"Actually, my dad called for me. I'll have to check with him."

"That would be a good idea," she said. "There were a number of players who committed late on Friday. Do you know what time your father called?"

"It was sometime in the morning." I felt crushed. It was becoming clear that I was not going to be able to play in the tournament. But I also felt terribly confused. I had earned my card. I was on the Tour. What the hell was going on?

Before two hours had passed, I had learned a great deal about how PGA events work. When my dad called the PGA office on Friday morning, he was told that I was in, but that did not really mean I was in. It meant only that as of that moment, I was in. Players have until five P.M., or thirty minutes after play ends on the Friday before a tournament, to commit, and there had been an unusually large number of last-minute commitments for Hawaii. Had I known about the procedure, I would have waited until Saturday before spending a small fortune on the airfare.

I also learned what the playoff at the end of the Q-School tournament was all about. I assumed that since I had earned my card, I could play in any PGA event I wanted to. It turned out that those of us who had finished in the top forty were well down the list of priority rankings that determined eligibility to play in tournaments. First on the list were all the players who had won the U.S. Open or PGA Championship prior to 1970, as well as players who had won one of the four majors, the Players Championship, or the World Series of Golf during the previous ten years. Second were those players who had won a Tour event during the previous two years. Third were about sixteen special exemptions. These included eight sponsors' exemptions, two foreign players designated by the commissioner, several PGA sectional pros, and four Monday qualifiers. Several of the players who were in the first category were seniors and no longer entered PGA Tour events, but if everyone in the first three categories wanted to play in a given week, they would take up more than two-thirds of the field.

And all of these people were ahead of the top 125 money winners from the previous year. There were about 65 players in the top 125 who were not in one of the preceding categories, so that brought the number of eligible players up to about 180. And the field for events scheduled before daylight saving time kicks in was limited to 144 players.

After the top 125 money winners come about a half-dozen special medical exemptions. These are followed by the top five money winners from the Nike Tour, and then we finally get to my category, the top forty from Q-School. The sixth through tenth leading money winners from the Nike Tour were mixed in with us, and our priority ranking was based on our finish. The winner of the 1994 tournament, Woody Austin, had the No. 1 ranking, and since I had won the sudden-death playoff, I began the year with a priority ranking of forty-second. At any rate, I learned there were approximately 220 players who were ahead of me on the eligibility list.

I discovered a few weeks later how John Adams could be so cavalier about making bogey on the first hole of the playoff. He had sponsors' exemptions for the first five events, so his ranking was irrelevant. The priority rankings for the Q-School graduates are reshuffled about every two months, with the new rankings de-termined by the amount of money won in those events. Needless to say, this put those of us near the bottom of the list in a tough spot. We could not get into events early in the year, so we had no chance of improving our position when the rankings were reshuffled.

After all of this was sorted out and I came to understand why I was not playing, I felt foolish. Several of my friends, I learned later, knew about these priority rankings. I suppose I should have known that not everyone who wanted to enter an event would be able to play, but I had spent so much of my time on the course on weekend afternoons that I never heard the television commentators talk about it.

My dad, in his typical military style, was furious about it.

When he called the PGA office that morning to find out what was going on, he had what he characterized as a "Marine conversation" with the official there. Later, he sheepishly admitted that the official didn't appreciate the Marines' style of communication.

When it finally settled in that I was out of the tournament, I said to Brett, "Well, I guess we might as well go back home."

He was feeling bad for me, but when he said "I suppose you're right," I could tell he did not really mean it.

"On second thought, let's not go back," I said. "We're already here in Hawaii, we've got a place to stay for the week, and it would cost us more to change our plane tickets than to spend the week here."

"You're right," Brett said. "I think we should do the smart thing and stay. After all, it's twenty degrees back home. You need to be here so you can practice, and I'm willing to stick around and do what I can to help."

I do not think it would be possible to imagine a worse way to begin my PGA career, but it turned out to be a good week nonetheless. Brett and I played golf every morning and spent the afternoons at the beach, surfing and relaxing. It would be some time before I would forget my disappointment, but surfing in Hawaii sure beat sitting at home, in freezing weather, waiting for the first minitour event of the year.

I was not able to get into the tournaments in Tucson or Phoenix, and I spent the two weeks with Chris Anderson, my friend from the minitour, in California. I practiced hard those two weeks, since I was confident I would be playing in the pro-am at Pebble Beach during the first week in February. It was played over three courses, which made it possible to have a larger field.

I drove up to Carmel on Sunday, and it was a nightmare. I had never been to that part of California, and it is hard enough to find your way around under ordinary circumstances. But they had heavy rains all winter, so several of the regular parking lots were closed. I had to park several blocks from the course and carry my clubs to the range. After dropping my bag off near the range, I realized I had no idea where to go to register. Everything was new to me, and I felt like a little kid who was off to summer camp for the first time.

I finally managed to get registered, only to learn that all the tournament courses were closed until Wednesday because of the rain. I was not pleased to discover that I would be playing in my first PGA event on two courses I had never seen before, Pebble Beach and Poppy Hills. I had played Spyglass in college.

I ran into Dicky Thompson, whom I knew from my minitour days, and we agreed to meet at Spanish Bay the following morning for a practice round. I would have preferred to play one of the tournament courses, but I was excited about playing Spanish Bay. I had heard a lot of good things about the course, and I was looking forward to seeing it.

Dicky and I had hit our tee shots from the first tee when the starter called out to us, "Hold up a minute, guys. I'm sending a twosome out with you. They'll meet you at the white tees."

"Great," I said to Dicky. "We'll probably get a couple of hackers and we'll spend the next six hours looking for balls."

We drove our cart down the hill and around the bend to the white tees, and I could not believe my eyes. It was Dr. J—Julius Erving, whom I had watched play basketball on television hundreds of times when I was a kid. He was playing in the tournament as an amateur. I jumped out of the cart to introduce myself. When we shook hands, his was so big that it seemed to wrap around mine twice.

The four of us hit it off immediately and we had a great time. Dr. J almost had an ace on the back nine. His eight-iron left the ball hanging over the lip of the cup. Near the end of the round he mentioned that he was announcing an NBA doubleheader on

Sunday. "But what if you make the cut?" I asked. The tournament did not end until late Sunday afternoon.

"I don't have much to worry about," he said. "I'm playing to a twelve this week."

We all laughed. While he was capable of hitting some good shots, he did not have much of a chance of breaking 90. After the round, I had a picture taken of the two of us, and he gave me a few autographed photos of himself that I could send to my cousins.

Later that evening, I called Brett to tell him about my first "official" practice round. He was as big a sports nut as I, so he was duly impressed with my meeting Dr. J. "Man, you've got life by the tail," he said.

"Yeah, I suppose I do." At that moment, I felt as if I was on top of the world. I would never have guessed that within weeks I could feel so differently.

I arrived at the course about nine the following morning for some serious practicing. I did not see any of the handful of guys I knew, so I went to the end of the range where I could hit balls in relative solitude. I hit about thirty wedges, then switched to an eight-iron. I had hit about ten balls when the man behind me hit his ball at the precise moment I made contact with mine. The two balls soared through the air within inches of each other, and at the apex of their arc, they appeared to brush against each other before falling back to the earth. They hit the ground at precisely the same instant, within inches of each other. I turned around to see who had hit the other ball, and it was Jack Nicklaus, the man I beat so many times during my childhood, imaginary matches.

"Did you see that?" he asked. "Wasn't that amazing?"

"Uh . . . eh . . . ah." I couldn't get a word out. Several very awkward seconds passed before I was able to say something clever like "Yeah, that was amazing."

All I could think about as I turned back to my eight-iron was that I was really there, I was actually on the Tour, warming up for a PGA event next to Jack Nicklaus. But a disconcerting thought crept into the back of my mind. I wondered if I really belonged there.

I was impressed with how easily Jack had spoken to me. Most people would agree that he is the greatest golfer ever, yet he gave me the impression that he would have gladly chatted with me had I enough presence to think of anything to say. I hoped I would have a fraction of his stature twenty years down the road, and I hoped that the new kids on the Tour would see me as being as approachable as Nicklaus appeared to be.

Thursday finally arrived, and I was scheduled to play my first round at Poppy Hills. As I looked down the first fairway, I said to my caddy, "Where the hell am I supposed to hit this?" The fairway looked like a narrow ribbon and the rough was at least five inches high. I had never played on courses like that. There were a few first-rate courses on the minitour and Hooters Tour, but the rough was never anything like what I saw that first day. As I would learn in the coming months, Poppy Hills was not an exception. Every week I would be playing tougher courses, under tougher conditions, than I had ever experienced.

Poppy Hills turned out to be an extremely difficult course for me. It did not have any bailout areas, it did not offer any options for playing it safe. You either hit perfect shots or you were facing the possibility of bogey or worse. Although I shot 74 that first round, I was not that disappointed. I played well to keep it to two over.

My second round was at Spyglass Hill, a course I had played in college. The first time I played Spyglass in college, I thought it was a great course, and Friday's round reinforced my opinion. Along with being a first-class test of golf, the course is absolutely beautiful. The first five holes are open, almost a links-type course. You can see the ocean, and the holes wind through countless dunes.

Beginning with the sixth hole, the fairways are lined by the huge trees so typical of California.

My definition of a great course is that it demands that you do everything well if you plan to post a good score, and Spyglass fits the bill perfectly. It quickly reveals any weaknesses in your game.

I played solid golf that Friday and finished with an even-par 72.

Saturday I played at Pebble Beach, and what more can I say about the course that has not been said before. It is as beautiful as any course in the world, and while not quite as exacting as Spyglass, it is an excellent test of golf. I felt fortunate to have the opportunity to play the course.

I was in the first group to tee off, and everything came together for me on the front nine. I hit the ball solidly, the putts dropped as expected, and I walked off the ninth green three under for the day. Suddenly, I had a chance to make the cut. After Friday's round, it looked as though one or two under would make it. If I could shoot even par on the back nine, the odds were good that I would be playing over the weekend. One under would do it for sure.

When we arrived at the tenth tee, we discovered there were still four groups waiting to tee off. Because of the short January days, they had to send people off the first and tenth tees and they hadn't counted on anyone playing the first nine in two hours. By the time I hit my tee shot on ten, forty-five minutes later, I had lost my rhythm. I played the back nine in three over and missed the cut by three strokes. I simply had too much time to think between nines.

The following week I was able to get into the Buick Invitational at Torrey Pines. I played well on Thursday, finishing with a 70. I had a good chance to make the cut, but my three birdies on Friday weren't enough to offset four bogeys and I missed the cut by two shots.

Patrick Burke was one of my playing partners for the two rounds. His first year out on tour was 1990, and he had to return to Q-School each year. We talked some about how tough it was to get established, to get to the point where you did not have the sense you were struggling to stay above water. He had not lost any of his determination to make it, however, and he did go on to have a good year and make the top 125.

It was clear to me I would have to improve if I was ever going to make a cut. I thought I had played well in my first two events, and yet I missed the cut in both of them. I was not so naive as to think I would set the world on fire my first month out, but I did believe that as long as I played my game, I would do okay. Obviously, "my game" was not going to get me anywhere. I was beginning to appreciate what it meant to compete against the best players in the world.

I just missed getting into the Bob Hope Classic, so I spent the week with Chris Anderson again. I took a couple of days off, but from Monday through Saturday I spent nearly eight hours per day at the course practicing. It was frustrating, because I was not sure exactly what I should be working on. I was doing everything pretty well, but I had to find a way to shave a stroke and a half off my scores. I talked to Butch a couple of times that week, and because he could not see me swing, he did not have much to offer. "Keep practicing. It will come around for you," he told me. And practice I did. I averaged hitting five hundred balls a day that week. I sure as hell was not going to fail from lack of effort.

I did get into the Los Angeles Open during the last week in February 1995. Corporate sponsorship of events mushroomed during the 1980s, and the L.A. Open was not immune. It became the

Nissan Open sometime during the late 1980s, but I never heard it referred to as that by any of the players. It will probably remain the L.A. Open for the players for another generation.

I liked Riviera a lot, and I thought it was the sort of course I could do well on. I do not know what happened, but I shot 77-76 to miss the cut by ten shots. Again, I did not have the sense that I played badly, but the breaks were not falling my way. I missed a half-dozen fairways by less than a yard, and another half-dozen greens by the same distance. And every time I was a yard off, I made bogey. It was frustrating.

That Friday night, after missing my third consecutive cut, the thrill of simply being out on tour was fading fast. I felt good about my first two tournaments. Missing the cut by only a couple of strokes indicated that everything would fall into place as soon as I became a little more comfortable out there. But missing the cut by ten shots was another story, especially since I had not played that badly. For the first time in quite some while, I felt discouraged about my prospects.

Talking to Heather that evening did not improve my mood. We had been together for more than two years, and we had always assumed that when the time was right, we would get married. I had talked to her every day since leaving for Hawaii, but she seemed to be growing increasingly impatient with my absence. I would have predicted that she would be my biggest supporter, but she was un-happy that I stayed in California during my two weeks off rather than returning to Columbia. I explained to her that even with the support of my sponsors, I had to be careful about costs. Also, the weather was too unpredictable in Columbia at that time of year to ensure that I would be able to practice every day. She said she understood, but her tone of voice made it obvious that she did not.

At any rate, the western leg of the Tour was over. I was confi-dent that my play would improve once we moved back east where I felt more comfortable. The grasses are different on the West Coast and I could never capture the same confidence, especially on the greens, that I typically had while standing over the ball back east.

I was not able to get into the tournament at Doral, so I had a week off before playing during the second week of March at the Honda, in Fort Lauderdale. My dad came down to watch me play, and it was nice to have a friendly face around. I had learned that the camaraderie that came so easily on the minitours and the Hooters Tour was not a part of the PGA Tour. Everyone was friendly in the locker room and on the course, but once the round ended, you were pretty much on your own. No one would get a bunch of the guys together to have a few beers and shoot a little pool. Perhaps it was because so many of the guys were traveling with their families. Maybe people took the PGA Tour more seriously than the minor leagues. Whatever it was, an exciting night for me was having a movie scheduled on HBO that I had not seen.

I hit a new low at the first round of the Honda—an emotional low, that is. I shot a big, fat, ugly 82. I could not believe it. I expected to shoot some low numbers in Florida, and instead I had my worst round of the year. Friday was a completely different day, but my one-under-par 71 was too little, too late. I missed the cut by eleven shots.

That night at dinner, my dad wanted to give my spirits a boost, but I wanted to talk about anything except golf. I made a few halfhearted attempts to get him to talk about the Hornets, the NBA team I adopted while living in Columbia, but he was not having any of it.

"Come on, Carl. You've only played in five tournaments. You can't get discouraged so soon."

"I know, Dad. But you can't imagine how much it hurts to be out of a tournament after the first nine holes. It's unbelievably frustrating."

"You know it always takes you a while to adjust when you move up to the next level. You've got to give yourself a little time. You made it to the Tour much sooner than anyone expected, and what you need more than anything right now is a little patience."

"I know. I'm trying. I just didn't know how hard it would be. Everyone out here is a great player. I'm not sure anymore that I'm in the same league with them."

My dad spent the next fifteen minutes trying to convince me of the folly of my self-doubt, and I appreciated his efforts. But he could not understand, not really. No one who had not spent some time beating his brains out trying to compete against the best players in the world could fully understand how difficult it was to be a stroke or two behind everyone else. It was especially hard since I believed that I had that stroke or two, maybe even more, within me somewhere and I just could not get it to come out.

The following week's event, at Bay Hill, was a popular one since Arnold Palmer was the host, so I had the week off. The week after Bay Hill was the Players Championship, so I had yet another week to work on my game.

During the last week in March, I was able to get into the Freeport-McMoran Classic in New Orleans. During Thursday's round, I hit the ball from tee to green as well as I had all year, but my putting was awful. It had been reasonably good all year, so I was surprised to have so much trouble on the greens. It was a new kind of frustration. I managed only two birdies against four bogeys to end the first round at a two-over 74.

I was feeling pretty low that evening when I called Heather. Before I had a chance to tell her about my round, she dropped a bombshell on me.

"I think we ought to start dating other people," she said.

"Why, what's wrong?" Her words made me tense, but I wasn't too concerned. She had been hinting at this for the previous month.

I assumed that with a little more time she would adjust to my being gone so much.

"Carl, I can't go on like this. When you're gone, I feel like I have no life. It scares me, and this is the only thing I know to do about it."

"But you knew it would be like this. You need to give yourself some time to adjust."

"No, Carl. I can't do it. I'm sorry." The line went dead. I immediately called back, but she would not answer the phone.

I was devastated. It felt as if someone had kicked me in the stomach. I loved Heather and I assumed we'd always be together. I did not know if I could handle this. But I did not have much choice.

The second round passed in a haze. I shot 72 and missed the cut by three shots.

With the Masters and the MCI Classic in Hilton Head coming up, I knew I would have a couple of weeks off, so I returned to Virginia Beach to spend some time with my parents. I especially wanted to talk to my mother about Heather. There was nothing she could say that would make the pain go away, but my mom has always been able to help me feel better. She has a much different perspective about my golf career than my dad. While my dad would be disappointed if I told him I did not like the life of a nomad and that I wanted to settle down and join him in his mortgage company, he would accept it, however reluctantly. He loves golf, and he loves having the opportunity to be my biggest fan. My mom, on the other hand, cares if I succeed only because she knows it is so important to me. She probably would be just as happy if I were to settle down so I could come over for dinner regularly.

It helped some to be home, but I missed Heather badly. We did talk on the phone every few days, but they were painful, sorrowful conversations. She was adamant that building a new life without me was the only way she could escape the abyss she had slipped into.

I decided to use the time off to switch irons. I had used the Ping Zing-2 since turning pro, and they were fine clubs. But I was looking for something that would give me a little more feedback as to how I was hitting the ball. Pings have so many self-correcting features built into them that as long as you hit the ball anywhere on the clubface, it is likely to be a decent shot.

Putting away the Pings wasn't an easy decision, since it meant that I would lose what for me was a sizable amount of money. Ping offered pros who were just getting started a nice bonus if they used their clubs in at least fifteen events.

I settled on the Mizuno MP29 blades. I liked the looks of the clubs and I felt comfortable with them in my hands. It seemed easier for me to work the ball with the Mizunos—from left to right, right to left, low, and high. Mizuno had a pool arrangement with players in my category. The endorsement fee would depend on how high we finished on the money list. Since my official winnings were a big goose egg, I was not expecting anything for using their clubs. I sure would not have minded, though, receiving a fraction of what they were paying Nick Faldo.

All golfers have the feeling they can improve just enough to beat the guys in their regular group if they can find the right clubs, and we pros are no different. I had already been through my share of clubs, and I was still relatively new at it. In my old room at my parents' house, I have four staff bags stuffed with clubs. One has three sets of irons, including two of the sets I played with as a kid. My very first set were MacGregor Tourney irons, and when I outgrew them I moved up to a set of MacGregor Nicklaus's. During high school I played with Taylor Made irons, and then switched to the Ping Eye-2 at South Carolina. Ping sponsored our golf team, so I had access to any of their clubs while I was there. The second bag is filled with putters and wedges. Currently, I use the Snake-Eyes wedges and the Titleist, Scotty Cameron putter. I carry three or four of his putters with me, all of which feel pretty much the same. Sometimes I want a different look to the putter, but I do not want it to perform differently. The third bag is filled with nothing but three-woods, and the fourth has another set of irons and about twenty drivers. I used a Taylor Made driver for some time, but the shaft broke off at the hosel. I tried about ten of their drivers that were supposedly identical to the one that I had, but none of them felt the same to me. I wish I could find another Taylor Made driver that performed like the one I had, because I loved that club. But I have not been able to, and consequently I have switched to the Great Big Bertha.

I have learned that pros can have widely different attitudes about clubs. Some are like me, and are reluctant to make a change. Others are constantly looking for something a little better and will change a wedge, a putter, or even a driver between rounds in the middle of a tournament. While some guys swear that equipment can make a significant difference, I believe they could give us all the same clubs and, after we had some time to get used to them, we would all play about the same as we had been playing with our own. If there is an advantage in equipment, it is mostly psychological. What I want most in a club is something that looks good to me and something that sets up to the ball well. I can have confidence in a club like that, and I need that confidence to play well.

My next tournament was the Shell Houston Open at the end of April. My opening round of 72 put me in a position to make the cut, but three consecutive bogeys during the middle of the second round put me out of it yet again. My score of 145 was two strokes off the cut line. I was beginning to wonder if I would go the entire year without playing on the weekend.

I spent the next two weeks in Virginia Beach working with

Butch. My game from tee to green seemed to be coming around, but my putting was getting worse. I reached the point where I felt grateful if I could get a five-footer into the cup. Of course, while Butch was watching me, I could not miss a putt of that length and he did not see anything wrong with my stroke. He talked to me about the importance of confidence, but how could I feel confident when I couldn't sink a putt to save my soul when it counted?

The third week of May 1995, I was able to get into the Buick Classic at Westchester. As usual, I flew in on Sunday night to play in the pro-am on Monday. The name pros are invited to play in the regular Wednesday pro-am, and those of us who are not yet household names have the opportunity to play in the sponsors' pro-am on Monday. The $500 fee comes in handy, and most tournaments throw in a courtesy car as well. My ability to enjoy anything related to golf had dropped precipitously over the previous two months, so the prospect of playing another six-hour round with high handicappers was not especially pleasant. But I made the best of it. I had met a number of really pleasant, interesting people and I already had quite a collection of business cards from partners who offered to take me to dinner the next time I was in town.

I played reasonably well on Monday, and even made a few par-saving putts. I hoped it was a sign of what might come later in the week.

I spent eight to nine hours at the course on both Tuesday and Wednesday. My routine for Tuesday was to play a practice round in the morning to learn what shots I needed to work on for the week. After lunch, I would hit balls on the range for a couple of hours, then spend another couple of hours chipping and putting. On Wednesday, I would spend all day at the course, practicing a solid seven hours.

By the time I dragged myself to bed that Wednesday night in New York, I was as miserable as I had ever been in my life. Not only was I not having any fun on the golf course, I was not having any fun anywhere. I did not like what had happened to me. I have always been a fierce competitor and I never have been able to accept playing badly. But in the past, I was always able to put my bad rounds behind me within a half hour of leaving the course.

I could not seem to do that anymore. I liked to think of myself as a gregarious person who was fun to be around, but I had become sullen and chronically unhappy. All I did was wake up, go to the course to practice or play, have dinner, and go back to the motel room to stare at the tube for a couple of hours before falling asleep. What kind of life was that?

I thought back to early February when I was so excited to be at Pebble Beach. I remembered Brett telling me that I had it knocked, and how enthusiastically I had agreed with him. I reminded myself of all the people who have told me that I was living out the fantasy of ten million guys who were struggling to break 90. How could have I let this happen to me? How could I have gone from being almost deliriously happy to feeling miserable and self-pitying in a few short months?

At that moment I made a promise to myself. I resolved to enjoy the rest of the year even if I did not make a single cut. After all, I was only in the second year of my five-year plan. I had lots of time to develop my game, and in the meantime, I was gaining valuable experience. My friends were right, it was probably true that there were ten million golfers who would gladly trade places with me, so I owed it to them, and to myself, to enjoy the moment. Even if I never developed to the point where I could be competitive on the Tour, I was collecting memories that would last for the rest of my life. And I damn sure wanted them to be good memories.

To act on my good intentions, I called an old roommate from

college, Morgan Beam, who was living in Philadelphia. I asked him if he wanted to come up to Westchester and watch me play and go out on the town Friday evening. He accepted my invitation with enthusiasm, and it reminded me of how much I missed seeing my friends. I would have never guessed that the Tour could be so lonely.

After I hung up the phone, I thought about my golf game. Despite my moments of self-doubt, I fervently believed I had the ability to be competitive on tour. I hadn't seen anyone capable of hitting better shots than I could, and I had seen a lot of guys who could not do some of the things with a golf club that I could do. True, my short game was not up to average, but it was steadily improving and I had no reason to think it would not continue to improve.

No, my problem wasn't that I didn't have the ability, my problem was mental. Had I played each round two strokes better, which I was fully capable of doing, I would have made a majority of the cuts in the events I had entered and I probably would have earned enough money to improve my priority ranking. Those two strokes per round had nothing to do with physical skills; they were all psychological. So the solution to my problems was not to practice more, as I had assumed, it was to learn to play smarter. And one aspect of being smarter meant to stop wearing myself out by spending seven or eight hours on the range on Tuesdays and Wednesdays. Hell, most weeks I felt exhausted by the time the tournament began on Thursday. I had to develop a more realistic practice routine. I would practice only enough to stay sharp and focus instead on playing with confidence. If I could let my potential break through, I would be fine.

There was one more thing I had to do if I was to turn things around. Heather and I had talked several times per week since she told me that she could not go on with our relationship. Every time I called her it was with the hope that she had come to her senses and we could be a couple again, but she showed no signs of relenting. It was a crazy way to end a relationship. I had to accept her decision and move on, and I would not be able to do it as long as we stayed in touch. A clean break was the only solution, and I called her to tell her so. I told her I loved her and that I understood how she felt. I hoped she would understand why I could not talk to her again. Who knows, I thought, maybe my commitment to being single again would bring some excitement to my life.

Westchester was not the sort of course you could score on unless you knew it well. I hit the ball okay, but I made enough mistakes to miss the cut by seven shots. It was a struggle, but I reminded myself that I was learning the course and that the experience would be invaluable in the years to come.

Morgan did watch me play on Friday, and that evening we took in a Yankees game, followed by a good dinner with lots of beer to wash it down. I laughed, I had fun. I could feel the old Carl coming back, and I didn't want to lose him again.

CHAPTER 6

*Rotella*

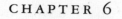

On the flight from New York back to Virginia Beach, I thought about what I could do to break out of my slump. An idea had crossed my mind several times over the previous month, and that was to see Bob Rotella. Over the years, I met several guys who played golf for the University of Virginia, where Rotella was a faculty member, and without exception, they had good things to say about what he had done for them. I also knew that he had worked with a number of the top Tour players, men like Norman, Watson, Faxon, and Price. He had the reputation of being the top sports psychologist in the business, and if I wanted to be the best, I had to work with the best.

I was entered in a Nike event the week after Westchester, the Dominion Classic, held outside Richmond the last week in May. I stayed with my folks in Virginia Beach, since it was only a two-hour drive from their house to the golf course. I spent Monday at Cavalier, working a little with Butch and practicing my short game, and when I got back to my parents' house that afternoon, I decided it was time for action. I called Rotella. He told me he would be glad to work with me, and as it turned out, he didn't have anything scheduled for Tuesday and Wednesday of the following week. He suggested I plan to arrive at his place in Charlottesville around ten-thirty Tuesday morning. I was pleased, since I expected it might be some time before we could get together.

I played well that week in Richmond. It was the first time all year that I played close to the way I knew I was capable of playing. My four rounds of 69, 71, 72, and 68 were good enough for a nineteenth-place finish and a check for $2,000. It was not going to have much effect on my tax bracket, but at least it meant I would not go an entire year without cashing a check. Perhaps the mere decision to do something about my mediocre play and to see Rotella was having an effect.

I spent the three-hour drive to Charlottesville wondering what seeing a psychologist would be like. I appreciated that at the Tour level, golf was 70 to 80 percent mental. No one could get to the Tour without the physical ability to shoot low numbers on a regular basis. So what separated the winners from the also-rans had to be mental toughness. I was skeptical, however, that anyone else could help someone like me make the transition from a struggling neophyte to a solid Tour player. It seemed to me that the mental toughness to do that could only be gained by experience.

But it was hard to argue with all those players who credited Rotella with helping them to get things to fall into place. Since there was so little that separated the winners from the hangers-on, perhaps it took only a slight adjustment to cross that line. I did not know what to expect, but I was excited about the possibilities. It sure could not get any worse.

Rotella's directions were clear enough that I did not have any trouble finding his house. He lived in a nice, heavily wooded neighborhood that was set in the rolling hills near the UVA campus. His daughter, who looked about twelve, answered the door. "You must be the professional golfer," she said. "Come on in. I'll get my dad."

Rotella came up from the basement a moment later. He looked more like a college football coach than a psychologist. At six-feet-two, he was several inches taller than I was, and he still had the build of an athlete at age 50. I heard that he was an all-American lacrosse player in college.

He put me at ease immediately. He had an easy, congenial way about him that made our small talk about my drive to Charlottesville seem unusually comfortable. His wife came into the foyer, and after introducing me to her, he invited me down to his basement.

It was obvious that he spent much of his time down there. It was almost like a separate apartment. The main room was comfortably furnished, complete with a small refrigerator and a television with a VCR. There was an exercise room, filled with a variety of machines and weights at one end of the house, and at the other end was a small bedroom with a private bath. Rotella sat down in one of the leather recliners and motioned for me to sit on the couch.

"Tell me about yourself," he said.

It was not a question I ever liked to answer, but I gave him a brief history of my golf career. I emphasized the point that it always seemed to take me a while to adjust to a higher level of competition, and that I was having a hell of a time adjusting to the competition on the Tour.

"What are your goals? Where do you see yourself going with golf?"

"I want golf to be my career," I answered without hesitation. "I see myself playing on tour for fifteen to twenty years. I want to win a lot of PGA tournaments, but my ultimate goal is to win majors. I want to be known as one of the best players in the world."

He nodded approvingly. Undoubtedly, he had heard similar comments before. "What do you want to work on? What areas of your game need improvement?"

"I think I need to work on my routine, especially with putting. I've been a pretty good putter most of my life, but I've been having trouble with it the past few months. I also need to work on the mental aspects of the game. I know I'm capable of playing much better than I have these past five months, and I can't practice any harder. It seems to me that I won't start playing better until I get my head on straight."

Rotella had an unusual way of communicating. After I answered a question, he would stare directly at me for fifteen to twenty seconds. I wondered if he wanted me to think hard about my answers or if he was thinking hard about them.

He had several more questions as to why I thought the psychological part of my game was in need of the most work. I did not know what else to say. I felt competitive with the other players on tour from tee to green. I had always hit my full shots well, and I was continuing to do so. But I was not scoring. My chipping was off just enough to leave me those dreaded six- to ten-footers for pars. And I had so little confidence in my putting that there were actually times, when I faced an eight-footer for par, that I told myself to leave the ball within tap-in distance for a bogey. It had to be mental, because I had not always felt like that. I have never been the greatest putter in the world, but until recently, I always had the feeling that I could make those six-footers.

Almost two hours into our conversation, he asked a question that really threw me. "What are you thinking about at the moment of truth? What thoughts do you have the instant you begin your swing or your putting stroke?"

It seemed like an easy enough question, but I did not have an answer for it. Rotella gave me plenty of time to think about it. He leaned back in his recliner and folded his hands behind his head. His gaze seemed to fixate on something several feet above my head.

"I'm not sure" was all I could come up with. "I suppose it's some mechanical thought; whatever seems to be working for me at the time. On my full shots, it may be to extend my arms, or to keep my left arm close to my chest on the backswing. When I'm on the greens, I remind myself to stay steady over the ball and to keep the tempo even throughout the stroke. I guess the best answer is that I don't have a consistent thought at the moment of truth."

He let a full minute pass in silence, perhaps to make sure I did not have anything to add. Finally, he said, "That's completely wrong. You are a professional athlete, and professional athletes do not, and cannot, think about the mechanics of what they are doing."

He let that sink it before continuing. "Do you think Joe Montana thinks about cocking his elbow when he throws a pass to Jerry Rice? No, of course not. He sees Jerry Rice running, picks out a target eight to ten yards ahead of him, and throws the ball to the target. Do you understand what I'm saying?"

"I think so," I said.

"Let me give you another example," he continued. "When Michael Jordan is about to shoot a free throw, do you suppose he thinks about his wrist position? He would have the lowest free-throw percentage in the league if he did. He focuses on the rim, probably a small spot on the rim, and releases the ball in precisely the way he has tens of thousands of times before."

"So you're saying I should swing at the ball without thinking about what I'm doing?" His ideas were so foreign to me, I was having trouble taking them in.

"Exactly. Let's talk about your routine on the greens, since that's where you're having the most trouble. After you have lined up your putt, what I want you to do is pick out a target by the hole. If it's a straight putt, it might be something in the hole—a discoloration in the cup, for example. If the putt has some break to it, your target will be on one side of the hole or the other. It can be a blade of grass that stands out, a spike mark, a dead bug, anything. As you stand up to the ball, take two practice strokes while you are looking at your target. After you've done that, position yourself over the ball, then look at your target one last time. Then move your eyes back to the ball, and the instant you have it in sight, begin your stroke. The only thing you should have in your mind is a mental image of that target. I don't want you to think about whether your putter face is square, about swinging with your shoulders, about the tempo of your stroke, about anything mechanical. The target should be the only thought in your mind."

"That's completely different from the way I've been doing things."

"Let me ask you this, Carl. Were you good at any other sports when you were a kid?"

"Yes, I was pretty good at most everything I tried. Next to golf, soccer was my strongest sport. I was good enough to play on southern California select teams and traveling teams. Why?"

"You're a natural athlete, Carl. And so is most everyone you're competing against. I think you'd be surprised to find how many of the guys out there were all-conference, all-state, all-something in basketball, baseball, tennis, or some other sport."

He was right about that. I was not sure if I could think of anyone I met on tour who had not excelled at another sport.

"The point I'm making," Rotella said, "is that you have the athletic ability to be a first-rate golfer. You've probably hit a million balls by now to groove your swing, and you have got to learn to trust it. You've got to learn to hit the ball like Montana throws a pass or like Jordan shoots a free throw. When you're out on the course, you have to pick a target, then trust that your natural ability and your hard work will allow you to react. You can't make it happen out there, you have to let it happen. Act and react, that's the key. You act by focusing on a target, and react when you trust your swing."

"What about full shots?" I asked. "Should I do the same thing?"

"Absolutely. What do you usually look at when you're standing on the tee?"

Again, a simple enough question for which I did not have an answer. "It probably sounds dumb, but I'm not sure. I think about whether it would be better to put the ball down the left or right side of the fairway and I set up to hit it to that position."

"So you don't have a target?"

"I'm not sure. I am thinking about hitting the shot down the right side of the fairway, or an iron to the left side of the green, stuff like that."

"How many free throws do you think Jordan would make if he were aiming in the general vicinity of the basket? Not too damn many, I can tell you that. You should always have a target, no matter what kind of shot, and the smaller the target the better. Rather than aiming for a tree at the end of a dogleg, for instance, focus on a branch on the tree. Or better yet, pick out a leaf on that branch. Instead of aiming for the left side of the green, pick out an edge of a bunker, or the crest of a knoll behind the green. You'll never reach your full potential if you continue to hit the ball in the general direction of where you want it to go. I don't want you to even think about hitting the ball until you've picked out a target."

"You've given me a lot to think about." I was excited by what he had told me, perhaps because it was so different from the way I had always approached the game. It was worth a try, though. Given my performance the first five months of the year, I sure as hell did not have anything to lose.

"What do you say we go out and try some of these ideas," Rotella said.

"Sounds good." I was eager to give it a shot.

We played at a course about thirty minutes from his house that was typically uncrowded during the week. It was a solid course, as difficult as many of the courses we played on tour. The rough, however, was playable, and the greens, while quick, were soft enough to hold shots.

Rotella clearly knew his way around the golf course. He played the back tees with me, and his score was in the mid-70s. He did not do anything spectacularly well, but he was extremely consistent. He must have practiced what he preached, since he seemed to get more out of his swing than most people could.

Starting on the first tee, I concentrated on doing everything Rotella had suggested. I picked a small target for every shot, and as I began each swing I tried to put everything out of my mind except a mental image of the target. It is not the easiest thing in the world to do. More than once I found myself thinking about "thinking about the target."

His approach seemed to work. I played as well as I had all year, finishing with a five-under 67. I made a fistful of putts of six feet or less, and I could feel my confidence returning as I stood over the ball.

Perhaps I took to Rotella's approach so readily because it was consistent with what Butch had been trying to teach me for ten years. Butch's motto had always been KISS—Keep It Simple, Stupid. He had reminded me hundreds of times that the best way to play golf was the way twelve-year-olds play it. They have not had time to clutter their minds with a thousand swing thoughts; they simply walk up to the ball and hit it, believing it will be the best shot of their lives.

About halfway through the round, it became clear to me that Rotella was telling me much the same thing, only with different words. The more things I tried to think about while I was swinging, the more likely I was to get in my own way. I had to free up my mind. I had to forget about mechanics while I was on the course. I had to swing with the same abandon and the confidence I had as a twelve-year-old.

We stopped for dinner at a pub near the campus on the way back from the golf course. Rotella was as much of a sports nut as I was, and we talked mostly about college football and basketball. I had the feeling that I had known him for years, and the time passed quickly.

When we arrived at his house, he motioned for me to follow him down to the basement. "I have some tapes I want you to watch," he said. The first one was of an interview with Nicklaus. The interviewer said to Nicklaus that he had never been known as a good chipper and wondered why that part of the game had been difficult for him. Nicklaus responded that he never felt he had to be a good chipper. He knew that if he could get the ball to within eight feet of the hole, he would make the putt. There was never any doubt in his mind that he would make those eight-footers to save par. And since he did not have to be very good at it to chip the ball to within eight feet, he spent the time on other parts of his game that might have a bigger payoff.

Some people may think Nicklaus was being cocky. After all, no one can make every single eight-footer. But I got the point—at least I think I did. Rotella was telling me that Nicklaus earned his reputation of being the best short putter in the game precisely because he did believe he could make it every time. That confidence—call it cockiness if you like—increased the odds that he would put a smooth stroke on the ball and knock it in the cup. Nothing ruins a swing more quickly than those doubts that have the annoying tendency to creep into the edge of your consciousness.

After watching a few more tapes of some of the best putters in the game, Rotella said, "You have got to remember that every week on the Tour is a putting contest. And you've got to remember that you're a part of it. Most importantly of all, you've got to love the idea of it being a putting contest. You've got to love every opportunity you get to sink a putt for birdie. If you're 130 yards away and you put a wedge fifty feet from the pin, you can't bitch and moan about your poor shot. You've got to love the fact that you have a chance to make that fifty-footer for birdie."

At some level, I knew that nothing he was telling me was new. Everyone knows that you cannot let your bad shots get you down. Everyone knows that you have to love what you are doing out there if you are to have any chance of doing it well. After all, is there a single player who has not said, "I'm going to have some fun out there," when asked how he intended to deal with the pressure of being in contention going into the final round? I know I have said those very words dozens of times, maybe hundreds. But somehow Rotella was able to put a fresh spin on these old, but reliable, ideas. He made it all seem so clear, so simple, and like so much fun.

"I guess you have to love it to the point where it almost makes you sick," I said, feeling his enthusiasm for the subject.

"No, not until you're sick. Would you be sick if you made every eight-footer you looked at? Would you be sick if you made $700,000 or $800,000 every year? Would you be sick if you were such a good putter that everyone else was either jealous or mad at you?"

"Actually, no. I wouldn't be sick. You're right, I think I could enjoy that."

It was past eleven when Rotella stood and said, "It's getting to be time for me to turn it. If you'd like, feel free to watch any of the tapes again. We'll get started about eighty-thirty in the morning." He gave me a pat on the back and headed up the stairs.

I was too excited about all the new ideas to sleep. I watched the tape of Nicklaus again, hoping that some of his confidence might rub off on me.

As promised, Rotella called for me precisely at eight-thirty. His wife and daughter joined us for breakfast, and I was impressed by how relaxed they were with the situation. I was, after all, a stranger to them, but they treated me as if I were a relative who dropped by for a brief visit. When Rotella told me I could stay at his house, I accepted only because I wanted to be gracious. I thought I would be more comfortable in a motel, but as it turned out, I was pleased to have the chance to get to know his family.

After breakfast, we talked for several more hours. He rein-forced many of the ideas we had discussed the previous day. As usual, he would ask questions and then pause after my answers. I realized he wanted me to give my answers with confidence. When I did not feel sure of what I was saying, I had a tendency to babble on. But when I was sure of myself, I gave my answer succinctly and waited for him to respond.

We played again at a different course that afternoon, and his ideas helped me to develop a fresh perspective that made the game more enjoyable. It was amazing to aim at a leaf on a tree 300 yards away and watch the ball fly directly toward it. It was even more fun to have the sense that I could sink every putt I attempted, and to have a good number of them actually fall into the cup. My 66 was one stroke better than my score of the previous day.

About halfway through the back nine, Rotella asked, "Have you ever wondered if you belong on the Tour?"

It was a difficult question. On the one hand, I knew if I was to have any chance of succeeding, I had to believe in myself. The competition was so intense, it left no room for self-doubt. I rarely missed a day without giving myself the pep talk that I could compete with anyone in the world.

But on the other hand, how can you go five months without making a cut and not wonder if you belong out there? Sure, those doubts crossed my mind much more than I liked, but I tried my best never to let them gain a foothold.

"Yes, I suppose I have," I answered simply.

"I'm going to say something to you that I've said to very few guys, so don't take it lightly. Not only do you belong on the Tour, you should be winning tournaments right now. Your game is that good."

I was stunned. I hadn't expected him to make any assessment of my chances of succeeding, other than the usual clichés about "if you work hard . . . ," etc., etc. I felt a surge of confidence. The feeling was so strong, it was as much physical as mental.

"Thanks. I don't know what to say" was all I could manage.

"I mean it, Carl. I won't be the least bit surprised if you accomplish all your goals, and then some. And I think you were right yesterday when you said that what you needed to do was get your mental game straight. I've given you a lot to think about. . . . The rest is up to you."

"You can bet I'm going to try."

After the round, we returned to Rotella's house so I could pack my stuff. After fifteen minutes, he came down to the basement, took two soft drinks from his refrigerator and handed one of them to me. We talked for about twenty minutes, reviewing all the points he wanted me to remember. He signaled that our time together had ended by standing and handing me a bag that included several of the tapes we had watched together and a copy of his book, *Golf Is Not a Game of Perfect.*

I had several days before I had to leave for my next tournament, and I used them to try to make Rotella's ideas a consistent part of my game. Even on the range, I would not hit a shot without first picking out a small target. His approach seemed to have the effect of making practice fun again. I played at Cavalier every day with some of my friends, and I made progress with putting mechanics out of my mind and swinging the way I did when I was twelve.

I could not wait to get back out there.

# CHAPTER 7

## Picking Up Speed

I had committed to play in the Nike Cleveland Open the week of June 14, and I saw it as an opportunity to have a "warm-up" using Rotella's techniques before trying them out in a PGA tournament. Nike tournaments are virtually the same as PGA tournaments except they are on a smaller scale—starting with the purse of $100,000. The largest crowd at a Nike tournament will not be nearly as big as a small crowd at a PGA tournament. There are fewer corporate tents, the equipment people do not have nearly the same presence, and the media are not as interested. There are fewer perks for the contestants on the Nike Tour: no courtesy cars, no breakfast or lunch at most events, no outings for the wives, and no day care for the kids. Also, the courses on the Nike Tour are not set up quite as hard as they are for the PGA Tour. The greens are usually firm and fast, but the rough tends to be less severe. On the PGA Tour, you can count on losing at least half a stroke, sometimes nearly a full stroke, if you hit it in the deep stuff. On the Nike Tour, the penalty is rarely as much as a half-stroke.

For me, the most noticeable difference between the two tours is that the fairways at Nike tournaments are not roped off, so people are free to wander all over the course. Most people are good about it; they stay close to the rough and never cut across the fairway as you're preparing to hit your shot. But there are a few people out there who could use a lesson in golf etiquette. One time a guy followed me down every fairway, and when I reached my ball, he set his folding stool about ten yards directly behind me.

Cleveland was not the successful experiment I had hoped for. I shot 74-72 to miss the cut by two strokes. I did not really play bad, but my driving was off a hair and I spent the two days hitting second shots from the rough, a yard or two off the fairway.

The following week was the Canon Greater Hartford Open, held on a TPC course in Cromwell. My first order of business upon arriving at the course on Monday morning was to find a caddy for the week. At the beginning of the year, Rick Adcock had caddied for me on the California swing. He spent most of the year as a caddy master in Cleveland and caddied in California only during the winter months. When I moved to the East Coast, Ray Branson took over for Rick. I met Ray in college; he was the assistant pro at a local course. He wanted to give Tour life a try, and I was glad to have a caddy I knew and felt comfortable with. Perhaps watching me miss all those cuts got to him, but after Westchester he told me he was not cut out for that kind of life and went back home.

I ran into Steve Gotsche, and he suggested I try Al Walker, a local man who caddied for him the year before. Steve said that despite his inexperience, Al had done a good job for him and he would have used Al again had he not hooked up with a regular caddy. I found Al near the practice green, and he accepted my offer enthusiastically.

There was a warm front stalled over Hartford at the beginning of the week, and by the time I reached the tee at one o'clock for the Monday pro-am, I was drenched with sweat; the thermometer was just shy of a hundred degrees. It was a typical pro-am; we finished the front nine in just under three hours. As we walked off the ninth green, Al told me he was feeling light-headed and dizzy. He did not think he could make it through the back nine. A few seconds later, he said he had to get to the first-aid tent soon, he was about to pass out. Fortunately, a friend of Al's was following us and offered to take over for him.

The heat was just as oppressive on Tuesday for my practice round, but the good news was that practice rounds rarely take more than four hours to play. This time Al made it through fifteen holes before heat exhaustion struck and he had to go in. A fourteen-year-old kid in the gallery offered to carry my bag for the last three holes.

I knew I had made a mistake. Al was in his early fifties and had been teaching math for the past twenty-five years. He was not in the kind of shape he needed to be in to carry a sixty-pound bag over a hilly course on hundred-degree days. I thought about looking for someone else, but I had no idea whom I could get the day before the tournament was to begin. Later that afternoon, I heard that cooler weather was on the way, so I decided to take a chance and stick with Al. With temperatures in the low eighties, I thought he might be able to make it around all eighteen holes. It was a good decision.

I played solidly the first round, but it was not reflected in my score. I was three over when I reached the seventeenth tee, and I thought I was well on my way to missing another cut. I pulled my tee shot thirty yards to the left in a mounded area that was legendary among the players. Hartford is known for its huge, enthusiastic crowds, and every year a group of regulars camps out for the entire week on those mounds to the left of the seventeenth fairway. They were known to indulge, with a great deal of enthusiasm, and they could be downright rowdy at times. As I reached my ball, a voice from the gallery said, "Hey, Carl. What are you going to do with that?"

"Try to put it on the green," I said. Since I was playing early, they had not had enough time to reach full speed, so it was actually quiet as I stood over the ball. I hit a great shot; my six-iron stopped a foot short of the pin. A roar of approval went up, and before I could give my club back to Al, someone was pounding me on the back, yelling, "Way to go, Carl." I sprinted to the safety of the roped-off fairway before I was knocked to the ground.

The birdie on seventeen, and a good up-and-down for par on eighteen, put me at plus two, and only a stroke off the projected cut line.

I played solidly again on Friday, and this time it was reflected in my score. I was two under as I approached the seventeenth hole. Once again, I pulled my tee shot to the mounds on the left. Since I was playing in the afternoon, the regulars there were more enthusiastic than they had been the day before, and by now they all knew my name. "Carl, good to see you again today." "Hey, Carl. Are you going to show us another great shot?" Everyone there had something to say.

They must have inspired me, because I hit another good six-iron, this time to twelve feet. I missed the birdie putt, but a solid par on eighteen put me at even for the tournament.

I made the cut!

My grin was so big, I thought my face would crack when I walked into the locker room. The first person I saw was Dicky Pride, whom I had known for years from college golf. "How'd you do?" he asked.

"Sixty-eight. I did it—I got the monkey off my back."

Dicky broke into a wide grin and gave me a high five. "Man, I know exactly how you feel," he said. "I went through the same thing last year."

It was a great feeling to play on Saturday, and I took advantage of it. I had my third straight solid round, finishing with a one-under 69. I hit my tee shot on seventeen to the mounds on the left again, and this time I was treated like an old friend. I was greeted enthusiastically, and heartily congratulated when I put the ball on the middle of the green.

Sunday, I played sixteen holes of solid golf. My downfall came on the seventeenth when I put my tee shot in the middle of the fairway for the first time all week. My friends from the mounds were disappointed. "Hey, Carl. Aren't you coming to see us today?" "What's the matter, Carl? Don't you like us anymore?" I gave them a wave and a tip of the hat in acknowledgment.

I was left with the perfect distance for an eight-iron, but then I went and chunked the damn thing. The shot was at least thirty yards short, and it landed in the middle of the pond guarding the front of the green. I was steamed as I was walking down the fairway, but I had to smile when I heard a voice from the mounds call out, "Hey, Carl. Next time remember to keep your head down."

I dropped a ball well behind the pond and chunked my sand wedge. It made it to the front fringe but slowly rolled back down the slope toward the pond. The ball stopped a yard short of the water and I promptly chunked yet another wedge, but this time the ball made it safely on the green, thirty feet short of the hole. Two putts later, I had a big, fat triple. My friends from the mounds cheered when I knocked in the last putt, so I gave them a bow to show my appreciation for their support over the four days.

I finished my round with a bogey at eighteen. No one likes to finish a tournament four over on the final two holes, and I was saying some pretty harsh things to myself as I entered the locker room. By the time I got out of the shower, however, I had recovered and was feeling good about playing my first four-round PGA tournament. My tie for sixty-sixth place had earned a check for $2,448, my first official career earnings.

I loved playing on the weekend. The pace of play was much quicker with twosomes, and I liked the three-and-a-half to four-hour rounds, as opposed to the five hours it took to play on Thursdays and Fridays. I hoped that now that the ice had been broken, I would be playing more often on Saturdays and Sundays.

Al made it through the week without another case of heat exhaustion. I knew he had retired from his teaching position and was interested in trying the Tour life full-time. He did a competent job and we got along well, so I asked him if he wanted to go to Memphis. He did, and I had a regular caddy again.

I hit it off immediately with one of my partners in the Monday pro-am in Memphis. His name was Nick Vergos, and we had our Greek heritage in common. Near the end of the round he said, "Guess what business I'm in."

"That's easy," I replied. "The restaurant business. All Greeks are in the restaurant business."

"Do you like ribs?"

"Sure, who doesn't."

"My place is called Rondeview Ribs. Why don't you ask a couple of your buddies to join you and I'll send a limo to pick you up to have dinner at my place?"

We settled on Tuesday, and as promised Nick sent a limo to take Joe Acosta, Scott Ford, and me to dinner. It turned out that Rondeview was one of the best-known restaurants in Memphis, and there was an hour wait when we arrived. We were promptly escorted to our reserved table and had a great dinner.

I had not arranged a practice round with anyone for Tuesday, so I hung around the putting green to see if one of my regular partners would turn up. John Cook walked by and noticed I was not too serious about what I was doing. He asked, "Do you have anything arranged for today?"

"No, I'm just kind of hanging around."

"Why don't you join me."

It was a thrill to play with John, a veteran with almost $5 million in career earnings. We both hit several shots into the greens, and he shared his strategy for playing the course. This PGA thing was turning out to be a lot of fun.

I played well and scored well on both Thursday and Friday. My scores of 67-70 made the cut by a bunch of strokes. Things did not go as well on Saturday. I missed too many fairways and my iron play wasn't sharp. It was a struggle to shoot 75. Sunday's round was better, and my 71 helped me climb all the way to a tie for sixty-fourth place and a check for $2,637.50. I felt great. I made two cuts in a row and I cracked the $5,000 barrier in career earnings.

The Western Open was the following week, and I was somewhere around the twenty-fifth alternate. I had no chance to get in the tournament, so I returned to Virginia Beach for the week. It would give me a chance to work with Butch and see my family again. My dad told me about a conversation he and my mom had with a couple of their friends. Their friends were expressing their sympathy for my slow start, and one of them said, "It's got to be really tough for Carl since he's playing all those courses for the first time. He hasn't had a chance to learn them."

"What's there to learn?" my mom asked. "One hole is a dogleg right, the next is a dogleg left." She's still working to develop an appreciation of the finer points of the game.


I was home alone on Thursday evening when the phone rang. "Carl?" a familiar voice asked. It was Heather. My heart began to pound, but I was too cool to let her know that.

"Hi, Heather. How're you doing?"

"I'm okay. I called to congratulate you on making the cut at Hartford and Memphis."

"Yeah, thanks. It was great." Man, was I cool or what?

She finally broke the silence. "I've missed you, Carl. I've missed you a lot."

"Why don't you come down to Mississippi. I'll be playing there the week after next." That was a little too quick to be cool.

"I'd like that."

We talked for another twenty minutes, and we agreed that Mississippi would simply be an experiment. We would see how things went, and if we both decided we wanted to resume our relationship, we'd take it very slowly.

Sure.

I was elated at the prospect of seeing Heather again, and I wanted to share it with someone. I did not know when my parents would get home, so I called Butch with some golf-related pretense and managed to work my seeing Heather into the conversation. Then I called Heather back to tell her about my conversation with Butch.

My next tournament was the Anheuser-Busch Golf Classic in Williamsburg, less than an hour's drive from my folks' home in Virginia Beach. I wanted to do well there, since all my friends and family would be following me. I was worried about Al, though. The tournament was held in the middle of July, and it is local lore that summer never arrives until the PGA comes to town. This year was no exception. It was in the middle nineties for the Monday pro-am and Tuesday's practice round, and the forecast was for the high nineties later in the week. The humidity, of course, was not far behind the temperatures.

Al and I both made it through Thursday and Friday in good shape. Al drank plenty of liquids, and I made the cut by three shots with a 70-69. Al was fine on Saturday, but the heat got to me—nothing dramatic, but I felt weak and a little spacey throughout the round. It was reflected in my score, a disappointing 74.

I felt fine on Sunday morning and I got off to a good start with solid pars on the first two holes. But as I reached down to pick my ball out of the cup on the third green, I almost passed out. Everything went black, and all I could see were thousands of dots drifting across my field of vision. I stood up slowly and waited for the dizziness to pass. The rest of the day was a struggle, and I was surprised that I managed to get through the round. As soon as I signed my card, I went to the first-aid tent. After thirty minutes I still did not feel ready to drive, so I called my dad and asked him to come get me. Given the circumstances, my 79 was not all that bad. It earned me a tie with Dicky Thompson for last place and a check for $2,167.

The following week was the Deposit Guaranty in Madison, Mississippi. It was held the same week as the British Open, so few of the big names were there. A friend asked me if I felt I had a better shot at a high finish and a big check with the top players in Scotland. My answer was no. It did not matter to me who was in the field. Every week there were relative unknowns who finished in the top ten, as well as a few name players who missed the cut. If I played well, I would do okay no matter who was in the field. And if I played poorly, I would miss the cut even if it was a Hooters tournament. The level of competition is that high.

I played well the first two days, shooting 70-69 to make the cut by three shots. I was proud of myself for keeping my concentration on Friday, since Heather was flying in that evening. Before heading to the airport to pick her up, I gave Butch a call. I told him I was having trouble with my Saturday rounds, and he told me what everyone says when they do not have a clear solution to the problem. He said I should relax, go out there and have some fun, and play like it was Thursday.

The thirty minutes before Heather's plane landed seemed interminable, but she finally arrived and we had a great reunion. We vowed to each other again that we would take it slow, but our actions belied our words. I never was very good at being cool.

Butch's advice was better than I had thought. My mantra while warming up on Saturday morning was "go out there and have some fun, go out there and have some fun." And did I. I birdied the first five holes, and suddenly I was ten under par for the tournament. The crowd swelled from about fifty to about 150. Two solid pars on six and seven were followed with another birdie on eight. I had a good up-and-down par on nine, and then made two-putt pars on ten and eleven. I knocked in putts of eight and twenty-five feet on twelve and thirteen for two more birdies to put me eight under for the day and thirteen under for the tournament. There was a scoreboard near the fourteenth tee, and I saw I had a two-stroke lead. The crowd had grown by another couple hundred people, and I also noticed that the guy with the Golf Channel camera was standing behind the tee. It was the first time the television people had any reason to follow me.

The adrenaline was pumping while I prepared to hit my tee shot. I was in a great position to go into the final round with the lead. That is, until I hit a big duck hook out of bounds. I doubled the fourteenth, three-jacked it for a bogey on fifteen, and hit it into the water at seventeen for another double. I was stunned as I stood on the eighteenth tee. I had a two-stroke lead, and four short holes later I had dropped from eight under to three under for the day. One of those learning experiences, I suppose.

Perhaps because I was numb and played the last hole without thinking about what I was doing, I hit two great shots and sunk a twelve-footer for eagle. I was back to ten under for the tournament and only three strokes off the lead.

I was not as nervous Saturday evening as I would have thought, and by the time I teed off on Sunday, I was feeling good. Nothing spectacular happened, but I was playing good golf and got it to two under for the day after sixteen holes. There was a scoreboard behind the sixteenth green, and I saw that I was two strokes back. I was thinking birdie-eagle as I walked onto the seventeenth tee.

The seventeenth hole had a split fairway. The safe route was to the left, but it meant a middle iron to a tightly guarded green. There was a narrow fairway to the right, and a good tee shot would leave, at most, a pitching wedge to the green. But if you went for the right fairway and hit it off line in either direction, you could end up wet. Since I had to have birdie to have any chance, I chose the riskier route. My two-iron faded more than I intended, but it hung up in the rough short of the water.

My heart sank when I got to my ball. I had absolutely no shot. It was tight against a tree, but I could not take an unplay-able because I would have to drop it in the deep rough and I was not sure I could get it to the green from there. I decided to chip it back to the fairway. I took a half-swing at the ball, but my club caught a branch on the way down and I whiffed it! I could not take a chance on doing that again, so I had no choice but to drop it in the five-inch rough at the edge of the hazard. I still did not think

I could get it to the green, but I had no choice but to try. I took a savage swing at the ball with a nine-iron and it came out pretty well. The ball landed about two yards short of the green and rolled back down the slope to the edge of the hazard. I chili-dipped my pitch, managed to scrape the next one to six feet, and two-putted from there for an eight. Everyone was sticking forks in me, I was so done. I limped home with a bogey to finish in a tie for thirty-fifth.

I had mixed feelings about the tournament. On the one hand, I was steamed about my finish, but I was excited by being in contention right up to the end. It was a great feeling, and I could not wait to experience it again. Morris Hatalsky came up to me early the following week and said, "Don't hang your head, kid, you did a good job. We've all been there, and you have to experience something like that a few times before you can win. Keep plugging away. Your time will come." It really made me feel good that a veteran would go out of his way to offer me encouragement. It made me feel as if I was one of them, that I belonged out there.

I took Heather to the airport that evening. Our planes were leaving at about the same time, hers back to Columbia and mine to Massachusetts. I was glad she was there to share the tournament with me, and maybe her presence was what kept me loose enough to get into contention. Before she boarded her plane, we reaffirmed our commitment to take it slow.

I am not sure whom we were kidding. I would propose to her in less than three weeks and she would accept.


After making four cuts in a row, I felt I had a rhythm going. When I talked to my friends, they would give me a hard time about the "rough life" I was leading, but in some ways it was rough. It certainly was exhausting, if nothing else. After finishing a tournament on Sunday, I would fly to the next city, and depending on time zone changes, it would be anywhere from nine in the evening to one in the morning before I would get in. It usually took at least another hour to pick up either a rental or courtesy car and get to the hotel, so an early night was close to midnight. I had to get to the course by nine on Monday morning to check in, get settled in the locker room, and have time to warm up for the pro-am.

I do not take the golf too seriously on Mondays. I try to relax, enjoy myself, and work the muscle kinks from the airplane out of my system. If I happen to get it to a couple under, I will start to grind a little more, but mostly I try to make sure my amateur partners enjoy themselves. I have met a lot of great guys on Mondays, and the contacts I have made could prove to be invaluable someday. Should I ever decide to leave the Tour, I bet I could have a good job with only a half-dozen phone calls. And since I was hovering around 230th on the money list, I did not mind the $500 I received for playing. The pro-am rounds typically take six hours, so by the time I've had dinner, I am ready to fall into bed.

Tuesday is my serious practice day. I get up about eight, have a big breakfast, and get to the course by nine-thirty. I like to play my practice round in the morning, especially if I have not played in the pro-am, so I can see what shots I need to work on for the week. I will have a light lunch after the round, usually a salad and a sandwich, and then spend a couple of hours on the range and on the practice green. I learned my lesson earlier in the year, and I vowed to never again practice for nine hours in one day.

Tuesday evening is the Tour's Saturday night. Since neither I nor the guys I hung out with had achieved sufficient status to be invited to play in the Wednesday pro-ams, we could go out, have a little fun, and sleep late the following morning. Joe Acosta, Scott Ford, and I would usually have a nice dinner, then take advantage of what the city had to offer. We might take in a ballgame or a rock concert, or—my favorite—find a bar with a pool table.

Wednesday is a light day for me. If I have an early tee time on Thursday, I get to the course by nine Wednesday morning, have a light practice session, and spend the afternoon sight-seeing or possibly doing a little fishing. A late Thursday tee time means that I find something fun to do in the morning, have lunch at the course, and follow that up with a ninety-minute practice session. I do not want more than twenty-four hours to pass between my last practice session and the first round of the tournament.

Thursdays and Fridays are full days. When I have a late tee time, I sleep as late as I can and have a big breakfast. I might spend an hour or two reading the paper or watching a little television before heading to the course. I do not like to loaf around too much before playing, because I tend to stiffen up. I try to get to the course about an hour before my tee time to have a light lunch and a forty-five-minute warm-up session. It is usually six-thirty to seven before I finish the round, and that only leaves me enough time for dinner and an hour or two to relax before getting to bed for the next day's early round.

On early-round days, I have to get out of bed by six to get to the course in time for breakfast and the warm-up session. I get off the course around two o'clock, have some lunch, and spend ninety minutes on the range. I might take in a movie before dinner, then it is back to the motel for the night.

Other than the fact that it is moving day, Saturdays can be relaxing. With the exception of Mississippi, my tee times have been early enough to give me time to do something enjoyable in the afternoon before dinner. Saturday night on Tour is really exciting and glamorous. I spend it packing for the next city. I leave out one change of clothes, which I take to the course on Sunday. A quick shower after the round is followed by a hurried trip to the airport to catch my connection to the next city.

Previously, I always chuckled when I heard guys say they

could play for only three or four weeks before taking some time off. I am more sympathetic now, and I am looking forward to the time when I am established and can pick and choose my spots. As it is, I do not have that luxury. I have to play in every tournament I can get in if I am to have any hope of making a move on the money list.

Sutton, Massachusetts was the site for the Ideon Classic, held during the last week of July 1995. The course, at more than 7,100 yards, was suited for my game, so I thought I had a chance to do well. And I played four solid, if somewhat boring, rounds. I had two or three birdies against a bogey or two each day for rounds of 69, 69, 70, and 71. I finished in a tie for forty-second, and earned a check for $3,400.

I was especially looking forward to the following week's tournament, the Buick Open at Warwick Hills, Michigan. I was staying with Rick Williams, a friend from college who had taken a job as an assistant pro in the Detroit area, and he told me that the course was built for my game. After the Monday pro-am, I agreed with him, even though I did not score especially well. I attributed my 75 to airplane swings and the distraction of a pro-am partner who could not stay out of the woods. I felt better after Tuesday's practice round. I hit two or three shots into each green and I was learning what it took to score well there. But Thursday and Friday were not much better than Monday. I had a pair of 73s to miss the cut by six shots, and I was not sure what had happened. I felt I played well enough to make the cut, but for some reason I couldn't put my finger on, I could not get the ball into the hole. I thought it might have been the bent-grass fairways. The ball seemed to nestle down a little more than usual. But the fact of the matter was that I had played well on bent grass before. It was very strange.

The following three weeks were the PGA Championship, the Sprint International, a very popular tournament among the players, and the World Series of Golf, so I had some time off. I spent a few days with Butch in Virginia Beach before heading back to Columbia to see Heather. Any pretense of taking it slow evaporated during those weeks, and we began to talk about marriage again, albeit in a somewhat vague way.

The three weeks' rest did wonders for my body and my spirits, and I was eager to get back out there. My next tournament was the Greater Milwaukee Open during the first week in September. I had a good opening round. My 70 put me inside the projected cut line of plus one.

The wind came up Friday afternoon, and it was a struggle for me. I came to the eighteenth tee three over for the day, two over for the tournament, so I was almost certain I needed a birdie to make the cut. It was doable. Eighteen was a relatively short par-five that I could easily reach in two with a good drive. I crushed my tee shot down the center of the fairway, leaving me only 235 yards to the green. A smooth swing with a three-wood was all I needed. I must have been a little quick, because I hit the worst shot of the week. It was at least twenty yards to the right of the green. A mediocre chip left me twenty feet for birdie, and I never gave it a chance. I was furious with myself. I had grinded hard in the wind to get myself in position, and I let it get away with a single swing.

My plan had been to spend the weekend in Milwaukee regardless of whether I made the cut, since I had a slight chance of getting into the Canadian Open the following week, but I was in no mood to stick around. I left for the airport immediately and paid the extra $100 to change my ticket. Heather would help me feel better.

On Monday morning, my decision to leave Milwaukee immediately looked like a good one when I learned that I was the twelfth alternate for the Canadian Open. There was no chance twelve guys would withdraw between Monday and Wednesday. To my surprise, I got a call from the PGA office Wednesday afternoon informing me that I was in. I was able to get the last flight out to Ontario.

I did not have a chance to see the course before my first round on Thursday, but I quickly learned that it was one tough layout. On the first four holes, I hit what I thought were eight perfect shots and I was four over par. I settled down after that, and my 76 still gave me a chance to make the cut. Thursday had been cold and windy, so the scores were higher than usual.

The weather Friday morning was not much better. The wind was blowing at least thirty miles per hour when I teed off, but I had learned a lot about the course the previous day. I played solidly, but the wind took its toll and I finished with a 75. I might have made the cut despite my 151 score, but the wind died down as the day went on and the afternoon scores were much lower. I missed by three shots.

Even though it cost me a small fortune to play those two rounds, I was glad I had the chance to play in the tournament. I loved Glen Abbey. It was probably the most difficult course I had played all year, but in my mind it ranked up there with Spyglass as a truly great course. It is a ball-striker's course, long with deep rough. The first ten holes are relatively flat, but from the eleventh tee, it is about a 150-foot drop to the fairway. Holes eleven through fifteen, which wind through a valley, are probably not as interesting as the others, but they are tough but fair. These holes can be especially challenging since the wind has a tendency to swirl in the valley. You might feel a slight breeze in your face, but if you look at the trees at the top of the rise, you get the impression there is a one-club wind behind you. The last three holes are simply tough, solid finishing holes.

I do not always agree with the other guys about courses, but I believe a great course is one that demands that you do everything well. And no one breaks par at Glen Abbey unless they have had a very good day with their woods, irons, and putter. You simply cannot score there if you have any weakness in your game. On the other hand, if you play solid golf, the course will yield a low score. I could not wait to play there again.

My mom had planned a big party for my dad's fiftieth birthday on September 12, and I thought I would have to miss it since the B.C. Open began two days later. But about two weeks earlier, an idea germinated in my mind and I decided to fly in for the day. My plan demanded that Heather be there, so I called her and told her how much it would mean to me if she could be there for my dad's big party. She agreed. Everything was set.

At about two on the afternoon of the twelfth, Heather and I were alone in my folks' house when the doorbell rang. I rushed to answer it before Heather got up, and as I expected, the engagement ring I had ordered from a local jeweler was being delivered. I took it to the kitchen, where I had hidden some yellow ribbon. I used the ribbon to tie the ring around the neck of our family dog, Albie, an aging golden retriever. I led Albie upstairs to where Heather was working on the computer, and said, "Hey, Heather, turn around and see what Albie has on her neck."

Before moving, she said, "It better not be anything gross, like a tick."

She turned, saw the ring, and said, "Oh my God."

I got down on one knee and said, "Heather, I love you. Will you marry me?"

"You know I will." She jumped into my arms and knocked me to the floor.

We talked about the best time for the wedding. I did not care about the exact date, but I did not want a long engagement. I thought we should allow enough time to plan the event and not put it off a day longer. I admit, I looked at the schedule for the following year and suggested a week when I thought I would be unlikely to get into a tournament. We settled on May 18, 1996, the week of the Colonial. I could not wait.

I left Virginia Beach Wednesday morning for Endicott, New York, and the B.C. Open. My opening rounds of 68 and 72 were good enough to make the cut by a stroke, but my 73 and 69 over the weekend were not good enough to improve my position. I finished in a tie for fifty-ninth and earned $2,160.

I played with Billy Andrade on Saturday. Billy had been on the Tour for about eight years and won consecutive tournaments back in 1991. He is a die-hard sports fan and he loves any team from Boston. He wanted to spend the entire round talking about the Red Sox and the Celtics. On Sunday I was paired with Howard Twitty. He is a twenty-year veteran who has more than $2.5 million in career earnings. All in all, it was a good weekend.

The Quad City Classic at Coal Valley, Illinois, was the next stop. Coal Valley is a suburb of Moline, which is right next to Rock Island, Illinois, and across the Mississippi River from Bettendorf and Davenport, Iowa. Thursday was a cold, rainy day, and I was grateful that I had an afternoon tee time. Play was suspended in midmorning and the round was canceled before I was scheduled to tee off. Nothing is worse than suffering through a steady rain, getting soaked to the skin, only to have the round canceled. Unless, that is, you have to finish the round and post your score.

The rain cleared out overnight, but it was cold enough on both Friday and Saturday to have frost delays of several hours—hard to believe, since summer had officially ended only a day or two earlier. Once we got started, I played my best golf of the year. I opened with rounds of 70 and 67 to make the cut by a full six shots. Despite the cold weather, D. A. Weibring somehow managed to post 64-65 to take a four-stroke lead. I shot a solid 69 on Sunday to maintain my position and earn a tie for twentieth place. The check for $11,650 was by far my best of the year.

After playing in forty-degree weather, I was more than willing to travel south to the Buick Challenge in Pine Mountain, Georgia. I fell in love with the course, Callaway Gardens, after the Monday pro-am, and after Tuesday's practice round I knew it was in the same class as Spyglass and Glen Abbey. Most of the guys liked the course, but I am probably in the minority when I put it in the "great" category. The first time you play the course, it may seem almost boring. It is not a typical resort course; it is relatively flat, with few water hazards, and no bulkheads made out of railway ties. But the rough is brutal, and you have to drive the ball long and straight if you are to have any chance of posting a good score.

At first blush, the greens do not look very dramatic, but after a round or two you come to appreciate that they were designed to provide a stern test of your iron game. The sixteenth hole may be the best example. It is a long par three, about 220 yards, with a green that is forty yards deep. The green narrows dramatically as you move from front to back, so when the pin is at the back of the green, you have to hit an extremely precise long iron to have a chance for birdie. What I love about the design is that the hole gives you a chance to play safe. You have a lot of room for error if you hit the ball to the front of the green, but then you are left with a challenging two-putt.

In my mind a great course gives you options, and that is exactly what Callaway Gardens does. Great shots will be rewarded with birdies, but the course gives you the option of playing it safe. If you play it safe, though, you do pay a price—such as the price of having to two-putt from fifty or sixty feet on the sixteenth hole.

I had my third solid tournament in a row. I opened with a pair of 70s to make the cut by three shots, and finished respectably with a 72-71. I earned a check for $3,600 and finished in a tie for fortieth.

Later that evening, it struck me how much I was enjoying myself. It had not been that long since I had concluded I was the most miserable human being on the face of the earth. But now, four short months later, I loved my life. I loved knowing that every time I played in a tournament, I would be competitive. I loved feeling confident of my ability, of knowing that I belonged out there competing against the best golfers in the world. Things were coming together for me. I was feeling more comfortable as the year went on, and the more comfortable I felt, the better I played. It was amazing how much difference a stroke or two per round can make on your perspective.

From Atlanta I went to Orlando, even though I was not sure I would get in the Disney. As of Saturday morning, I was the fourth alternate, but I thought the odds were good enough that four people would withdraw and that it made more sense to go on to Orlando than back to Columbia. If I did not get in, I would not have considered it a tragedy. I had played in five consecutive tournaments, and I was beat. I did not think I would be able to play at Las

Vegas, since the tournament had a large purse and consequently was a popular event, but I was pretty sure I would be able to play in the final full-field tournament of the year, the Texas Open. My plan was to rest up for a couple of weeks and then use the Texas Open as a warm-up for Q-School. I was somewhere around the 220 mark on the money list, so I knew I would be playing in the Fall Classic once again.

My estimate of the odds proved accurate, however, and I was relaxing by the pool on Tuesday when the PGA office called to tell me that Jonathan Kaye, another first-year player, had withdrawn. I was in.

My opening-round 62 was an incredible experience. I knew I was capable of putting together a round like that, but it came at such an unexpected time. My two days of lounging around the pool had not been enough to recharge my batteries, and I felt as if I was dragging while I warmed up for the round.

When I called my dad to tell him about the round, he was so excited he decided to come down for the rest of the tournament. He, my mom, and my uncles Lou and Bill jumped in the car Thursday evening for the twelve-hour drive to Orlando.

A 62 can have remarkable regenerative powers. I felt full of energy when I got up at six o'clock that Friday morning for the second round. Scott McCarron and I stopped at Shoney's for the breakfast bar, and I arrived at the course around seven-thirty to warm up. Walking onto the range that morning was an experience I will never forget. I heard "Good round, Carl" from several of the guys. From the guys I knew well, the comments were more like "Hey, Paulson. What happened to you yesterday?" or "I hope you get back to your regular game today, Paulson, and give the rest of us a chance." I was with the best golfers in the world, and they were acknowledging my play. "Unbelievable" was all that I could say to Al as we walked to the end of the range.

I got off to a fast start on Friday, with birdies on four of the first six holes. I could not believe it. I was fourteen under par for twenty-four holes. I did not see a scoreboard, but I had to be three, maybe four shots up on the rest of the field. I began to have thoughts about what a win would mean. The check for $180,000 would be great, of course, but the victory was much more important. It would mean that I did not have to worry about Q-School for at least two years, and maybe never again. It would mean I could plan my schedule at the beginning of the year and play in the tournaments I enjoyed most. And best of all, it would establish me as a player to be reckoned with on the PGA Tour.

All this passed through my mind in a few seconds, and I knew I had to put an end to it. I could not get ahead of myself. I had a lot of golf left. I turned to Al and said, "Let's take it one hole at a time," to emphasize the point to myself.

I cooled off after that. I hit the ball solidly, but I was not getting it close to the pin. I parred the next eight holes.

It began to sprinkle as I was preparing to hit my second shot into the fourteenth green, and by the time we putted out, it was coming down hard. We took our time getting to the next tee, and just as we walked on the tee box, the horn sounded, indicating that play was postponed. The rain did not let up, and an hour later the course was unplayable. We would have to finish our rounds in the morning.

I had mixed feelings about the rain. I hated having to quit before my round was finished. I was hitting the ball well and I thought I could get at least one, and possibly two, birdies on the remaining holes. But on the other hand, I was not disappointed that the tournament would be reduced to three rounds. It was not that I did not have confidence in my ability, because I did. It was a simple matter of the odds. After two hot rounds, most everyone expects to cool off some. And someone else in the field was bound to get hot and make up a lot of ground. The odds were that I had a better chance of maintaining my lead over one round than two, and I believe everyone else would feel the same way, even if they would not admit it publicly.

That Friday evening, as hard as I tried to think about something else — anything else — my mind kept returning to my opportunity to win the tournament, or, at the very least, to make a huge jump on the money list. Before Disney, I had won slightly more than $30,000 for the year and was 220th on the money list. The projection was that it would take from $145,000 to $150,000 to make the top 125 and fully exempt status for 1996. Winning the tournament, of course, would mean an exemption for two years, but even a second-place finish, worth nearly $130,000, would do it for me. Third place was worth $85,000, so with two tournaments left, that would be enough to give me a shot at the top 125.

At the end of every year, only ten to fifteen players of the forty who earned their card at the previous Q-School have earned enough money to make the top 125. To be among those ten to fifteen guys would be an unbelievable accomplishment, especially for those of us who were playing on the Tour for the first time. Guys like me, who finished far down the list of forty qualifiers, had a tough time getting into tournaments early in the year. So while we were sitting at home watching the Phoenix Open on television, the guys we were competing with were building up a lead that was insurmountable for most of us. That, taken together with the fact that everything was new to us, including the courses, made it nearly impossible for those of us who finished in the bottom third of the Q-School qualifiers to make it into the top 125. It is no accident that a majority of the veterans have been to Q-School more than once.

But I had a chance to do it, to be one of the very few rookies to make it into the top 125. All I had to do was hang on. I did not have to shoot any more 62s, I just had to play good, solid golf. I was fourteen under for thirty-two holes. I figured I only had to get four or five birdies, six at the most, to win the damn thing.

It took me longer than usual to fall asleep that night.

There was a light drizzle coming down Saturday morning. The forecast for the weekend, which called for intermittent showers, worried me. Since the tournament was being played over three courses, we had to get three rounds in for the tournament to be official. It would be a disaster to end up the winner of an unofficial tournament.

The sky cleared some by the time I arrived at the course. I had a good warm-up session and I thought I could get another birdie or two on my remaining four holes. It did not happen. I hit all four greens in regulation, but I could not get any of the putts to drop. I finished the day at fourteen under, tied with Brad Bryant for the lead. That son of a gun shot 63 to make up a lot of ground. Brad was a journeyman pro. He had been on the Tour since 1978, had almost $3 million in career earnings, but had never managed to win a tournament.

I was tight from the time I finished my round on Saturday right up to my tee time on Sunday. There is no doubt about it. Because Disney was a pro-am, I probably did not feel as much pressure as I would have otherwise. Even though Brad and I were tied for the lead, we were not in the same group. I was playing with my three amateur partners on the Magnolia, while Brad was over at the Palm course with his group of amateurs.

On the first hole, I hit a good drive down the right side of the fairway, leaving a seven-iron to the green. The adrenaline was pumping, though, and my shot cleared the green and landed in a back bunker. A so-so explosion shot left me with an eight-foot putt for par. I burned the left lip but had to settle for bogey. It was not the way I wanted to start my round.

I could not make anything happen the rest of the day. I was hitting my tee shots solidly, but my irons were off just a hair. They were good enough to hit most of the greens in regulation, but I could not get the ball close enough to the hole to have any realistic chances for birdies. On the sixteenth, I did stick a seven-iron to within a foot to get me back to even for the day, but routine pars at the seventeenth and eighteenth holes finished off what turned out to be a boring round. Brad shot 68 to win his first PGA tournament.

I finished tied for seventh, and my check for $31,275 doubled my earnings for the year. I was excited by the top-ten finish. Sure, I would love to have shot 67 and won, but it was the first time I had gone into the final round with the lead, and I thought a solid, even-par round was not too shabby. I kept my emotions under control and I took good swings. All in all, it was a good day. And it would prepare me to do even better the next time I went into the final round with the lead.

Thirty minutes after the tournament was over, I learned how big my birdie on sixteen was. Had I parred the hole, I would have finished in a tie for fourteenth, but my top-ten finish meant that I could play in Las Vegas the following week. I was playing some of the best golf of my life, and the tournament had a purse of $1.5 million. I still had a shot at the top 125. Three hours later, I was on a plane headed west.

I thought I had a chance to do well at Las Vegas. I heard the courses were long and open, so they played to my strength. I did get off to a good start with a 69. The scores were always low there, so I had some work to do to make the cut, but two more rounds like that would do it for sure. Like Disney, Las Vegas was a pro-am, but it was a ninety-hole tournament with the cut coming after fifty-four holes.

I played the second round at the Las Vegas Hilton course, the only one of the three that was short and tight. I could not keep my tee shots in the fairway and finished the round three over for the day and even for the tournament.

The projected cut was seven under, so I was relaxed when I teed off for the third round. I did not think I had much of a chance, but it turned out to be one of those days when the ball had eyes. I could not miss a putt, and after twelve holes I was right at the cut line of seven under. I slipped with bogeys on thirteen and sixteen, but I reached the eighteenth tee with a chance to make it. It was a medium-length par five that I could reach with two solid shots. I crushed my drive and hit a solid five-iron to thirty feet for eagle. I put a good stroke on the ball, and it caught the right lip. But it had a little too much speed and spun out two feet from the cup. My birdie left me one shot shy of the cut line.

My plane reservation for Texas was for Sunday, and since there was no point in going there early, I hung around Las Vegas. I was staying with Scott McCarron again, and he had a good start. He had about $40,000 for the year, so he did not have much chance to get into the top 125, but a solid finish might get him into the top 150. The top 150 was important, because it meant an exemption from the first two stages of Q-School. Anyone who had played on the Tour certainly had the ability to make it to the final stage of the Fall Classic, but golf is too fickle to depend entirely on ability. A couple of bad swings in the wrong places could eliminate anyone from any stage. He knew he needed two great rounds to make it, but he was playing as well as he had all year and he was excited by his prospects.

Scott played great on Saturday. He shot 64 and was only five strokes off the lead. He was still a long shot to make it to the top 150, though. There were quite a few guys ahead of him, and he needed about $75,000 to make it. A fourth-place finish would probably do it.

Scott played great again on Sunday. He finished with a 65, and as he walked off the course he was tied for third with Mark O'Meara, who was a hole behind him. Mark could birdie the eighteenth and Scott would still make the top 150.

By the time Scott reached the locker room, Mark had hit his approach on eighteen to twenty-five feet. He thought his downhill putt would be faster than it was, though, and he left it three feet short. There were a dozen guys watching O'Meara on the tube, and Patrick Burke had done some quick calculations in his head. "Hey, Scott. If O'Meara misses this putt, you keep your card." Patrick was right. If O'Meara missed, Scott would finish in third alone and earn $102,000. That would put him in the mid-140s, right around the bubble. Scott had never seriously considered the possibility that he might make the top 125.

Scott told me later that he could not breathe while he watched O'Meara. Anyone would have to be out of his mind to bet that Mark would miss a three-footer, but stranger things have happened. And miss it he did. He did not hit it firmly enough and it slid by the left edge.

The instant the ball passed the cup, a deafening roar went up in the locker room. Everyone was thrilled for Scott. Finishing in a tie for fourth rather than a tie for third didn't mean a thing to Mark. He already has had a great career and he has a zillion dollars in the bank. But to Scott, it meant everything. It meant he would not have to play in the dreaded Fall Classic.

I have read dozens of times that if a player tells the guys in the locker room that he shot 78, half of them will not care and the other half will wish it had been 79. Perhaps there is some truth to that, but it has not been my experience. Yes, I realize that 90 percent of the guys out there couldn't care less what I shoot, but you do make friends on the Tour, friends who are happy to share your triumphs. The guys in the locker room that Sunday afternoon were genuinely excited for Scott. I was truly happy for him, even though he jumped from thirty places below me on the money list to sixty places above me. I would, of course, have been even happier had it happened to me, but since it did not, I am glad it was Scott.

Scott's experience illustrates how fine the line is between success and failure on the PGA Tour. Had Mark made that three-footer, who knows what might have happened. Clearly, Scott has the ability to be a consistent winner, but hitting a cart path instead of the rough only inches to the left washed me out of Q-School on my first attempt, and something like that could happen to anyone. As it turned out, Mark did miss the putt, Scott kept his card, and then, early the following spring, he won his first tournament and earned a two-year exemption.

It made me think that if God gave me two inches to play with on the greens at Disney, I could easily have earned enough to keep my card. Hell, I would have won the tournament. Two inches. The entire year came down to two lousy inches. It is enough to drive you crazy if you let it.


The final stop of the year—at least for me and the other guys who were not among the top thirty money winners who qualified to play in the Tour Championship—was the LaCantera Texas Open, held during the third week of October 1995. Had I not believed there was an outside chance I could finish in the top two or three, I would have skipped it. I had played in eight straight tournaments, and I was exhausted.

After the practice round, I almost wished I had gone back home. The course was definitely not suited for my style of play. On one par four, I hit eight-iron, sand wedge to the green. I do not mind a few holes that demand that you play conservatively off the tee, but an eight-iron is a little too conservative for my tastes.

It was also a tough course to walk. It was quite hilly, and the distances between the greens and the next tee were several hundred yards. On a few holes the walk was so long, they provided us with shuttle service between the green and the tee. I felt sorry for anyone in the gallery who tried to follow a particular group. There was no way they could keep up, and there was a chance they could get lost out there.

I had a good round on Thursday, although my 71 was seven shots off the lead. Given the type of course it was, however, I knew I had no chance to finish high enough to make any difference. On Friday, I was dead tired by the time I reached the eighteenth green. I played okay, but I was two over for the day and was facing a twenty-footer to save par. I was too tired to walk all around the green to get all four angles, so I settled for a quick look at the line from behind the ball. The damn thing went in, and as it turned out, I needed that putt to make the cut.

I dragged myself around the course on Saturday, and my score of 81 reflected it. I did my best on every shot, but I was just too tired to put a consistent swing on the ball.

My score put me seventy-ninth in the field of eighty, so I was in the first twosome to go off on Sunday. Bruce Lietzke was my playing partner, and he was struggling as much as I was. He bogeyed the first four holes, while I started par-double-double-par. As we walked to the fifth tee, I said to him, "It looks like we've got quite a battle going for next-to-last place."

"Yeah, I guess we do." He thought for a few seconds and then added, "You know, that might be the only thing I can win today. Let's see who can win 'next to last.'"

"You're on," I said.

Bruce has been called a legend in his spare time. He is a twenty-year veteran who has thirteen wins on the Tour, but golf is about the fifth priority in his life. He hasn't played in as many as twenty tournaments a year since his kids were toddlers. My favorite story about Bruce is that his caddy simply did not believe Bruce's claim that he did not practice during those four- to six-week stretches when he went home to see his family and do a little fishing. As his caddy was packing Bruce's clubs for a trip back to Texas, he put a banana inside the headcover with his driver. And sure enough, when Bruce came back out a month later, that banana, somewhat aromatic, was still there.

Bruce played the next twelve holes better than I did, and he had a two-stroke lead on me going into seventeen. But I picked up three quick shots when he doubled the hole and I birdied it. Suddenly I was a stroke up. On the eighteenth hole, Bruce put his approach shot within easy two-putt distance, while I caught a bunker with my second shot. I hit a nice recovery shot, leaving myself four feet for par. As expected, Bruce two-putted, so I needed that four-footer to beat him. I lined it up carefully and as I positioned myself over the ball, he said, "Hey, Carl, you know you need that to beat me, don't you?"

I smiled, shook my head, lined up the putt again, and knocked it in. I had to give him a hard time about stooping so low to keep from losing to me.

On the flight back to Columbia, I had plenty of time to review my first year on the Tour. My earnings of $64,501 put me 183rd on the money list. That may not sound like much, but it did put me ahead of about one-third of my fellow Q-School graduates. Of the forty-six guys who graduated with me, only twelve of them earned enough money to keep their card. Woody Austin, who won the 1994 Q-School tournament, had a great year, finishing with $736,497 to put him twenty-fourth on the money list. His victory at the Buick Open was the only win by a rookie.

I was pleased that two of the guys I roomed with during the year were among the twelve who made it. Along with Scott McCarron, Joe Acosta reached the top 125 on the strength of a third-place finish at Milwaukee and a fourth-place finish at Disney.

I played in twenty-one tournaments and made the cut ten times. That in itself wasn't bad. I have not seen any stats about rookies, but I bet ten out of twenty-one is above average. Even more encouraging was the fact that I had made nine of my last thirteen cuts. Had I been able to get off to a halfway decent start, I would have had a good shot at keeping my card.

The year provided me with invaluable experience. Next year, I would not have to wonder where the course was, where I had to go to register, or even where I had to go to use the bathroom. Having seen the courses before would give me an advantage over the next crop of rookies. I would not be tempted by as many sucker pins, and I would know when to keep my driver in the bag.

Yes, I had paid my dues, and my game had progressed as well. My short game was still not where I wanted it to be, but it was getting closer with each passing week. I felt confident that 1996 would be my breakthrough year. All I had to do now was make it through the Fall Classic.

# CHAPTER 8

# Back to School

I did not do a thing for the first week I was back in Columbia. I was dead tired, and even had I felt the need to practice, I am not sure I could have summoned the energy to do so. I lay around the apartment, drank a fair amount of beer, watched a lot of movies on television, and read a couple of spy novels. It was a luxury to know there was nothing I had to do.

The second week I practiced some with the golf team at South Carolina. Steve, my old college coach and Butch's brother, wanted to hear all about my year, and I enjoyed playing the role of the wise old PGA pro who had come back to visit his alma mater and to provide a few words of wisdom to Steve's current crop of players. There was nothing I really needed to work on, so I practiced just enough to stay sharp.

Since I had played on tour, I was exempt from the

first stage of Q-School, and I elected to play second stage at Greenlefe in Haynes City, Florida, the same course that hosted the final stage the previous year. I liked the course, and I could not argue with the success I had there in '94. Dad met me down there, and I insisted we stay in the same motel we had stayed in the year before. I admit, I am a little superstitious—but nothing like my dad. He packed precisely the same clothes he had worn the year before.

Al agreed to come down from his home in Massachusetts to caddy for me. Since my fortunes changed dramatically for the better after I hooked up with him at Hartford, I wanted him there. I am not sure if I wanted his good luck or his ability to help me stay on an even keel. Whatever the reason, I knew it could not hurt to have him there.

The tournament began on Tuesday, so I arrived Sunday evening to get in a practice round on Monday. I played with Scott Ford, whom I had roomed with the second half of '94, and I took him for $10. We wanted to hit some balls after our round, but a twenty-five-mile-per-hour wind was blowing dead into our face on the range. No one likes to practice under those conditions, because you have a tendency to press a little too hard to compensate for the wind. And since hitting into the wind exaggerates fades and draws, you can get the feeling your swing is off when it is fine.

Rather than fight the wind on the range, we decided to play nine more holes. We were not taking it seriously; my dad might even say we were goofing off. At one point, I jumped out of the cart before it had stopped and I wrenched my back severely. I could not take a full swing. There was nothing to do but go back to the motel, take several aspirin, put a heating pad on it, and hope it would loosen up before the morning.

There is nothing around Haynes City, not even a movie theater. So I spent the rest of the afternoon and the evening playing gin with my dad. I gave him the $10 I had won from Scott along with another $40.

My back was slightly better in the morning, but it still hurt when I took a full swing. I wore a back brace and it helped some, but I was losing everything to the right on the range. I would have to play very conservatively and hope that I would not dig myself a hole too deep to climb out of.

The conditions were tough for the first round. The wind was blowing twenty to thirty miles per hour and the course was playing hard and fast. I stuck to my game plan and tried to avoid doing anything stupid. My tendency to lose shots to the right stayed with me throughout the round, so I played for the left side of the fairways and greens. It worked out well enough. Two bogeys and a birdie gave me a 73, two shots above the cut line.

My back was much better the second day, but I wore the brace to play it safe. My swing was much more fluid than it had been the day before, and everything was going my way. I had four birdies on the first seven holes and finished the front nine in 32.

The tenth hole may have been a turning point in the tournament for me. It was a tight driving hole, so I decided to take my driver out and blast it over all the trouble. I swung too hard and hit a bad pull hook. When I looked up, there was no doubt in my mind that the ball was out of bounds. But just before it crossed the white stakes, it hit a tree and bounced back into play. I had a small opening through the trees, so I punched a five-iron under the branches in the general direction of the green. It was a good shot, but I hit it a little too hard and the ball ran over the green and down a five-foot slope. From there I hit a great pitch that landed in the fringe and trickled five feet past the hole, then I knocked it in for par. Had my tee shot missed that tree and gone out of bounds, my momentum would have been broken and anything could have happened. But the ball stayed in and my roll continued. I finished with a 65, which gave me the lead and put me ten shots above the cut line. I know better than to ever think in absolutes, but I did not see how I could fail to make it to the final stage.

I did not take any chances the third and fourth days and played good, conservative golf. My pair of 73s were good enough for a second-place finish behind Ernie Gonzales. Ernie is one of only five left-handers to win a PGA tournament, the Pensacola Open in 1986. He lost his card in 1987 and he has been struggling ever since to get it back. I hoped this would be his year.

When I returned to Columbia, I rested for a couple of days and then practiced hard for a week. Heather and I left on Wednesday for my brother's place in Atlanta for Thanksgiving. I mostly relaxed for four days. We did go to the Georgia–Georgia Tech game, and I found an hour each day to hit balls.

I left for the finals the following Monday. They were being held at Bear Lakes Country Club in West Palm Beach. They had two courses, the Links and the Lakes, with the Links the easier of the two. The greens on the Links were well mounded, so the course demanded good approach shots, but it was wide open off the tee. No matter how wild you were, you could not get into too much trouble.

The Lakes is an interesting course. The first time I saw it I thought it was a typical resort course, one with water on more than half the holes. But after my practice round I realized that it was a ball-striker's course—something clearly in my favor. The water may have made the course challenging for the snowbirds and tourists, but it came into play on only a couple of holes for us. The course was long, but three of the par fives were reachable in two, and the fourth was a possibility if there was a trailing wind. It was a course that was perfectly suited for my game.

My feeling about the tournament was completely different from what it had been the previous year. In '94, my goal was to make the cut and earn a Nike card. This year I was shooting for a high finish. I wanted to be in the top ten so I could get into more of the tournaments early in the year and get off to a faster start. It is hard to make the top 125 when you're spotting everyone else three months and ten tournaments.

My first round was on the Links course, and it was a tough day. The wind was blowing twenty miles per hour, and there was a light rain throughout most of my round. Still, I managed a solid, two-under-par 70. I spent only about a half hour on the range after the round; I did not want to get tired, since I had five rounds ahead of me. When I checked the scoreboard, I was surprised and concerned by how many low scores there were despite the rough conditions. My 70 put me at about the top-third mark. I did not like the idea that it might be one of those tournaments where you had to have a bucket full of birdies to make it. Despite Rotella's advice that I had to learn to love the idea that each week was a putting contest, I still preferred courses that placed a premium on ball-striking; they gave me a much better chance.

My second round was on the more difficult Lakes course, and I had my best round since Disney. I missed only one fairway, where I made bogey, and I was knocking down the pins with my approach shots. Eight birdies, together with the one bogey, gave me a 65, and I jumped all the way up to tenth place. I was especially happy with the round because it took away the pressure of making the cut. All I had to do was have two more solid rounds and I was a shoo-in.

Later that evening, I overheard Michael Christie, with whom I was rooming, talking on the phone to our friend, Chris Anderson. "Carl is playing so well, the rest of us are competing for thirty-nine spots. He's hitting the ball great, and there's no doubt he'll qualify. I think it must be a nuisance for him to have to be here."

It made me feel good to hear Michael talk about my game

that way. Golf is a funny game, one in which confidence can make all the difference in the world. My confidence was good already as a result of making most of the cuts during the second half of the year. But hearing what Michael had to say pushed it a notch or two higher. I liked that, because I do not think it's possible to have too much confidence in your game.

It was back to the Links for the third round. Since it was the easier of the two courses, and given my play the previous day, I thought I could shoot a real low number. But my approach shots were a yard or two farther from the pin, and my putts were lipping out instead of diving into the hole as they had the previous day. Still, I played well, and my 69 put me in a good position. I was only two strokes off the lead, so I did not even have to think about the cut.

It was back to the Lakes for the remainder of the tournament, and my fourth round was almost a duplicate of my second. I got off to a fast start with birdies on four of the first six holes. It seemed as if everything I looked at on the green went into the hole. I came to the last hole six under for the day. The eighteenth was a difficult par four, about 440 yards with water down the left side of the fairway and guarding the front of the green. The hole had a double green, sharing a pin with the ninth. It was so large that it was easy to put the ball in three-putt range. Since there was a breeze behind me, I used my three-wood off the tee. About 300 yards out, the fairway sloped steeply down to the pond in front of the green, and I did not want to take any chances. I caught the three-wood flush, and I was a little worried when I saw the ball bound over the crest of the hill. But it stopped twenty yards short of the water. I had only a sand wedge left, and I put it to within three feet for an easy birdie. My second 65 gave me a two-shot lead over Kevin Sutherland.

I was excited about having the lead, but I was also happy that Michael Christie, my teammate from South Carolina, made the cut too. Another old friend from college golf, Jerry Wood, the guy who came from four down with four to play to beat me in the semifinals of the Virginia State Amateur, missed the cut by a single stroke. But he finished high enough to earn his Nike card, and he was excited about that. The three of us went to dinner with Heather, my mom, my dad, and my uncles Lou and Bill, who had come down to watch the tournament. We had a great time. It was a thrill to be leading, and it was made even better by having two of my best friends do so well.

My solid play continued into the fifth round. I was hitting the ball closer to the pins than I had the day before, but the putts weren't dropping. Still, I managed to get it to four under after ten holes. The eleventh was a 170-yard par three, dead into a fifteen-mile-per-hour wind. I hit my six-iron solid, but just as I made contact with the ball, the wind died and the ball flew into the trap behind the green. It was an extremely difficult shot. I had a downhill lie, and the green sloped sharply from back to front, with a pond in front. If I caught it fat, I might not get out of the bunker, and if I caught it thin, I would be wet for sure. I hit it exactly as I intended, but the ball still trickled across the green, stopping just short of the fringe. I two-putted for bogey.

My game flattened out after that. I managed to par the next five holes, and I felt confident I could birdie the seventeenth, the shortest par five on the course. But my tee shot caught a bunker on the left and all I could do was punch it out, fifty yards short of the green. I hit my pitch thin; the ball hit about pin high before skipping over the green. My chip was too tentative; I was worried about it rolling off the front of the green and I left it six feet short. I missed the putt and made six. I was pissed. I hate making sixes anywhere, but I had just made one on the easiest hole on the course.

The tee at the eighteenth faced into the wind, so there was no need to worry about the pond in front of the green. I caught my driver a little thin, and left myself 190 yards to the pin. I hit a great four-iron fifteen feet left of the hole, and knocked it in for birdie and a three-under-par 69. Kevin, who was playing with me, shot 68, so my lead was cut to one stroke.

I was a little disappointed with my score. I thought I had played well enough to be a couple of strokes lower, but I was pleased that I put myself in a position to win. I knew I would finish in the top ten, which would allow me to get into more tournaments during the winter months, so now I could focus on winning. I wanted it badly.

The first hole of the final round was wild. I hit my drive solidly, dead center of the fairway, but Kevin's drive was the worst shot I had seen him hit in two days. His ball was in the middle of the ninth fairway, at least seventy yards to the right of his target. I never pay much attention to what my playing partners are doing, but this was more like match play and I could not help but feel encouraged that I had handled the first-tee jitters better than he had. Kevin hit a great second shot to the left fringe, and I started my wedge directly at the flag. It came up a little short, tried to make it to the top of the two-tiered green, but rolled down the slope thirty-five feet away from the cup. Kevin hit his chip to within inches for a sure par, while I left my approach putt six feet short.

It seems like that happens all the time. I had a clear advantage after our tee shots, and now I had to sink a testy little putt to keep from losing a stroke. The putt looked as if it was going to die on the lip, but it managed to make that one last quarter-rotation and fall into the hole. I sighed with relief.

We both made routine pars on two before heading to the third tee, a short par five and a definite birdie hole. I pull-hooked the tee shot and thought it was probably out-of-bounds. I hit a provisional, but there was some chance my first ball got caught up in the rough short of the stakes. It was in bounds by a yard, and I salvaged my par. Kevin birdied the hole to pull even with me.

I birdied the second par five to regain the lead. After that, Kevin had several solid pars while, for the first time all week, I could not hit a green. It seemed that I had to sink a four- to five-footer on every hole for my par. I was able to maintain my one-shot lead when we reached the ninth, a 465-yard par four and the most difficult hole on the course. We both hit good drives into a stiff wind, leaving ourselves long irons into a shallow green. Kevin hit his second shot a little fat and his ball bounced once before disappearing into the pond fronting the green. I hit my shot a little thin, but it managed to clear the pond, hit the bank, and hop up to the front fringe. Kevin took his drop eighty yards from the green and hit a great wedge to within five feet to save his bogey. I made yet another four-footer for my par to take a two-stroke lead.

On ten, I hit my second shot wedge to within a foot for birdie and a three-shot lead. I felt good. My irons were not as sharp as they had been all week, but I still had it two under and had extended my lead.

We both parred eleven, twelve, and thirteen and I was confident my game was back on track, since I had hit all three greens in regulation. The fourteenth was a long par three, and Kevin and I both hit good shots pin high, thirty feet to the right of the flag. The only problem was that there were two fingers extending from the back of the green and a five-foot swale was between our balls and the pin. Kevin was away by a couple of inches. He putted his ball down the slope. It barely had enough steam to make it back to the top of the swale, but then it trickled to within inches of the cup. I tried the same shot. I hit it with the right speed, but I did not allow enough for the break and my ball ended up six feet below the hole. I felt confident about the putt. I had been making six-footers all day, and this one was easier than most; it was straight uphill. But I pushed it slightly, and it caught the lip and spun out. My lead was down to two shots.

I made two more quick bogeys on fifteen and sixteen when two poor iron shots caught bunkers. Not only did I fall back to even with Kevin, my three consecutive bogeys probably let some other guys back in the hunt. I was feeling discouraged as I approached the seventeenth tee. I said to Al, "I might end up bogeying the rest of the way in."

"I don't think so," Al said in his typically calm voice. "I think you've got a couple of birdies left in you."

Kevin hit his drive down the center of the fairway on the short par-five seventeenth, and I pulled mine into the left rough. Kevin hit a great four-wood over the trees guarding the corner of the dog-leg. His ball was on the green, and it looked as if it could be close. I was blocked out by two small trees, and my only chance was to hook the ball around them. I put a great swing on the ball with a four-iron, but it had a touch too much hook on it and caught the bunker on the left of the green. I was in trouble.

There were not any scoreboards on the course, so I did not know how things stood. My dad was checking with the Golf Channel people to see what they knew. He learned that Steve Hart had eagled seventeen minutes earlier to move ahead of both Kevin and me by two shots. My dad decided it was best not to tell me.

I hit a good bunker shot, but I left myself with another six-footer for birdie. Kevin's shot was close; he did not have more than fifteen feet for eagle. His putt burned the right edge but refused to go in, so I had a chance to stay even with him. I do not know when I last grinded so hard over a six-footer, but somehow I managed to get it in the hole for my birdie. We were going to eighteen dead even.

Kevin did not take any chances with the water and bunkers on the left and hit his tee shot well to the right. It was in the fairway, but it left him with a long iron to the green. I wanted to have a short iron in, so I aimed down the left-center of the fairway. I pulled my three-wood slightly and saw that it was headed for a bunker on the left before I lost it in the setting sun.

I turned to Al. "What happened to it?"

"You must be living right" was all he said.

"What do you mean?"

"The ball couldn't have cleared the bunker by more than a foot."

Kevin hit to the back fringe. It was a good shot; there was no way he could keep a long iron on the shallow green with the wind at his back.

I breathed a sigh of relief when I got to my ball. It had stopped in the only level area within twenty yards, among some scraggly rough on firm sandy soil. Considering where I had hit it, it was the best possible lie I could have. I had 165 yards to the pin with a slight breeze at my back. The adrenaline was really working, so I thought an eight-iron would be enough. The moment it came off the club I knew it was a good shot. It was right at the pin and came down twelve feet below the hole.

Kevin hit a good chip four feet past the cup, so I knew that if I could sink my birdie putt I would beat him. I did not know where anyone else stood, but my dad had learned that Hart had three-putted eighteen for bogey to drop back into a tie with Kevin and me. We were the last group on the course, so all 800 people who had come to watch the tournament had their eyes on me as I lined up my putt. It was as easy as a twelve-footer can be, uphill with a slight right-to-left break. It was in all the way.

When the crowd roared, I knew I had won. I experienced a sense of relief more than anything else. The tournament had been mine to win, and I almost let it slip away with those three bogeys on the back nine. The birdies on seventeen and eighteen, though, proved that I had become a lot tougher mentally. I was ready to break through in the big time.

Both the Golf Channel and a crew from *Inside the PGA Tour* wanted interviews, and I was happy to oblige. While I was talking, I could hear a familiar voice in the background yelling, "Do they want to talk to the winner's dad?"

There was no presentation ceremony and I did not get a trophy, but the number-one ranking among the Q-School graduates for the beginning of the 1996 season and the check for $15,000 were more than adequate. I would probably be able to play in any tournament I wanted for at least the first couple of months, and the $15,000 would be more than enough to finance the Tour's West Coast swing.

After I finished talking with the handful of media who were covering the tournament, I was approached by four or five agents who had come for the final two rounds looking for new clients. I had signed a contract with an agent the previous June, so they were not persistent. A representative from IMG, superagent Mark McCormick's group, did promise me they would take good care of me if I ever wanted to make a change.

The best thing about the win was the shot of confidence it provided. There were eight former Tour winners who did not make the cut, and another half-dozen who finished behind me. My score of twenty-three under par set a new Q-School record. I also couldn't help but think about Woody Austin, who had won the previous year's Fall Classic and went on to win a tournament and three-quarters of a million dollars in his rookie year. I had proved to myself that I belonged in that category. The following year, 1996, would be my year to prove it to everyone else.

## CHAPTER 9

## Déjà Vu All Over Again

During the weeks following my Q-School victory, I felt like an old veteran—at least compared to the year before. I was not drifting off in the middle of conversations wondering what it would be like out on the Tour; I knew what it would be like. I was not wondering how I would find my way around two dozen new cities; I was the old pro, I would manage just fine. And most important, I was not wondering if I would be competitive out there; I knew I was competitive. Anyone who wins the Fall Classic, a tournament played under the most intense pressure possible, has the ability to win anywhere. I was not going around predicting I would win a tournament in '96, but I did not rule out the possibility, either.

I experienced something else for the first time that December—my phone was ringing. Because I tied for the last spot in the '94 Q-School, and because I managed to stay anonymous until nearly the end of the year when I shot 62 at Disney, I had not had many offers for endorsement contracts. I did receive about $10,000 for the '95 season for wearing the shirts and hats made by a small clothing company, but they were apparently having financial problems and they did not pay me until my uncle Lou, an attorney, let them know I would appreciate my money.

I received several calls from both equipment and clothing companies following my victory, and I signed with Snake Eyes and Izod. I agreed to use the Snake Eyes wedges and to display their logo on my bag and hat, and to wear Izod Club golf shirts. I also received a small retainer from Titleist to use their balls, gloves, and shoes. A few months down the road I would begin to wear a Sharpie office-supplies logo on my shirtsleeve as well. Taken together, these contracts would cover the $75,000 it would take to play the Tour for the year. The contracts included performance clauses, so if I had a good year, my income from the endorsements could double.

It is expensive to play on the Tour. I spent nearly $12,000 on plane fares in 1995. Since I began so many weeks on the alternate list, I usually did not know if I would be playing in a tournament until a few days before it started. That meant, of course, that I had to pay the full fares. I expected to save some money on plane fares during the first few months of 1996, since my high priority ranking meant I could plan ahead and buy my tickets for the West Coast swing a month early. Overall, though, I expected to spend considerably more on plane fares for '96. When Heather began to travel with me in May, the cost of tickets would double. Also, I expected to play in about ten more tournaments in '96 than the twenty-one I played during 1995.

For my 1996 budget, I estimated I would average about $700 per week for travel. The standard fee for a caddy was $500 per week plus 3 percent of my winnings if I made the cut, 7 percent if I finished in the top ten, and 10 percent for a win. When I split a hotel room with a friend, I spent from $40 to $50 per night, but that would also double beginning in May. The tournament entry fee was $100, and I usually gave the locker-room attendant $50. Add in another few hundred bucks for meals, entertainment, and incidentals and it cost me from $1,700 to $2,000 per week to travel alone. Come May, after Heather and I were married, that would jump to $2,200 to $2,500 per week.

Since I could count on another $20,000 in income from the Monday pro-ams and a few corporate outings, I began the year knowing I would finish in the black even if I never made a cut. I was lucky to be in the position of not having to give the money a thought, but it did annoy me when I read articles about professional golfers being spoiled. I finished 1995 183rd on the money list, and I did little more than break even. The 183rd highest-paid baseball player probably made a couple of million dollars, and he did not have to make his own plane reservations, much less worry about paying for them. And if he had an off-year, his multiyear contract meant that he did not have to wonder where he would have to go to earn a paycheck the following year.

I, like most of the guys, take pride in the fact that professional golf is a merit system in its purest form. If you play well, you do well. If you play poorly, you are gone. But I think professional golfers are the least spoiled and the lowest paid of any professional athletes. I honestly do not care about the lowest paid part. As long as I earn enough to support my family in a comfortable way, the money does not mean much to me. I care about the competition. I am out there to win tournaments, and someday, to win majors—not to make a million dollars.

The week before Christmas, I sat down with a tournament schedule to plan the first part of the year. I called the PGA office and committed to play in all the tournaments beginning with the Nortel Open in Tucson through the BellSouth Classic in Atlanta, with the exception of the Hawaiian Open during the middle of February. That schedule would have me playing in five consecutive tournaments before a break during the week the Tour was in Hawaii, and then five more consecutive tournaments. I would have off the week of the Players Championship—unless I happened to win one of the first ten tournaments—before playing in the BellSouth. I recorded the commitment numbers for each tournament that the PGA office gave entrants to eliminate the possibility of mix-ups. Had I wanted to, I could have committed to all the tournaments for the entire year, but my strategy was to plan about one-third of the year at a time. That way, if something good happened (like winning a tournament, maybe) I could make adjustments to my schedule. I hoped I could get off to a better start than the year before so I would not have to play in every tournament I got into. When I could pick my spots, I was sure it would feel like a luxury.

I left Columbia for Tucson on a Sunday afternoon. While I was excited about getting the year started, I was concerned about my game. December was unusually cold on the East Coast, and there were very few days when I could hit any balls. I do not like cold weather, and I am sure there are guys who practice in conditions I would find intolerable. But when the temperature is in the twenties with high winds, I would have to wear so many clothes, it might do me more harm than good to practice.

When I arrived in Dallas to make the connection to Tucson, I saw Curtis Strange waiting for the same flight. He had come from Newport News, the airport closest to his home in Williamsburg. He congratulated me on my Q-School win, but mostly we talked about how cold it had been. Like me, he was concerned that he did not have much of a chance to prepare for Tucson.

When we boarded the plane, Curtis took his seat in first class while I continued to the rear of the plane. A few minutes before we took off, a stewardess asked, "I saw you talking to Curtis Strange. Do you know him?"

"Yes, I'm Carl Paulson, one of the guys on tour whom you've never heard of."

"There are some extra seats in first class. Would you like to sit with him on the flight?"

"Sure." I did not have to think twice about that. I did not know firsthand, but I heard a rumor that the food was better up there, and it would sure be a lot easier to catch a nap in those roomy seats.

So the promising Tour sophomore was on his way to the first tournament of the season—first class, no less—and asking Curtis Strange to pass the sugar. What a life.

The weather in Tucson was perfect for a golf tournament, and I could not wait to get out on the course and get the year started. I actually hit the ball decently on Thursday during my first round at Starpass, but I could not sink a putt. In the frustration of the moment, I blamed the greens—which, in fact, were awful. I heard they had been just as bad the year before and the superintendent was given a year to get them in shape. He did not make it and was fired the Monday after the tournament. My late starting time did not help. I saw spike marks that were—I swear to God—an inch high. But the fact of the matter was that not everyone had nearly as much trouble as I did. Still, had I not doubled the seventeenth, I would have been in pretty good shape. As it was, my seventy-four put me in danger of missing the cut.

I felt good about my chances on Friday, though. I was playing at Tucson National, which was my kind of course: medium long and relatively open. It was one of the easier courses we played all year, and I thought I could shoot a low number and still make the cut. Once again I hit a lot of solid shots, but I could not get the ball in the hole. My one birdie was offset by a single bogey, and I missed the cut by three shots. It was not the start I had hoped for, but I was pleased I hit the ball as crisply as I did. Given my limited opportunities to practice in early January, my game could have been much worse.

The Bob Hope would be a better week, I was sure of it. I liked the courses and I was staying with Chris Anderson, my friend from the minitour. Pete Jordan, a third-year Tour player, and I played a practice round at Indian Ridge on Tuesday, and on the fourth hole we saw Tom Kite coming up behind us. I hoped he would ask to join us, but there was not much chance of that. Tom rarely played practice rounds, and when he did, he liked to play alone. But I would have loved the opportunity to pick the brain of the man who was second on the career money-earning list.

He drove his cart up to ours and said, "Hi, guys, do you mind if I play through?" I hopped out of the cart and said, "Hi, Tom, I'm Carl Paulson." We had met before, but I wasn't sure if he remembered me.

"Sure, I know you, Carl. Say, you put some pretty good numbers on the board in West Palm Beach. That should get people to sit up and notice you."

"Thanks. I'm surprised you know about that."

"Of course I know about it. I watched the last round on television."

I was amazed that Tom would have any interest in the tournament. Clearly, he loves golf as much as anyone if he spends his days off watching Q-School. I was also flattered that someone of Tom's stature would remember me and compliment me on my play.

As expected, Tom did play through, and within a couple of minutes we lost sight of him.

I got off to a good start for the first round of the tournament on Wednesday. My 69 put me in the top half of the field, but I was disappointed with my putting again. Had I putted average, my score could have been three or four strokes lower.

Thursday I played at Indian Ridge, and my irons were hot. It seemed as if I had a fifteen-footer for birdie on almost every hole. The only problem was that I could not get any of them to drop. On eighteen, I had it to within six feet for birdie and I yanked it to the left of the cup. It was the eighth putt of fifteen feet or less that I had missed during the round, and I was seething. With my head hanging, I walked to the edge of the green and heaved my putter toward the center of the lake. I momentarily forgot it was the hole where they had floated two cars in the water. When I looked up, my putter was flying directly toward the first car. "Oh my God," I thought, "I'm going to break a windshield." I could not hit anything all day with that putter, so I should not have worried. It cleared the first car by a good ten yards and splashed several yards short of the second car. It was a dumb thing to do, and I could have been fined for it, but I was in the last group, the television cameras were long gone, and there could not have been more than ten people in the stands.

About six months later, one of the guys who work and travel with the Tour told me he went in after my club and had been putting great with it. I was happy for him. It never did a damn thing for me.

I went into Friday's round in good shape at four under. But I had trouble with more than my putting that day, and I finished with an ugly 74. I dropped back to two under par for the tournament.

The cut at the Hope came on Saturday, after four rounds, so I still had a chance. The projected cut was five, maybe six under, so it would not take a miracle to post a score good enough to get me to Sunday. The first hole at Tamarask was a short par five, and I put my four-iron second shot to within a foot for eagle. On the second hole, I nailed a seven-iron to a foot again, this time for birdie. Suddenly I was back to five under and in good shape to make the cut.

I am not sure what happened on the next seven holes. I was shell-shocked by the time I walked off the ninth green. Somehow, I had managed to take my three-under start and turn it into a three-over 39. I was out of the tournament.

I did hit one memorable shot on the back nine. On the seventeenth, I pulled my drive into the left rough. The ball was 140 yards from the green, but it was nestled against one tree and behind another. Since I did not have much to lose, I turned my six-iron over and tried to hook the ball around the tree, left-handed. I made good contact with the ball, but it went dead straight. Somehow it managed to get through the branches cleanly and it landed five yards short of the trap guarding the front of the green, skipped through the sand, and stopped ten feet from the pin. I saved my par, went on to birdie the eighteenth, and finished with another 74.

My putting was rapidly becoming a serious concern. I hit the ball well enough to make the cut in my first two tournaments, but here I was, batting oh for two. During the last round at Bob Hope, I noticed that my loss of confidence in the putter seemed to be working its way through the rest of my game. I was beginning to shoot at pins I had no business going for, but I was afraid I could not get a birdie unless I hit it to within a couple feet. It was so bad, I was beginning to worry about two-putting when I was more than thirty feet out. I had to turn things around.

The confidence I brought with me to California was virtually gone.

Phoenix, the last week in January, was the next stop, and it battered my confidence even more. I managed a 72 in the opening round, then ballooned to a 78 on Friday. Not only couldn't I get my putts started on line, I could not even see the line. The common wisdom was that everything would break toward the valley, but I could not bring myself to believe it half the time. Perhaps it was the kind of course I could learn to play with experience, but the greens remained a mystery to me after two rounds.

Before the first round on Thursday morning, I went to the back of the range to warm up since it was close to the first tee. After ten minutes or so, Tom Watson walked up with a shag bag of balls, dumped it on the ground, and began to hit two-irons. "Hey, Tom," I said. "Don't you think you should limber up with some wedges?"

"No, if I can hit my two-iron, I can hit anything in the bag," he said as he rifled another shot 220 yards down the range.

During my first year on the Tour, I was able to see almost all the guys hit balls—at least on the range—and I would say that Tom is the best ball-striker out here. And from what everyone tells me, he has not lost a thing over the twenty-five years he has been playing. Indeed, some claim he has become even better with his driver. He is absolutely amazing. Needless to say, I would not mind a bit if my career paralleled his.

I suppose everyone tries to come up with reasons why their particular strengths are more important than their weaknesses, and I am no exception. My ball-striking ability is clearly better than my short game, and I have to believe that it will be my ball-striking that will allow me to succeed. I have heard it said that great putting can get you to the top of the money list for a couple of years, but it is great ball-striking that can keep you competitive on tour over the long haul. That certainly seems to apply to Watson. Even though he will be eligible for the Senior Tour in a few years, and even though he has played in only fifteen or sixteen tournaments a year for the past ten years, he is consistently in the top fifty money winners. And during those years when his putter was hot, no one could beat him.

I did not have anywhere to go after missing the cut on Friday, so I hung around the clubhouse that evening. They have a lounge there called the Bird's Nest, and it is always pretty lively during the week of the tournament. I ended up at a table with several guys, and Roger Maltby joined us. He had endless stories about the old days on tour, and I was fascinated by them. I could not help but feel better listening to him, and before I left two hours later I was laughing as hard as everyone else. I made a mental note to tell my dad some of Roger's stories when my mom was not around.

From Phoenix I went to the AT&T Pebble Beach, and again I felt good about my chances. I had not missed the cut by much the year before, I had seen the courses, and I loved playing both Spyglass and Pebble Beach. They were both courses I could score on. Spyglass, in my mind, is one of the truly great courses we play, and Pebble Beach offers the most breathtaking views. It was weeks like this, when I was able to play two such great courses, that I appreciated how fortunate I was.

My only concern was Poppy Hills. I would have trouble there. For the life of me, I cannot see the landing areas when I am standing on the tee, and the course doesn't offer any bailout areas. You either hit perfect shots out there or you make double. If I could get by Poppy Hills without blowing up, I would have a good chance of doing well in the tournament.

Poppy Hills got me again. My 75 put me far down the leader board, but not so far that I could not make it up.

By the time I got back to my room that evening, I knew I was coming down with something. My muscles ached, and I had a sore throat and a headache. I took three aspirin and hoped I would feel better in the morning.

I did not. I felt worse. It was obvious by this time that I had a bad case of the flu. I thought about withdrawing from the tournament, but I did not want to miss the chance to play at Pebble Beach.

Friday was a cold, rainy day, and my symptoms got worse as the round progressed. I felt so bad by the time we finished that I did not even care that I shot 82. I would have withdrawn immediately, but the forecast was for more rain, and if Saturday was washed out, I might feel better by Sunday.

The weather on Saturday was bad, and my flu was worse. The rumor Saturday evening was that the tournament might be canceled. I knew I could not play and was about to withdraw, but if they canceled the tournament everyone would get a check, and I could not afford to pass that up. Finally, about nine o'clock that evening we got word that the tournament was over and we would all get $5,000. I was never so pleased to see a round washed out.

I was feeling much better by Tuesday of the following week, so I knew I would be ready for the Buick Invitational near San Diego. I was, however, becoming desperate to make something happen. I could not believe what was going on. I began the year with such high expectations, and it was turning out to be 1995 all over again. The first month of the season was gone and I still had not come close to making a cut.

Nothing happened in San Diego on Thursday. I shot 74, which put me out of the tournament since it looked as though the cut would be four under par. I called Butch that evening to ask for his help. He agreed to fly out with Heather and my mom and dad, who had planned to come out for a few days.

My goal for Friday was simply to get it under par. I did not have any illusions about shooting 66 and making the cut; I just wanted to have my first subpar round in a month. I managed two birdies to go with two bogeys, and I reached the eighteenth tee even for the day. The last hole was a short par five and an easy birdie hole. I was sure I could do it. I could get birdie for 71 and maybe that would be enough to break my slump. But I hooked my drive in the woods, had to chip out, and settled for par.

After the round, I was feeling as low as I had the year before. Maybe even lower. The previous year I had no reason to believe I would get off to a fast start, but 1996 was supposed to be my year.

Butch and I were on the range by nine on Saturday morning. He watched me hit about a half-dozen balls before he said, "Carl, I've never seen you so tense. You've got to loosen up. You've got to stop putting so much pressure on yourself."

I understood what he was saying, but I am not sure he could understand how hard it would be for me to do what he was asking. If someone is afraid of snakes, how much good will it do to say, "Don't be scared, just relax," while dangling a python in front of him? That's how I felt. I knew I was tense. I knew I felt unbearable pressure. But I could not change simply because Butch told me I should.

"How do I do that?" I asked.

"Listen, Carl. You're in a slump right now and I know it feels like the end of the world. But you'll get past it, just the way you did last year. And once you get past it, you'll look back and ask yourself why you made yourself suffer so. What I'm telling you is that it's not the end of the world. Right now you may feel like it is, but you have to stop believing that. Now, let's see what we can do to get your swing back on track."

We spent the morning working on developing a more fluid transition from the backswing to the forward swing. My swing has always been compact; I hardly ever want to take the club back past three-quarters. But Butch saw that I had become even shorter and quicker.

Nick Faldo was hitting balls next to us, and he seemed to be interested in what Butch was saying to me. A few times he paused and openly watched as Butch was giving me instruction on the position of my hands at the top of my backswing. After Nick left, Butch said, "You see how lucky you are to have me for a teacher? Even Faldo listens when I talk."

The Tour went to Hawaii the week after San Diego, so I had a few days off. Butch and I spent the mornings working on my swing, and the rest of the day my folks and Heather joined us and we played the role of typical San Diego tourists. The zoo really is as great as everyone says, and the city is packed with great seafood restaurants. I am sure the traveling gets old for the guys who have been on tour for a number of years, but I was having a great time. I had never traveled much before, and the Tour stops at some of the nicest places in the country. I was especially looking forward to Heather joining me so I could show her all the sights I had experienced the previous year.

My family and Butch left for home on Tuesday evening and I left for Los Angeles. I was staying with George and Patty Pappas, whom I met at the pro-am in San Diego. Our Greek heritage gave us an instant connection, and they were a great couple.

At the beginning of the year, I planned to skip Hawaii to give myself a break and to save a little money on the airfares. As it turned out, I needed the time off to work on some of the things Butch and I had talked about. By the weekend, I felt as if I was making progress. My swing was feeling a little smoother and I thought I felt some glimmerings of confidence when I had the putter in my hands.

I was looking forward to the following week and the Nissan Los Angeles Open, because I loved Riviera. It was both a demanding and interesting layout, and I placed it just a notch below Spyglass and Glen Abbey.

Thursday and Friday were both disappointing days. It was obvious that the changes Butch had tried to get me to make had not taken hold. I shot 74-75 and missed the cut by four shots. I could not blame my putting for my poor scores. My entire game was giving me trouble, and I began to wonder if my slump would ever end. It seemed to be getting worse, not better.

I paid the extra money to change my plane reservation and left for Columbia on Saturday morning after missing the cut. I wanted to get back east as fast as I could. I had enough West Coast golf to last me for quite some time.

It looked as though I would have the week off, since I was tenth on the alternate list for the Doral-Ryder Open. I needed the break. Maybe I could use it to get my game together. Because I had yet to win any money, I was rapidly losing the advantage that my win at Q-School gave me. They reshuffled the rankings about every two months, and after failing to win a dime during that time, my number was dropping like a rock.

The Honda Classic was held in Fort Lauderdale the first week of March 1996. As usual, I arrived on Sunday evening to give myself time to prepare for the busy week. I played a practice round with Mike Donald on Tuesday, and we talked about how we both felt more comfortable on the East Coast.

"A couple years ago, I decided to skip San Diego," Mike told me. "I have never played worth a damn there, and I told myself I wasn't going there only to frustrate myself again." That was unusual for Mike, because he lives to play golf and he almost never skips a tournament he's eligible for.

"Well, come Thursday morning, I was feeling guilty," he said. "After all, you never know what's going to happen in a given week."

I gave him a sympathetic smile.

"Then, on Saturday morning, I looked in the paper and saw the cut was five under," he continued. "I said, thank God I didn't bother. I couldn't shoot five under there if my life depended on it."

I am not sure why so many guys have trouble playing on the coast opposite the one they grew up on. And it isn't only guys like Mike and me who have trouble adjusting. Phil Mickelson, one of the very best players on the Tour, would not win his first tournament east of the Mississippi until later in the year.

It is difficult to understand. Sure, the grasses are different on the two coasts, but they do not really play all that dissimilarly. It seemed to me the difference between Bermuda and bent greens, both of which are common in the southeastern part of the country, is more dramatic than the difference between East and West Coast greens.

Maybe it all comes down to confidence. That certainly is a possibility, since putting is mostly attitude.

At any rate, I was glad to be in Florida, just a few miles down the road from where I had played so well in December.

I played halfway decent golf on Thursday and Friday. My scores of 71 and 72 were good enough to make the cut by two shots. The monkey was finally off my back for 1996. I hoped 1995 would repeat itself and Honda would be the first of a string of tournaments in which I made the cut.

My only disappointment was that I was staying by myself that week so I did not have anyone to share my excitement with. After Friday's round, I celebrated my first cut of the season by going back to my room and watching a pay-per-view movie.

I was paired with Vijay Singh for Saturday's round. It was fun to play with him, because he hits the ball as long as, and maybe a little longer than, I do. He finished 1995 fourth in driving distance with an average of 283 yards, while I finished eighth with an average of 278 yards. I could keep up with him most of the time, but into the wind, no one could hit it farther than Vijay. He has such a low, boring trajectory that his ball seems to cut right through the wind. And if the fairways are firm, he will outhit his playing partners by thirty or forty yards—unless, of course, he is playing with John Daly.

The first hole at Weston Hills was dead into a thirty-mile-per-hour wind. I caught my drive solid and I was only about fifteen yards behind Vijay. I had 145 yards to the pin, and it took every bit of a four-iron to get it to the front fringe. Vijay's approach shot ballooned into the wind, drifted a few yards to the right, and came down in a little swale beside the green. He had an impossible third shot. The wind had dried out the greens, and they were lightning fast. The pin was on the short side of the green, which sloped away from him. There was no way Vijay could keep his chip on the putting surface.

He walked back and forth from his ball to the left side of the green several times. "What the hell am I supposed to do with this?" he asked. As he positioned himself over the ball, he said, "I guess the only thing to do is hit the pin."

His ball motored as it approached the hole, but the damned thing hit the flagstick squarely, took a little hop into the air, and dove into the cup. I hit my chip five feet past the cup and made it coming back for par.

Both of our rounds seemed to continue in a similar fashion.

We played almost exactly the same, but Vijay got a couple of good breaks to finish with a 70 while I got a couple of not-so-good breaks to finish with a 74.

I thought a lot about our rounds that night, while I spent another evening alone in my hotel room. On the scoreboard, the difference between a 70 and a 74 is enormous. It means the difference between making and missing the cut. It means the difference between earning a check that helps you pick up some ground on the money list and a check that barely covers your expenses for the week. Yet on the course the difference between a 70 and a 74 can be so small. Vijay's chip hits that flag, mine trickles five feet past the cup, and I have lost a stroke to him, just like that.

It seemed to me that two possibilities could account for my posting more 74s than 70s. Maybe my slow start resulted from bad luck. Maybe I was losing those three to four strokes per round because I could not get a break. There was some comfort in that thought, but I was probably the only one who could believe I got only bad breaks for two months running.

It seemed more likely that Vijay had something I did not, something that let him turn a mediocre round into a 70. Maybe it was his experience, maybe it was his mental toughness. But whatever it was, I knew I had to pick it up soon or I would be playing in the Fall Classic for a fourth time.

Sunday's round was a little better. I shot 71 to finish in a tie for forty-fourth and earn a check for $3,837.

Tim Herron ended up winning the tournament, only two months into his rookie season. He played on the Nike Tour in 1995, where he finished twenty-fifth, and earned his card for 1996 when he finished twelfth at Q-School. Since we were low guys on the totem pole, we both received the late-morning and afternoon tee times the first two days of tournaments and we were always running into each other.

I was happy for Tim, but it made me wonder why I was struggling so. Tim had a great amateur career; he won all three of his matches in the 1993 Walker Cup. As a professional, he had not had any more success than I, yet he came out of nowhere to win a tournament. If Tim could do it, why the hell wasn't I doing it?

Arnold Palmer's tournament at Bay Hill the following week was popular with the players, so I had the week off. Paul Goydos became the second consecutive first-time winner when he shot thirteen under to earn the first-place check. Jeez, everyone was breaking through except me.

I was able to get into the Freeport-McDermott in New Orleans the following week. I requested housing through the tournament, and I was placed with a family who lived not more than ten minutes from the course. It is always an option to stay with a family who has volunteered to take a player into their home for the week, and I had done so a couple of times the year before. Unless you are willing to spend more than $100 per night, it is not possible to find a place to stay in New Orleans that is reasonably close to the course and give you confidence that you would not be mugged in the middle of the night.

The weather was terrible for the practice round on Tuesday. It was cold, and the wind had to be at least forty miles per hour. When I got out of bed on Wednesday morning, my neck was so stiff I could hardly move my head. It had happened to me a few times before, and I knew it probably would not get better before the week was out. I spent most of Wednesday in the physical-fitness trailer at the course, taking massages, heat, and a whirlpool, trying to loosen it up. It did not help much. The man I was staying with was a physician, so Wednesday evening he gave me enough pain pills to get me through the next two days.

On Thursday morning, it did seem a little better. I could move my head to the right pretty well, but I still couldn't move it to the left at all. When I hit my first wedge on the range, I realized I was in for a tough day. Because I could not move my head to the left, I could not keep my eye on the ball throughout my backswing. There was a split second when I simply lost sight of it.

It never got any better as the round progressed, but I played surprisingly well given the howling winds together with my losing sight of the ball on every shot. I came to the eighteenth hole two over for the day, which would be a respectable score in the tough conditions. I nailed my drive down the center of the fairway, leaving myself a full wedge to the green. The shot was dead on line and came down six feet short of the pin. Then I watched in horror as the ball spun sharply back, made it to the slope in front of the green, and continued to roll until it dropped in the pond guarding the front of the green. I had hit what I thought were two great shots and ended up with a triple. The 77 put me out of yet another tournament.

My neck had not improved by Friday, and I limped in with an 81.

Going into the week, I told myself that I had reached bottom—things could not get any worse. Missing the cut by thirteen shots proved that I was wrong.

Scott McCarron was thirteen under for the week, which was good enough for the win. He had become my closest friend on the Tour, so I was very happy for him. But I also felt a rush of frustration. I thought about all our Tuesday practice rounds when I had taken him for fifteen or twenty bucks as often as not. Still, he had been able to put four good rounds together while I was having trouble putting together two mediocre rounds. Yes, he was a good player, good enough to win. But so was I. I knew it, Scott knew it, several of the other guys knew it. Why was I having so much trouble showing everyone how good I was?

The Players Championship was the last week in March and I did not come close to qualifying, so I returned to Columbia for a week of rest and practice. I left Sunday afternoon for Atlanta and the BellSouth Classic. My dad met me there and I looked forward to having a friendly face around, even if he happened to bring one of his dirty, good-luck shirts.

Thursday's round was a roller coaster. I had seven birdies, but still managed to shoot only even par. My driver was giving me fits that day. Almost every bogey resulted from missing the fairway off the tee, and the rough was severe enough that I could not get it out and onto the green. After a birdie at thirteen, I hooked another tee shot on fourteen to a spot that almost guaranteed another bogey. In frustration I snapped the driver over my knee. As I handed the pieces to Al, I said, "There. I won't be tempted to use that club again today."

On the fifteenth, a par three, I hit my tee shot to four feet for birdie, and as I walked off the green I was thinking I could still get it to two or three under for the day.

The seventeenth hole seemed to be typical of much of the year. I hit a good drive, and what looked like a perfect nine-iron for my second shot. It was a couple of yards short, though, and buried in the front trap. I could not do much with the shot and got it only to the front fringe. I thinned my chip and ran it twenty feet past the hole. Then I knocked in the twenty-footer to save my bogey. The two dozen people who had stayed around late enough to see me play gave me an enthusiastic round of applause. I was steamed by letting the round get away from me, but there was something almost humorous about my pathetic display around the green. I turned to the largest group of people and said, "My dad will be around to collect sixteen ninety-five for the exciting show I gave you." They laughed, and I felt a little better.

The weather was bad on Friday, and by the time I finished the front nine, the cut was projected to be three over. I managed to keep it to two over on the front nine, and I was actually pleased with my play. I was having a tough time with the wind, but I was able to get it up and down more times than not to stay in the tournament. I made a few more bogeys early in the back nine to put me at four over, but I started grinding, trying to get back into the tournament. I was making those four- and five-footers for the first time in a long while, and it was fun.

My tee shot on the par-three fifteenth hole was dead at the pin. The wind caught it, however, and held it up just enough so the ball caught the bunker guarding the front of the green. I hit a good trap shot to four feet, but the ball was above and to the left of the cup. I knew it would be fast coming down the hill, and I knew I had to have it if I were to have any chance of making the cut. There was enough break to make me unsure of what the ball would do if I tried to die it in the cup, so I decided my best chance was to hit firm to the center of the hole. I did hit it firm, but it missed the right lip and did not stop until it was twenty feet past the cup. I two-putted from there, and the double put me well outside the cut line. I was going home early again.

I had committed to play in the Nike tournament in Florence, South Carolina, the following week, the week of the Masters. I knew a lot of people in the area from my college days, and I liked the course. Also, I thought with some of the pressure gone, I might find a way to get things turned around.

I had played the course so many times that I did not need to have a practice round, so I did not leave Columbia for Florence until Thursday morning. I played well the first two days, and my 68-70 put me close enough to the top of the leader board that I thought I had a good chance to do something over the weekend.

Saturday was not my day, but I stayed in it and managed to get through the first fifteen holes even par. Then I finished double, bogey, bogey. It was maddening. I had worked so hard to make the most of what I had that day, and then I let it get away from me. I had been letting it get away from me all year.

Sunday was a good day. I burned up the front nine for a 31, then held it together on the back for a five-under 67. It was good for a sixth-place finish and a check for $9,000. Maybe I had turned the corner.

I learned the following Monday that I was in for the MCI Classic at Hilton Head. I got there in time for a practice round on Tuesday, and while the course was not designed with my game in mind, I thought I could do well. Harbour Town is a beautiful course, and it demands a variety of shots. There are a number of holes where you could be in the fairway and still not have a clear shot to the green. You had to be able to put your tee shot in one side of the fairway or the other, and you had to be able to work the ball, depending on the demands of the particular hole.

I played about as I expected on Thursday, with the exception of one hole on which I set a personal record for high score as a professional golfer. Somehow, I managed to get a nine on a par-four hole. My three-wood off the tee drifted into the right rough among the trees. It was an easy chip back to the fairway, but I rushed it a little and hit the ball too high. It caught a branch dead center and caromed over my head. The ball landed in a bush, so I had no choice but to take an unplayable lie. I dropped the ball in a position to chip it out to the fairway, but caught a branch again. This time it dropped straight down into deep rough.

Heather had come to Harbour Town to watch me play, and later she told me she was dying the whole time I was struggling to get the ball back to the fairway. After my fourth shot, a man standing next to her observed, "This guy really sucks."

Heather was not about to let my honor go unchallenged, so she told him, "Watch it, asshole, that's my fiancé you're talking about."

"I didn't mean anything by it. I was just saying 'this sucks' that he's having a tough time." The man was obviously embarrassed.

Heather was too angry to be mollified. "I heard what you said" was her only response as she turned and headed toward the green.

I did not play badly after that, but it was far too late. My 80 gave me no chance to make the cut. Friday was about the same—although I did not make a nine—and my 74 saved me from being dead last. I finished two strokes ahead of Robert Gamez, who shot 77-79.

Sunday I received word that I was in at Greensboro for the following week. After the practice round, I felt good about my chances. The course had good length and reasonably generous landing areas off the tees. The rough, though, was something else. It was among the most severe I had seen yet in my eighteen months on the Tour. Some of the guys were saying that it was every bit as tough as what you would find at a U.S. Open.

I got a bad break with the weather. I was playing late-early the first two days, and a cold front was due to come through the area around noon on Thursday. And sure enough, the morning was calm, but the wind picked up to twenty-five miles an hour by the time I teed off at two o'clock.

I hit the ball solidly on the front nine, but I could not get a break. On the second hole, a 180-yard par three, I hit my five-iron on the button. It came down not more than a yard from the flag, then bounced into the deep rough behind the green. I was not more than twenty-five feet from the pin, but I was lucky to get my pitch to within fifteen feet. Bogey. I bogeyed another hole late in the nine when my drive went through the dogleg by a yard and I could not get it to the green out of the deep rough.

I hung in there. I birdied the par-four tenth with an eight-footer, and got another shot back on the par-five twelfth with a good up-and-down from a miserable lie. I was feeling good. I had not given up, and if I could keep to even, it would be a good score for the afternoon.

The thirteenth was a medium-length par four with water well to the right. I decided to play it safe and hit a two-iron off the tee. I did not finish the swing; and the ball squirted to the right and caught the edge of the hazard. I lost my patience after the drop and tried to put in on the green from a terrible lie; I managed only to slash it into even deeper rough. It took me two more shots to get on the green, I two-putted for a triple, and I was done for the day. I limped home with a 79.

My dad and Butch were coming down from Virginia Beach to watch me play on Friday, and I was so discouraged and so down, I thought about calling them and asking them not to come. I was experiencing 1995 all over again, and I did not want to talk to anyone. Finally, the hope that Butch might be able to help got the best of me and I didn't make the call.

Friday was a repeat of Thursday, complete down to the brisk winds and the triple bogey. Again, I felt I was hitting the ball good, but I was a yard off the fairway here, a yard off the green there, and the bogeys continued to pile up.

I wanted to go to the range immediately after the round, but Butch insisted that we wait until the morning. "You look like you need a break more than you need to hit balls," he said. After a movie and a nice dinner, I felt I could get through the weekend without biting someone's head off.

We were on the range by nine on Saturday morning, and before I had hit the first ball, Butch said, "I saw your problem on the first tee yesterday. You've let your left-hand grip get too weak."

"But I've been hitting the ball sweet," I protested. "I've just had some bad luck, and the couple of bad swings I have to expect during every round have been costing me dearly."

"It's more than that. With such a weak grip, all you can do is slap at the ball. That's why you're getting into trouble. You can't count on your swing when you slap at it. Go ahead and warm up, but I want to see three knuckles on your left hand."

"You mean my grip has become that weak?" I really hadn't noticed.

"Yes, it has. And you just can't hit the ball consistently with such a weak grip. Why don't you try it my way for a while."

I knew I had a tendency to let my left-hand grip get too weak, but three knuckles simply did not feel comfortable. I did as he suggested, however, and moved my left hand well to the right before hitting some wedges. Typically, I liked to see two and a half knuckles on my left hand, but after playing for four or five weeks in a row, the golf muscles get stronger and it feels more comfortable to hit the ball with a weak grip. Maybe Butch was right. Maybe I had let it get too weak. I could barely see one knuckle. But my driving had been good the past two days; it was a few bad irons that caused the rounds to get away from me.

I had worked my way down to the driver when Butch asked, "How does that feel?"

"It feels like crap," I said angrily.

"I'll tell you what. I'm always willing to compromise. I'll settle for two and a half knuckles for the driver, but I want three knuckles for everything else."

I made the slight adjustment, and it did feel a little better. But compared to the grip I had been using, it still felt like crap. I had to admit—to myself, at least—that I was hitting the ball solidly. I wanted Butch to compromise one more time, but he was adamant.

The grip change may have been complicated by my switching drivers. I had experimented with several since the Taylor Made that I loved so much went out of service, and on Tuesday I asked the Calloway rep if I could try some Big Berthas. He brought out a dozen or so, and I really liked the feel of the titanium Great Big Bertha. I decided to go with it, he told me the fee I would receive for each tournament in which I used the club, and I was set.

After two days of working at it, the grip still did not feel comfortable, so I did not have high hopes for Houston, the next stop on the Tour. I wanted to weaken the grip a little more, but I had to trust Butch. He had played a major role in my development as a player, and it would be foolish of me to begin disregarding his advice at this point. I called him after the practice round, and as soon as he said hello, I told him, "It still feels like crap."

"Maybe it does," he said. "But it's something you'd better get used to if you want to hit the ball with any consistency."

I played good, solid golf and finished the first round at 69, three under. It was the first time I had been in the 60s since the Bob Hope, more than three months earlier. I could not wait to tell Butch, but the first thing he asked was "How does it feel now?"

"It still feels like crap," I answered.

"What did you shoot?"

I told him my score.

"You know, Carl, I'm really mad at you."

I was surprised. "Why?"

"Last week at Greensboro, you told me you were hitting the ball sweet and you shot 79. This week you tell me it feels like crap, and you shoot 69. It seems to me that my crap is ten shots better than your sweet."

I laughed, but I got the point. I would not be so resistant to his suggestions again.

My front nine on Friday was a solid, one-under 35. But two bogeys early on the back nine put me to one over for the day and two under for the tournament. The cut looked as though it would be one under, and I could feel myself letting it slip away once again. On the sixteenth hole, I hit my seven-iron second shot directly at the pin. But it cleared everything and plugged into the back bunker. "Oh, my God," I said to Al. "Here we go again." My explosion was the best I had hit in weeks, and it stopped a foot short of the hole for an easy par. I was still in it.

On seventeen, I hit a solid six-iron to the green just to the right of the pin. It landed on the fringe, not more than twelve feet from the hole, but it must have hit a sprinkler head. It took a huge bounce twenty yards over the green. Maybe I was not meant to make a cut, I thought. But my pitch back to the green was nearly perfect, leaving me an easy four-foot uphill putt for par. Just one more par and I would make my first cut in two months.

I pushed my tee shot on eighteen into a fairway bunker and behind a tree. I managed to hit the shot I envisioned and sliced an eight-iron to the left fringe of the green. Two putts later, I had my par. I would be playing on the weekend once again.

Saturday and Sunday were okay, but a long way from great. I shot a pair of 73s to finish in a tie for forty-eighth, good for a check for $3,694.

Something interesting happened during Saturday's round. I had hit my tee shot on the par-three fifth hole and was walking to the green when I noticed a familiar face in the gallery. Without thinking, I said, "Scott Arbach, what the hell are you doing here?"

I had not seen Scott since I was twelve years old. He had been one of the few kids I knew in California who played golf, and we spent a summer together on the course. He was visiting his brother in Houston, and he happened to notice my name in the paper. I made arrangements to see him after the round, and that evening we had dinner and went to a private party held by one of the club manufacturers. It was great fun.

The following week was the Byron Nelson, which turned out to be my best tournament of the year. It was strange, because I still did not feel comfortable with the grip change and I did not feel as if I had hit the ball all that well either. Maybe I was learning how to score. I shot 69-68 to make the cut easily, then finished off the week in high style with 70-68. It was good enough for a tie for thirty-sixth and a check for $7,219.

I had called Rotella a few weeks earlier and he had told me he would be in Dallas that week and would make a point of trying to get together. He followed me for nine holes, and they turned out to be my worst nine holes of the tournament. Twice, I popped my driver up not more than fifty yards from the tee. He reminded me to "go with what you've got when you're on the course."

I was having trouble concentrating that week. Heather and I were to be married the following week, and I could not stop thinking about it. Maybe that is why I played so well. My preoccupation with the wedding made it possible for me to stop analyzing everything to death. I was excited about the marriage, and I was really looking forward to her traveling with me. The Tour can be a very lonely place.

Heather was there to greet me when I arrived in Columbia late Sunday night. If possible, she was more excited about the wedding than I was, and she had a million things to tell me about the plans. After talking nonstop for ten minutes, she paused and said, "Oh, by the way. Congratulations on your great tournament."

The week flew by. All my friends and relatives came for the wedding, Al brought his wife down from Massachusetts, and Scott McCarron and his wife, Jennifer, were there. It meant a lot to me that Scott came, since he had to withdraw from the Colonial, one of the more prestigious tournaments of the year, to attend.

The week was one nonstop party.

I did have to spend one day during the week taking care of some business. Unlike most newlyweds who are concerned about finding a place to live and furnishing it, Heather and I were giving up our apartment and putting all our belongings in storage. Our schedule was such that we would spend, at most, three weeks at home for the rest of the year, and it was too much of a hassle to keep an apartment. It can be a real pain to get the bills paid when you go six or seven weeks without checking your mail. It would be easier to use my parents' house as our home address and to spend our off weeks with either them or Heather's mom.

My enthusiasm for the wedding held steady until the last moment. George, my brother and best man, and I were waiting in a small room off the back of the church for the ceremony to begin. When a woman stuck her head in the door and said, "It's time," my heart began to pound. I turned to George and asked, "Is it normal to feel like running away?"

"You're ready," he said. "Let's go."

When I saw Heather walking down the aisle, the last remnants of doubt vanished. Not only was she stunningly beautiful, I remembered that she had been my best friend for the past several years. It was a combination I liked.

We had a typical PGA Tour honeymoon—the Kemper Open outside of Washington, D.C. We did splurge and spend the week at the Ritz-Carlton.

I suppose I never had a chance to play well that week, and after a 79 on Thursday, I was out of the tournament. I played better on Friday, finishing with a 72. I was still flying high from the wedding, so I was not concerned about missing the cut. My good attitude seemed to come without effort, and I felt confident I would not miss many cuts the rest of the year.

The first week in June was Nicklaus's Memorial Tournament, so I played in the Dominion Open, a Nike event outside Richmond, Virginia. My play was solid the first three rounds. Three 69s put me in the all-too-unfamiliar position of having a shot at a victory.

I got off to a good start on Sunday, with birdies on two of the first four holes to put me eleven under for the tournament. Then disaster struck at the fifth. I hit my drive in heavy rough, and all I could do was punch it out in the direction of the green. It rolled into the front bunker, close to the front lip. It left me with an awkward stance, with one foot in and one foot out of the bunker. I bladed it over the green, but then managed to hit a great pitch to four feet below the hole. I missed the damn thing and finished the hole with a double. I could not put it behind me, and three-putted the following hole for bogey. In twenty minutes, I had gone from two under to one over for the day.

I settled down after that and got it back to one under for the day by the time I reached the eighteenth tee. Olin Browne, the man who had made it through Q-School for the first time on his tenth attempt the previous December, had finished an hour earlier. He had burned up the course and had the lead at twelve under. The eighteenth was a medium-length par five that I had reached in two all three days, so I was thinking eagle and play-off. I crushed my drive down the left side of the fairway, leaving only a five-iron to the green. The pin was front right, not more than twenty feet from a pond that guarded the right side of the green. I told myself to go for the pin, and I am not sure exactly what happened. I think I got cold feet at the last instant and hit the shot to the left, and safe, side of the green. I got it up and down for birdie, but finished a stroke behind Olin. I was pleased, though, with the second-place finish, to say nothing of the check for $15,500.

The following week, Heather returned to Columbia to finalize the details of giving up our apartment and moving our things into storage. I stayed with Tom and Nancy Reese for the Buick Classic at Westchester, a couple I met the year before when I requested housing from the tournament. They were such a great couple, I looked forward to seeing them again.

Westchester is a very tough course. It is not unusual for the cut to be three or four over, but for some reason unknown to me, there were a lot of low scores this year. To me, the course seemed as tough as ever. My opening two rounds of 70 and 72 made the cut by four shots, but I was not even close to the leader, Ernie Els, who was burning up the course.

I had a solid 72 on Saturday, and I was holding my own on Sunday until late in the round. But I had a couple of doubles on the back nine to finish with a 76. My 290 was good for a tie for sixty-second, and $2,520.

It always leaves a bad taste in your mouth to finish the way I did, but overall I was pleased with the tournament. Every cut I made was another piece of evidence that I was coming out of my slump. Although I was so far down the money list I could not even get a sniff of the top 125, I knew a strong second half of the season could still get me there.

Besides, what was there to be unhappy about? I was married to a beautiful woman, I was playing golf for a living, and my next stop was the U.S. Open.

CHAPTER 10

# *The U.S. Open*

**M**ajors are different. No one remembers how many tournaments Bobby Jones won, but every golfer knows that he won four U.S. Opens and finished his career in 1930 by winning the U.S. and British Opens and Amateurs. Only a few historians could tell you how many tournament victories Jack Nicklaus has, but who does not know that he has won twenty majors? Fair or not, majors are the yardstick by which golfers are measured.

On the other side of the coin, many people bring up the name of Greg Norman. I believe he is one of the very best—if not *the* best—golfer of his generation. He has had an amazing career, finishing number one on the money list and in scoring average several times over the past fifteen years. And when he has not finished at the top, he has been damn close to it. But Greg has won only two majors, exactly the same number won by Andy North. I have heard people predict that twenty years from now he will be thought of as a step below the likes of Watson, Nicklaus, and Trevino. That puts him in very good company, with players like Strange, Crenshaw, and Kite, but I have the sense that is not how Greg wants to be remembered. But the fact of the matter is, it takes about seven or eight majors to be considered one of the truly great players. This may change as time goes on, since the level of competition is so much higher than it was thirty or forty years ago. It is becoming increasingly difficult to win multiple majors.

I want to win majors. I want to make my mark as one of the very best. It may sound cocky, even presumptuous, to say that, but I do not see the point of trying to be something less than the very best.

I entered the U.S. Open every year, beginning my junior year at South Carolina. I never made it through the first round of qualifying, so when I sent in my application along with the $100 entry fee in the spring of 1996, I was not counting on it to be my year for a breakthrough. Because the U.S. Open is truly an open—anyone with a handicap of two or less is eligible—there are more than seven thousand entries each year. With so many people trying to qualify, it takes only a slightly off day to be eliminated. You can count on at least a few of those seven thousand players to have the round of their lives to beat you if you are not playing your best.

Qualifying for the Open takes place in two stages. The first stage, called local qualifying, is only an eighteen-hole tournament. I was good enough to make it past this hurdle back in my junior year, but with so many people entered, anything can happen in eighteen holes. I always found a way to have a mediocre round that day, so I had not made it past local qualifying in three attempts. The second stage, called sectional qualifying, consists of a thirty-six-hole tournament.

I elected to play the local qualifying round at Florence, South

Carolina. It was held on the same course as the Nike Tournament, so I had played there several times. Steve Liebler, my college coach, volunteered to caddy for me, and we left Columbia for Florence on the morning of the round; it was only an hour's drive. I wanted to make it to the second stage, of course, but I was realistic enough to see that the odds were against me. Only five or six players from a field of about eighty would go on to the sectionals, so even if I had a solid round, a few of the other guys could get hot and I would be gone. I would bet on myself to win if it were a seventy-two-hole event, but a single round makes it possible for all sorts of fluky things to happen.

Everything went right that day. Steve made sure I never hit before I was ready, and I put together six birdies against a single bogey for a 67, good enough for medalist honors. I was going to the sectionals.

I elected to play the sectional qualifying in Ohio, near Nicklaus's Muirfield course. The Memorial was held at Muirfield the week before, so Ohio was where most of the Tour players went to qualify. I wanted to play there because the top thirty scores qualified, whereas only the top five or six scores at the other sites made it.

The sectionals were thirty-six holes, held on Monday with the two eighteens on different courses. I had not seen either course before, but I heard that one was short and tight, while the other was more open and had some length to it.

I felt good about my chances. I was coming off a second-place finish at the Nike tournament in Richmond, where I had four solid rounds. I wanted to play in my first major badly, but it was not like Q-School. If I failed to qualify, I would still be able to tee it up the week after that.

I had a slight disadvantage for the qualifying rounds. Most of the guys were already in Columbus for the Memorial, so they had a good night's sleep before the tournament. I flew in from Richmond, and it was nearly two in the morning before I got to bed. Since Monday was a thirty-six-hole day, I had to get up at five-thirty A.M. to give myself enough time for breakfast and a warm-up session. I was so tired, I felt delirious at times. Al had it even tougher. He drove in from Richmond and was able to get only a couple hours of sleep.

I played the short, tight course in the morning and had a solid, one-under-par 71. I was pleased with the round, since I had not seen the course before and it did not play to my strengths. It was good enough to put me in the thick of things.

I began the afternoon round confident I could make up some ground on the longer course, but I could not make anything happen. Two early bogeys put me one over for the day, but I birdied the ninth hole to get back to even. After pars on the tenth and eleventh holes, the sky opened up and the rain came down in buckets.

We returned to the clubhouse, certain that play would be canceled for the day. But after twenty minutes, the sky cleared and they sent us back out. No one was happy about it, since the fairways were soaked and there was more rain on the way. It seemed pointless, and, I admit, I bitched and moaned with the best of them. But the officials were adamant. They wanted to get the thirty-six holes in. Everyone's schedule is so tight that a rain delay means that a number of guys will not be able to keep previous commitments and most everyone else will be inconvenienced in some way. The officials would get a lot more flak if they did not send us back out and the second storm missed us.

I went back out to the twelfth hole, a medium-length, par-five. I crushed both my drive and three-wood, and the ball stopped three feet below the hole. The eagle put me two under for the day.

It began to sprinkle while I was lining up the eagle putt, and before we got to the thirteenth tee, it was pouring again. This time they did postpone play until the following day.

Tuesday morning began with two solid pars on thirteen and fourteen. On fifteen, a relatively short par five, I hit driver, three-iron to ten feet and made the putt for another eagle. That put me at four under for the tournament, and I was pretty sure I was in if I could par out. I began to feel the pressure over the three final holes, but I hit solid shots all the way back to the clubhouse and made my three pars.

It turned out that I made it by a single stroke. I was in the U.S. Open! I could not get to a phone fast enough to tell my folks.

The 1996 Open was held at Oakland Hills, about twenty miles northwest of Detroit. I was pleased that my first major would be at a course with such a rich history. Designed by Donald Ross in 1916, Oakland Hills hired Walter Hagen as its first club professional. Hagen stayed for only a couple of years, since he apparently had little patience for giving lessons.

The course hosted its first U.S. Open in 1924, when Englishman Cyril Walker shot 297 to beat Bobby Jones by three shots. As an indication of how much professional golf has changed, Walker earned $500 for his victory, but apparently neither the money nor being a former U.S. Open champion was enough to guarantee his financial security. He spent his later years working as a caddy, and he died in poverty. Thirteen years later, a twenty-five-year-old Sam Snead had his first of four second-place Open finishes at Oakland Hills when Ralph Guldahl beat him by two shots. In 1951, Ben Hogan proclaimed the course a monster, but he did manage to win his third Open there. As I was to learn, he was not exaggerating how difficult the course was. The two most recent Opens at Oakland Hills were held in 1961 and 1985, with Gene Littler and Andy North the winners. Andy North was the only champion to break par there, and he did it by a single stroke.

The week of the open, Heather and I flew into Detroit late Sunday night, she from Columbia and I from Westchester. It was close to midnight by the time we picked up our luggage and found the counter where Open contestants could pick up their courtesy cars. We were about tenth in line, and Tom Kite was immediately ahead of us. Heather and I were so excited to be there, we were oblivious to our surroundings, but after a few minutes Tom turned to us and said, "Have you noticed that it's taking fifteen to twenty minutes for each person? At this rate, we won't get our car until after three in the morning." This was old hat for Tom, and all he wanted to do was get to bed.

Scott McCarron had qualified as well, and it was his first U.S. Open too. We decided to do the week up right and rent a house together. We got one about two miles from the course, and it was perfect. It was like being at home, and the McCarrons took turns with Heather and me preparing dinner.

Scott and I went to Oakland Hills Monday morning to register and play our first practice round. As soon as we drove through the gates, it was obvious that the Open was something special. It was only a Monday, and early on Monday at that, yet the place was already jammed with people. When we registered, we were offered tickets for a number of attractions in the area. Scott and I took the baseball and music park tickets.

They had had heavy rains the week before, so the course was playing much softer than the USGA would have liked. While it was nice to be able to get the ball to hold on the greens, the course was playing unbelievably long. I was not used to hitting long irons into par-four holes. Despite the soft greens, the course was extremely difficult. I could not remember ever playing a harder course. The fairways were narrow and the rough was so deep that it was a full shot penalty for anyone who hit it there. The only option was to pitch it back to the fairway with a sand wedge. The contours on the greens were as severe as I had ever seen, and despite the rain, the greens were fast. I could not imagine what they would be like later in the week if they dried out.

I had my share of bogeys that first round, but I thought it was the sort of course on which I could be competitive. However, I would have to keep my tee shots in the fairway, something I was not famous for.

It was strange to play a practice round with so many people watching. In my experience on tour, a large gallery consisted of two hundred people, so I could not believe it when the tees and greens were lined with people two or three deep for a Monday practice round.

After the round, I noticed Ben Crenshaw in the locker room. On impulse, I walked up to him and said, "Do you have anything set for tomorrow? If not, you're welcome to join us."

"No, I don't have anything arranged," he said. "I'd be glad to play with you guys."

It was great. I was at the U.S. Open, and I was playing a practice round with Ben Crenshaw. How could life get any better?

On Tuesday morning, I teed off with Ben, Scott, and Brant Jove. Brant had played college golf at UCLA with Scott and had been to Q-School a couple of times. When he did not get his card, he went to Japan and played on their tour, and he loved it. He was doing so well there, he did not much care if he got his card or not.

If possible, the crowd on Tuesday was larger than it had been the day before. There was a huge throng of people around both the practice green and the driving range, and they were at least four or five deep around every green on the course. It had been a long time since I had seen so many people at a PGA tournament. It was a strange but somehow enjoyable feeling to know that people were watching everything I did. It was all so new to me. On the course, after we had putted out and were walking to the next tee, all of us would be asked for autographs or our ball. That might happen on a Sunday in a regular event, but not during a Tuesday practice round.

It was a thrill to play with Crenshaw. He is one of the most down-to-earth, nicest guys on the Tour. Everyone likes him, and his moniker, Gentle Ben, fits him like a glove. Watching him putt was a pleasure. I had never seen the ball roll so smoothly. With Ben, you never see those couple of small hops at the beginning of a putt that you do with most everyone else. After finishing a hole, we would pick the toughest spot on the green to putt from, and see who could get it closest to the hole. Needless to say, Ben won more than his share. We were like a bunch of kids, just having a blast. The only difference was the thousands of eyes watching our every move.

After the eighth hole, the sky made good on its threat and it began to pour. I was disappointed at not having the chance to finish the round with Ben, but we had no choice except to go in. When we got back to the clubhouse, we were told that the forecast was for a three- to four-hour delay, so Heather and I went with the McCarrons to see *The Rock,* starring Sean Connery and Nicolas Cage. My anticipation of the week's events made it difficult to focus on the movie.

It was pouring when we went into the theater at about two in the afternoon, but the sun was shining by the time we got out. Scott and I hurried back to the course to hit some balls and put some time in on the practice green. We met Michael Christie there, and he asked us if we wanted to go off the back nine with him. It sounded like a great idea.

On the tenth tee Scott and Michael piped their drives down the middle, and as I was preparing to hit my tee shot, Scott yelled to the three hundred or four hundred people who were in the area, "If you guys like golf, watch this swing." The crowd laughed, and my hands trembled slightly because I knew they were waiting for a second, good laugh. That Scott, he will do anything for five bucks.

Without planning it, I lunged at the ball, putting the worst-looking, fake swing on it I could. The crowd roared. Then I relaxed and crushed it down the center, twenty yards past Scott's. He would not get my money without a fight.

Thursday morning, it was obvious that this was not just another week on the Tour. The atmosphere was different; it was almost bigger than life. I was excited about the prospect of playing, and I could not wait to get started. But my tee time was third from the last, 2:50 in the afternoon. It was an awful time. The morning seemed to go on forever, and I knew the greens would be spiked up something terrible by the time I teed off.

My goal for the tournament was to make the cut. I did not come simply to be able to say I played in a U.S. Open; I wanted to do well. I wanted to have a respectable showing in the first of my many majors.

I do not think there has been a close second to how nervous I was on the first tee that afternoon. It is an indescribable feeling to be playing in your country's national championship. My heart must have been beating 140 times per minute as I walked onto the tee, but when the announcer said, "Next on the tee, Carl Paulson, from Virginia Beach," it shot up another forty beats per minute. I touched the bill of my cap to acknowledge the gallery's applause and forced a small smile. I could feel my legs tremble as I stood over the ball, but somehow I managed to catch it solid and put it in the fairway. I was off the first tee in good shape.

I was pleased with my play for the first fifteen holes. I hit a number of good shots and even had a couple of birdies. I missed a few fairways, which meant automatic bogey, and I found myself shooting at some pins that I should not have. I was three over when I walked onto the sixteenth tee, which meant I was still in the tournament.

I hit a good drive down the left side of the fairway on sixteen, leaving myself a little nine-iron to the green. I thought I hit it solidly, but it came up a little short and plopped into the water. Double bogey.

I doubled the seventeenth, a long par three, when I put my tee shot in the deep rough, barely got it out, hit a poor chip, and two-putted from ten feet. From the eighteenth tee, I put my drive in the deep stuff, had to pitch out to the fairway, and finished with a bogey. My 78 was disappointing, to say the least.

I thought I had a chance going into Friday. The cut was projected at eight over, so an even-par round would get me to the weekend. My early tee time meant that the greens would be a little softer and I would not see many spike marks. I could do it.

After a par on the first hole, I hit driver, three-iron to eight feet on the 540-yard, par-five second hole. I made the putt to get back to plus six for the tournament. I was in good shape. All I had to do was play solid golf for the remaining fourteen holes and I would make the cut.

It was not meant to be. A double on eight and four bogeys against a single birdie on the back gave me a four-over 74. As predicted, the cut was 148.

The week was interesting, because there was such a contrast between how I felt off the course and how I felt while playing. When I was on the range or on the practice green, or even just walking from the parking lot to the locker room, the sense of excitement was pervasive. The crowds were enormous, and it seemed as if most of them wanted to know who I was. When I told them my name, they wanted my autograph even if it was the first time they had ever heard it.

The excitement I felt off the course contrasted sharply with the emotions I experienced while playing. The course was so difficult, so physically demanding, that I felt exhausted by the time I finished my round. I did not feel the same pressure I experienced at Q-School, but in some ways the Open was a more mentally challenging experience. You had to think about where you wanted to hit it on every shot, and you knew that if you did not hit it precisely, you would lose another stroke. The course had a way of taking its toll on you.

A few weeks after the Open, my dad told me an interesting story he heard from one of his friends, a man named Jim. Jim was watching the Open on television, hoping to catch a glimpse of me, when his wife, Meredith, walked in the room just as Johnny Miller was talking about Jack Nicklaus's unbelievable record of having played in forty consecutive U.S. Opens. Meredith heard the comment and said to her husband, "You mean Jack Nicklaus hasn't missed a U.S. Open in forty years? That's really amazing."

"Yes, it is amazing," said Jim, surprised by his wife's appreciation of Nicklaus's accomplishment. She was not much of a golf fan.

"It's amazing," Meredith continued, "that for forty years he never had other plans for that week."

I am not sure if Meredith's comment reflects her failure to appreciate the importance of the Open, or if it indicates our failure to view golf from a realistic perspective.

My week in Detroit taught me that U.S. Open golf is clearly different from PGA golf. The Tour sets up courses so they are demanding, but they make it possible to get birdies if you are on your game. I think the USGA views birdies as anathema. They set up the course so you have to be on your game to get pars.

I had the feeling that the USGA was looking for more than the best golfer—they wanted to identify the best person. They begin by making the course so tight and fast that it demands that players hit extremely precise shots, and hit them under the pressure of a major championship. To win the Open, one must have incredible self-discipline and patience. The course is set up so that 90 percent of the time you have to shoot away from the pin. You have to be willing to wait for those two or three holes per round when you can get a little aggressive and try for birdie. If you hit it in the rough, you must have the self-discipline to pitch it back to the fairway and accept the loss of a stroke with equanimity. As I learned all too well, if you get greedy, if you try too hard to force things to happen, you can make double in a heartbeat. You have to learn that par is always a great score at an Open.

I was disappointed that I did not make the cut, but I left Detroit with a feeling of satisfaction. Simply qualifying to play in the tournament was an accomplishment I could be proud of, and I was confident that it would not be the last time I would do so. I have always been slow to adjust to new challenges. It has always taken me some time to move up to the next level. But in the end, I have always learned my lessons well, and the Open would be no exception. Yes, I was off to a slow start once again, but I would be back. And I would be ready to prove that I was capable of moving up to the next level, the level of major championship play.

# CHAPTER 11

## Learning to Score

I hoped the U.S. Open would serve as a fresh start in much the same way as my visit to Rotella had the previous year. I had to do something to keep the year from being a disaster. Over the first five months, I had played in fifteen tournaments and made only three cuts. The $14,000 I had earned for the year put me so far behind the top 125, I could not even see their dust.

The first stop after Oakland Hills was the FedEx St. Jude Classic, held the third week in June in Memphis. It was a good place to start the second half of the season, since I had played well there in 1995.

On the Tuesday before the tournament, I called Nick Vergos, the man I met in the previous year's pro-am. He was happy to hear from me and invited me to his place, the Rondeview, for dinner. He did not send a limo this time, but Heather and I were able to walk directly past the half-block line to our own table. It was great to see him. And to taste his ribs again.

The tournament did not go as I had hoped. I shot 72-75 to miss the cut by a bunch.

After Friday's round, Al told me he needed some time off. His right foot was bothering him enough that he had trouble making it around the course the past two days. I understood, of course, and hoped he could get back out soon.

From Memphis, we went to Hartford for the Canon Greater Hartford Open. Upon arriving late that Sunday night, Heather and I were struggling with our luggage at the airport when Heather noticed a man whose cart was overflowing with suitcases. He was having trouble keeping everything on board while he pulled the cart over a bump. Heather walked over to him and asked, "Do you need some help?"

"That would be great," he said. It was John Cook. He had just arrived from Memphis, where he won the tournament with a score of 258, only one stroke away from the all-time record set by Mike Souchak in the 1955 Texas Open. I could not help but shake my head at the sight. Here was someone who was in the top twenty in career earnings, someone who had blown away the competition in a tournament that had ended only hours earlier, and someone who was having a tough time getting his luggage to the curb so his caddy could pick him up. I wondered if any of those sportswriters who wrote that professional golfers are spoiled have ever seen Michael Jordan, John Elway, or Barry Bonds doing battle with a luggage cart in an airport.

I suspect that John's struggle with his luggage explains why professional golfers, as a group, are different from other athletes. Professional athletes from other sports tend to be insulated from the day-to-day hassles of the real world. All they have to worry about is being on time for the bus that takes them to the airport, and when they arrive at their destination, someone gives them their room key and they can count on having their luggage delivered to their room shortly after they get there. If something does not go their way, they can complain to the team gofer, so I have heard, and more than likely the problem will be solved for them.

Well, we have to make our own travel arrangements. We have to get our own luggage and equipment to our motel room. And we do not have anyone to complain to when things do not go our way; we have to solve problems for ourselves. I think having to deal with the nitty-gritty details of making it through each week keeps us grounded. We rarely forget that we are just ordinary people who happen to have one extraordinary skill.

Professional golfers are by no means perfect human beings. We have the same frailties and limitations as everyone else. But I do not think it is simply a coincidence that drug, sex, or violence scandals, so common in baseball, football, and basketball, are virtually unknown at either the college or professional levels of golf. We have never had the message communicated to us that we are so special that the rules do not apply to us. And struggling with our luggage in airports reminds us on a regular basis that we are like everyone else, except for those few hours each week when we are out on the course.

I was looking forward to the tournament in Hartford, since it was where I had broken through in 1995. Perhaps for that reason, the local paper, the *Virginian-Pilot,* sent a reporter and a photographer to follow me for the week. I did not know how literally they meant that business about following me. After my round on Monday, both the reporter and photographer followed Heather and me into our hotel room. I had to change into my T-shirt and shorts in the bathroom, and when I came out, they wanted some pictures of us relaxing. They printed one of Heather jumping on the bed while I was trying to take a nap.

My first job on Monday morning was to find another caddy, but I was not having any luck. I had breakfast and hit some balls on the range, all the time keeping my eye out for someone who was looking for a loop for the week. Finally, an hour before my tee time for the pro-am, I saw a familiar face near the practice green. It was Tim Broadman, a veteran caddy, who had not been out in a while. "Hey, Tim. Do you want to go today?"

"Sure." He walked over to my bag and began to wipe the irons clean.

The pro-am round that afternoon seemed to go on forever. When you are not playing well, it is a lot tougher to enjoy the day and to be congenial with your partners. I had learned, though, that they were likely to remember everything about the round, and I wanted them to have good memories of me. And I enjoyed giving them a few swing tips and asking about their work. It seemed to mean a lot to them, and it was a good way to break the ice so everyone would enjoy himself.

When I first began to play in the pro-ams, it was a strange and somewhat uncomfortable feeling to know that what I said and did was so important to my amateur partners. These guys were always much older than I and were quite successful in their businesses, and yet I was the one in the group everyone was trying to impress. It was something I got used to, and when things were going well, I got a real kick out of making the round fun for them. Hartford, however, was one of those days that required a concerted effort.

Tim did a good job for me during the pro-am round, so I offered the job to him for the rest of the week. He accepted without hesitation.

That evening at dinner, Heather said, "I think I'll have seafood tonight."

"Where are we?" I asked. I was wondering if the seafood would be fresh, so I tried to remember how close to the coast we were, but for the life of me, I could not remember what city we were in. The constant travel can be disorienting, and about half the time I did not know where I was when I first awoke in the morning. Most of the time, though, I had figured it out by dinner.

The first round on Thursday was solid. I shot 70 and was well within the cut line. Friday, however, did not go as well. The bogeys were piling up and I doubled seventeen, the hole where I had made so many friends the year before. My five-over-par 75 was two strokes shy of the cut.

John Maginnes, a good ole country boy from North Carolina, had an encounter with a group of regulars who planted themselves on the hills to the right of the eighteenth fairway. During Friday's round he hit his tee shot in their area, and since it was late in the afternoon, they were especially rowdy. John was on the bubble, and he needed a par to make the cut. The group went right on talking and laughing while he was preparing to hit his shot. He turned to them and said, "Hey, guys, can you give me a break? I need to par this hole to make the cut."

"If you can't make par with a little noise in the background, you shouldn't be out here," one of the group shouted.

John was so disconcerted by the response, he put his approach in the bunker to the right of the green. He hit a great trap shot, though, to a foot from the pin.

"Attaboy, John. You're on your way to the big time now," he heard someone yell from the hills. John tapped in his putt for par. He was playing on the weekend.

I could not get into the Western Open the following week, so Heather and I went to Clover, South Carolina, to spend some time with her mom. I practiced a couple hours each day, hoping to find a way to get back on track. I was off by only a hair, but that was enough to make the difference between playing on the weekend and moving on down the road.

Next was the Anheuser-Busch Golf Classic, renamed the Michelob Championship at Kingsmill, and Heather and I were back in Williamsburg for the second week in July. My parents live less than an hour away, but they decided to rent a condo on the course for the week. My gallery in Williamsburg usually included a couple dozen friends and relatives, and my folks thought it would be fun to have a place for everyone to meet after the round. My dad had three dozen bright, coral-colored T-shirts made up with "Paulson's Pilgrims" printed on the back for everyone to wear on the course. I was thankful he could not find a matching golf shirt.

Tim decided not to follow the Tour, so I was faced with finding another caddy for the week. On Monday morning, I ran into Keith Clearwater's caddy and asked him if he had any recommendations. He told me that Anthony Wilds, who sometimes caddied for Stan Utley, might be available, so I went looking for him. I found him near the clubhouse, and he said that he did not have anything firmed up with Stan so he would be glad to carry my bag. I was looking forward to it, since he would be, by far, the most experienced caddy I had worked with. He was about forty years old and had been on tour for almost fifteen years. He had caddied four times for tournament winners, twice with Gary Hallberg and twice with David Peoples. The most noticeable thing about him, though, was his striking resemblance to David Letterman. Anthony, however, was addicted to cigarettes rather than cigars.

Thursday was another tough day. Again I was just a little off, but it cost me dearly. I made four bogeys against only a couple of birdies for a two-over-par 73.

It became clear to me early in the round that Anthony was a very different caddy from Al. Al never offered advice. He would only give his thoughts about club selection if I asked, and to be honest, that is the way I liked it. No one else knew my game as well as I did, so I did not want a caddy telling me what I should do. But Anthony was not one to remain silent if he believed I was about to make a mistake. He had strong opinions about how I should play certain holes, and he never hesitated to give them to me, although he might do it in indirect ways. On the sixteenth, for instance, I had 159 yards downhill to the green for my second shot. "What do you think?" I asked.

"It looks like a six-iron," Anthony said.

"Are you sure?" I said, surprised by his advice. "It's only 159 yards and it's downhill."

"Maybe you're right. Why don't you go with the seven."

I put my seven-iron twelve feet to the left of the pin. As we were walking to the green, I asked, "How could you think that was a six-iron?"

"I didn't. But I could see eight-iron written all over your face, and I couldn't let that happen."

Anthony would take some getting used to, I thought, but maybe he would be good for me.

I was not all that eager to play on Friday. The forecast was for rain all day. Hurricane Bertha was headed directly toward the Williamsburg area, and there was some chance the tournament would be canceled. It was cool and cloudy when I teed off shortly after eight-thirty, but it looked as if the rain could come at any minute. I hated the idea of playing a few holes and having to come in for the day.

Friday turned out to be a very different day from Thursday. Wonderfully different. I began with a two-putt par on the first hole, and a good up-and-down for par on the second. From there I went on a tear, with birdies on three, four, six, and seven to finish the front nine with a four-under-par 32. The back nine had a shaky start. After a great drive on ten, I left a wedge in the bunker. But I came out well, and knocked in my three-footer for par. I knocked in an eight-footer for birdie on twelve to go five under, then on the par-three thirteenth I hit my tee shot about two yards to the left of the green, pin high but in deep rough. It was a tough chip even with a good lie. The green sloped sharply away from me, and I had very little room to work with. I decided to take my medicine rather than risk double bogey by getting too cute and failing to get the ball out of the rough. I hit the pitch firmly, and as expected it ran twenty feet past the hole. Bogey. I was still four under, but I was steamed at giving a shot back. I hated the idea of letting my great front nine slip away.

I got the stroke back when I hit a wedge to four feet on fourteen. I was back to five under for the day, and in the middle of my best round of the year.

The fifteenth hole was a medium-length par five, but a tight driving hole with out-of-bounds on the left and a hazard on the right. I was hitting the driver well, so I took it out again and absolutely crushed it down the left side of the fairway. My five-iron second shot was directly at the pin and actually damaged the lip of the cup before settling twenty-five feet past the flag. I could see the line as clearly as if someone had chalked it out for me, and the putt dove into the center of the hole for eagle. I was seven under par with three holes to play. I had to kneel down and take a couple deep breaths before I could tee off on sixteen.

Sixteen, a difficult dogleg right, yielded a routine par.

Seventeen was a 175-yard par three with an extremely narrow green. The tee shot had to be precise, since it was difficult to make par if you missed the green on either side. The adrenaline was going strong, so I took a seven-iron and put it twelve feet below the hole. The birdie putt melted into the left side of the cup.

The excitement got to me on the eighteenth tee, and I hooked my tee shot to the edge of the hazard. It stayed in play and I was able to get it close to the front of the green. A good up-and-down saved my par.

My 63 was the low round of the day by three shots, and it turned out to be the low round of the tournament. I made a huge jump on the leader board and finished the day only four strokes off the lead.

Later that evening, I had a thought about Anthony. On Thursday's round, when I was struggling, he wanted to talk about every shot. On Friday, when I was going great, he did not say a word to me the entire round. Maybe he was the sort of caddy who could help me.

We got lucky with the weather. We did have an on-and-off light rain all day Friday, but it did not begin to pour until the last group was coming up the eighteenth fairway. Bertha passed through during the night, and the eye was far enough to the east to preclude any serious damage to the course. Starting times were delayed for a couple hours on Saturday to give the groundskeeper a chance to clear up the debris, but the tournament was safe. Thank God.

I had a solid round on Saturday. It was one of those days when I hit the ball from tee to green about as well as I can, but the putts were determined to stay out of the hole. Nonetheless, my 69 kept me in the thick of things. Scott Hoch was burning up the course, but I had a good shot at a top ten finish.

Sunday began much the same as Saturday had. I was playing solid golf, and I managed to get it to two under for the day and ten under for the tournament by the tenth hole. A couple more birdies and I had a chance to finish in the top three or four and make a big move on the money list.

The pressure got to me. My swing got a little quick and I bogeyed four consecutive holes to finish with a 73. I finished in a disappointing tie for twenty-third, but my $10,042 check was my largest of the year. I was not happy when I finished the round. Each one of those bogeys cost me $8,000, and I knew I had no one to blame but myself for letting it get away from me. An hour later, though, all I was thinking about was that I just had my best finish of the year. Friday was the first day I had played really well all season, and I was sure it was a sign of things to come. I still had time to make the top 125.

From Williamsburg it was on to Madison, Mississippi, for the Deposit Guaranty Golf Classic. I had good feelings about the tournament, since I had been in the lead briefly the previous year. I continued my good play and had four solid rounds of 71, 68, 70, and 70. Given my score of nine under, I was a little disappointed with the thirty-third-place finish and $5,063 check. Many weeks a score like that would have earned a top-ten finish.

Anthony and I were getting along very well. He was more conservative than I, and at several points during the tournament he convinced me to play it safe. And I believe it paid off. He had a standard response when I hit a poor shot that I found reassuring. If I hit it in the deep rough, he'd say, "Let's go try from there." If I buried it in a bunker, his only comment was "Let's go try from there." After the round ended, he told me, "Look, you just made $5,000 and you haven't even sniffed feeling good about your play. Let's go try again next week."

I liked Anthony, I thought he was good for me, and I wanted him to be my regular caddy. "Sure," I said. "We'll get 'em next week."

The only problem was that Al was due to return the following week. Al was more than a caddy, he was a friend. And he was a good caddy. He was completely trustworthy and dependable, he was always waiting for me when I arrived at the course, and he handled the mechanics of caddying as well as anyone. But the truth of the matter was, I felt Anthony was doing more for me. His experience made it possible for him to help me score in a way that Al could not. I hated to do it, but I had to call Al.

"Al, this is Carl," I said when he answered the phone.

"Hey, Carl. Are you coming in on Monday?"

"Listen, Al. I've had to make a business decision. Anthony and I have had some good success the past couple of weeks, and I hate to have to tell you this, but I think I should stay with him."

There was a brief pause before Al said, "I understand. I know it's a tough decision for you, but I wish you all the luck in the world. I hope you do great the next few months."

Al was a gentleman to the end. He could not have been more gracious, even though I knew he was disappointed. I promised to put his name out, and I told him I hoped to see him out there soon. Within two weeks, Kevin Sutherland hooked up with him and Al was back on the Tour. It made me feel a little better about the situation.

The CVS Charity Classic outside Boston was our next stop. My good streak continued, and I opened with 71-67 to make the cut easily.

I got off to a good start on Saturday with three pars and a birdie and reached the fifth hole five under for the tournament. I ripped it off the fifth tee, but when I looked up I was surprised to see the ball fading to the right. I could not understand it. The ball felt like a 290-yard shot but it went only about 240 yards. I made bogey from the rough, and since the only explanation I could come up with for the strange tee shot was a defective ball, I tossed it to a kid in the gallery on the way to the sixth tee and took out a new one.

The sixth hole was a long, dogleg left, and I ripped it again. The ball started down the left side of the fairway, but about 170 yards out began to bend sharply to the right. Something had to be wrong. I looked at my shoes (I have no idea why, but at the time it seemed like the place to start), my glove, and finally at the driver. The writing on the shaft was a quarter-rotation away from where it had been on the first tee. I grabbed the head of the club, gave it a twist, and it came off in my hand. I had been trying out a new driver that week, and it must have been bad epoxy. Fortunately, a friend of Anthony's was following us, so he was charged with sprinting back to the car to get my Great Big Bertha. He did not make it back until the ninth hole, which gave me time to make two more bogeys. I finished the day with a three-over-par 74.

Sunday was a solid day. Nothing spectacular happened, but I did manage three birdies against a lone bogey for a 69. I finished in a tie for thirty-second and earned a check for $5,714. I was more than a little steamed when I thought about how much the bad epoxy on the driver might have cost me.

I left that Sunday evening for Detroit and the Buick Open, held the first week in August. It would be a good week, if for no other reason than Heather and I were staying with my old friend Rick Williams. He had called me a few days earlier to let us know that he had tickets for a Lions preseason game and a Tracy Chapman concert.

I was determined to do something with the course this time. It seemed like one of the easier courses we played, and the other guys did not have much trouble with it, but it gave me fits the year before.

Despite my good intentions, '96 was an instant replay of '95. I shot a pair of 74s and missed the cut by a mile. I could not understand it. I seemed to hit the ball well, but again, I just could not get it in the hole.

I was ready for some time off, and with the PGA coming up the following week, I got it. I returned to Virginia Beach, worked a little with Butch, but mostly took it easy and regrouped after a month of motel rooms.

I hoped to get in the Sprint International in Colorado the week after the PGA, since I thought the format was made for my game. The tournament used the modified Stableford scoring system where eagles counted five points, birdies counted two points, and you lost only one point for a bogey. I was second only to Tom Watson in the rate I made eagles, and I always made my share of birdies, so I thought I could rack up the points. But I never made it past sixth on the alternate list, so I had another week off.

I did get into the Greater Vancouver Open the third week in August. When I got to the course Monday morning I was excited to learn I would be playing in the pro-am with Paul Coffey, a member of the Team Canada hockey team. It turned out that he had a groin injury, so I did not get to meet him. The day was a good one nonetheless. One of my amateur partners chartered a boat on Tuesday and took Heather and me fishing.

I had a late tee time for Thursday and the conditions were tough. The wind was up and the greens were firm and fast. I played well, but had to grind for my three-over-par 74. It was not a great score, but I was satisfied with it given the conditions. Only two or three guys who played in the afternoon were under par.

The course was easier for me on Friday, with my early tee time. The wind had slowed to a gentle breeze, and the dew softened the greens enough to hold approach shots. Again I had a solid round, and finished three under at 68. I was playing on the weekend again.

On both Saturday and Sunday, I played as solidly as I had all year. I missed very few greens, but I could not get the putts to drop. Anthony reminded me frequently to remain patient, but it never happened for me. Still, my pair of 69s was not too shabby. I earned a check for $6,950 and a tie for twenty-eighth.

Guy Boros won with a score of 272. Guy was in his third year on the Tour and he was another first-time winner. My time had to be coming. I was playing well, and Anthony was helping me learn how to score on those days when I was a little off. It had to be just a matter of time before everything fell into place.

The last week in August meant Milwaukee and Tiger Palooza, as Heather called it. Tiger Woods had turned pro after his third consecutive U.S. Amateur Championship and was joining the Tour for the Greater Milwaukee Open. Needless to say, there was a lot of talk about his professional debut, and I did not hear anyone predict that he would burn it up the rest of the year. No one doubted he was a great player with a great future. But he had missed the cut in most of the pro tournaments in which he had played, and there was no reason to believe he would do much better after turning pro. There is a big difference between match play, where you can blow out a few holes without its being fatal, and medal play, where every single stroke counts. I saw the Nike commercials in which Tiger asked, "Are you ready for me, world?" My question was "Are you ready for us, Tiger?" He showed us he was.

Maybe Tiger Palooza inspired me. I got off to a great start, shooting 68-64 the first two days. The 64 could have been lower. On the last two holes, I lipped out short birdie putts.

On the weekend, I could not seem to get my driver in the fairway. I was off just a hair, but it was enough to make me grind for pars the entire thirty-six holes. With Anthony's help, I played smart golf and finished the tournament with 71-70, even though I had not played my best. I was pleased that my tie for thirty-fourth and my check for $6,060 were better than Tiger's. Maybe soon people would be talking about Carl Palooza.

I was happy to get into the Canadian Open, since Glen Abbey was one of my three favorite courses of the year. In '95, I did not have a chance to see it before the tournament, but I had learned a great deal about the course and I felt good about my chances.

The tournament has an interesting history. The first Canadian Open was held in 1904 at the Royal Montreal Golf Club and was won by John Oke with a two-round score of 156. For more than half a century, many people thought of it as a major, just a step below the U.S. and British Opens. Then, in 1994, it became the Bell Canadian Open and today it is just another stop on the PGA Tour.

It is amazing to me how differently a golf course can look when you are playing well compared to when you are playing poorly. During the midst of my slump, when I looked out at the course from the first tee, all I could see was the enemy. I saw water, traps, and rough, all eager to gobble up my ball.

I had been playing well for a month, so when I looked out from the first tee at Glen Abbey, I was struck by the course's almost preternatural beauty. I loved the subtle contrast between the various shades of green as my eye moved from the rough to the fairway to the putting surface. I loved the crisscross pattern on the green that resulted from the double cutting. And when I looked at the water and the bunkers, I marveled at how well the architect had used them to frame the hole. It was one of those rare moments when the sheer beauty of my surroundings made me appreciate how lucky I was to be alive.

Perhaps it was the harmony I felt with the course, because I played the front nine in five under par. While I played solid golf on the back, I did not get any more birdie putts to drop, so I had to "settle" for a 67 on a very difficult golf course. My dad called the scorer's tent shortly after I made the turn, and when he asked, "How's Carl Paulson doing?" he was told, "He's kicking ass out there."

A cold front moved through the area Thursday night, so the second round was canceled. It was windy and cool on Saturday, but my solid play continued, and I was pleased with my even-par 72, given the conditions.

Sunday was one of those days when it felt like a struggle. I was not hitting the ball crisply, and I had to grind hard to get my pars on the first seven holes. On eight, I crushed my drive down the center of the fairway and had the perfect distance for my five-iron left to the green. I made solid contact with the ball, and when I looked up I saw it flying directly toward the flag. I waited for it to come down close to the pin, but it simply disappeared. For an instant, I was afraid that I had flown the green, but the roar from the crowd told me the damn ball had landed in the hole for an eagle two. I went back to grinding after that hole and managed to make a lot of pars. I bogeyed the fifteenth, but then got the stroke back with a birdie at eighteen to finish the round two under par. It was good enough for a tie for twelfth place and a check for $31,500. I picked up a lot of ground on the money list, and the top 125 was in sight again. There were six tournaments left in the year. I was playing as well as I had in two years. I could still make it.


I did not make it at Coal Valley in the Quad City Classic. I struggled for the entire thirty-six holes. My one-over-par 71 on Thursday gave me a reasonable shot at making the cut, and I grinded hard on Friday. I came to the eighteenth hole two over for the day and three over for the tournament. I was fairly certain the cut would be plus three, so I needed a par on eighteen to make it. It was the toughest hole on the course, a tight, long, dogleg-left par four, but there was no reason to think I could not make par. I used a three-wood off the tee to keep it in the fairway, but I hooked the shot deep into the woods on the left. I had no choice but to hit a sand wedge out to the fairway, and another wedge put me fifteen feet from the cup. The putt never had a chance, and I missed the cut by a single stroke.

I was as upset as I had been in a couple of months. I was in the homestretch, and I could not afford to miss any cuts if I wanted to avoid the Fall Classic. Time was running out.

The B.C. Open in Endicott, New York, was the next stop. I had played well there the year before, so I had a good chance of making up some ground. My first two rounds were solid. I shot 69-68 to make the cut handily, and 69 on Saturday to finish the day in seventeenth place. I was pleased with the round, since it put me in position to make a move on the money list. A good round on Sunday could mean a top-ten finish.

When I teed off on Sunday, it was cold and breezy, with a fine drizzle coming down. It was encouraging, since it meant the scores would be higher and I would have a better chance of making a move. As it turned out, though, I was among those who were making it possible for the other guys to make a move. I was three over par after eleven holes. My best shot at a good finish at that point was a hard rain and a canceled final round. My rain dance produced results, and play was suspended before I putted out on the twelfth green. That allowed me to maintain my seventeenth-place position, which was good for a check for $16,000. That gave me over $90,000 for the year, with four tournaments left. It looked as if it would take around $160,000 to make the top 125, so I had a realistic shot at it. One third-place finish or a couple of top tens would do it for me.

After it became obvious they would not be able to finish the final round, they sent Fred Funk and Pete Jordan, who were tied after the third round, out on the course for a sudden-death playoff. I liked Fred a lot. He was one of the veterans who would stop to chat when our paths crossed, and he never failed to compliment me on my good rounds. But Pete was one of my regular-practice round partners. He was in his third year on the Tour and had yet to make the top 125. Fred had already won several times, so I could not help but root for Pete to earn his first victory and secure his card for the following two years. Fred, however, birdied the first playoff hole and won for the fourth time.

I was really looking forward to the next stop, the Buick Challenge, at Callaway Gardens in Georgia. Not only was the course one of my three favorites of the year, I was going to have my fifteen minutes of fame. Scott McCarron had been invited to host a segment of *Inside the PGA Tour*, which was to be filmed that week, and he asked me to do the show with him. We had a great time. We spent much of the show riding mountain bikes around the bike paths by the resort, and generally acting goofy. Scott showed an impressive streak of creativity during the filming. We were given a script, but he was full of ideas for improving it, and I think the show turned out well. I was given a nice T-shirt for helping them out.

The golf, however, was something of a struggle. On both Thursday and Friday, I got off to a slow start, getting it to two over early in the round both days. I could see my hopes of making the top 125 slipping away, but on both days I came back strong. I shot 69-70 to make the cut easily, and was looking forward to the weekend. Despite the few poor holes I had early in both rounds, I was playing good golf and I knew I could improve my position.

A front moved into the area Friday evening, however, and I never got a chance to move up the leader board. The final two rounds of the tournament were rained out.

My friend John Maginnes was in a five-way, sudden-death

playoff for the victory, which he ended up losing to Michael Bradley. But John's tie for second and the check for $66,000 boosted him into the top 125. John has such an appealing, self-deprecating way about him that he was constantly doing interviews the following week. He talked about how he had to develop a unique swing because it was difficult to get his short arms around his big belly, and about how he could finally get a good night's sleep after knowing he had his card for the following year.

I did not believe John about the sleep thing. He is such a laid-back guy that I doubt he has ever worried about anything to the point where it kept him awake. And while John might make fun of his swing, he is one hell of a golfer. He keeps his tee shots in play, he hits his irons close to the pin, and he's a first-class putter. I expect him to do well for a long time.

I have learned that you cannot judge a player's game or his potential by his swing. I have seen dozens of players in college and on the minitours who have more graceful and athletic-looking swings than many of the guys out here, but having a graceful, athletic swing is not enough to get you on the Tour. You have to know how to score, and that ability seems to be independent of the aesthetic virtues of one's swing.

Everyone who makes it to the Tour has a swing that is good enough to allow them to score, even if it is not technically perfect or the prettiest in the world. The difference between the guys who are consistent winners and those who are struggling to stay out here is repeatability. The guys who can repeat their swings, especially under pressure, are the ones who do well. Jim Furyk, who has been described as having the Tour's most unorthodox swing, is the best example. His swing is indeed unorthodox, and it is not especially graceful. But Jim can repeat that swing as well as anyone, and that is why he has had so much success.

Butch has worked to make my swing as simple as possible for

that very reason. It seems reasonable that the simpler the swing, the easier it will be to repeat it. I am making progress, but I cannot explain why guys like Jim have more success repeating their unorthodox swings than guys like me, with much simpler swings. I suppose, though, golf would not be so endlessly fascinating if we could explain everything.

The following week's tournament, the Las Vegas Invitational, was critical. With a purse of $1.5 million, it offered me the best chance to make a big move up the money list. But I dug myself a hole on the first day of the tournament that would be difficult to climb out of. I shot 73 on the Las Vegas Hilton course, the only one of the three courses used that was not suited for my game. I needed to get by that round no worse than even par, but at one over, I had a lot of ground to make up if I was going to make the cut.

I played solid golf on Thursday and Friday, but I had trouble with the short stick again. My scores of 68 and 70 were respectable, but I lost count of how many ten-footers for birdie I missed. Had I putted reasonably well, both rounds could have been several strokes lower. As it turned out, I missed the cut by four shots.

Tiger won the tournament when he beat Davis Love on the first hole of a sudden-death playoff. I guess Tiger Palooza was more than mere hype. He really is that good.

I did not have much hope of doing anything the following week at the LaCantera Texas Open. The course was not suited to my game, and when you do not feel good about a course, it makes it all the more difficult to post good scores. Incidentally, the course must not have been suited to the games of Ben Crenshaw and Tom Kite, either. Even though they are both from Texas, they passed up the tournament.

I hit the ball as badly that week as any PGA pro ever has. I topped one drive and popped up another one. I left a bunker shot in the trap and sculled a chip across the green. Somehow, though, my opening rounds of 73 and 71 were good enough to make the cut by a stroke. I finished the weekend with rounds of 72 and 75 to finish in a tie for sixty-sixth, good enough for a check for $2,424.

The high point of the weekend was when Mark Weibe, my playing partner on Saturday, aced the third hole. He had gotten off to a terrible start, and when he took his scorecard out on the fourth tee, he said, "Let me see my scores. Seven . . . six . . . one."

I was beginning to appreciate Anthony's unfailing optimism. Since I can get down on myself when things are not going well on the course, he served as a much-needed counterbalance. When I was limping home on Sunday, feeling discouraged about shooting 75, Anthony said, "How much do you figure your check will be?"

"I don't know. Two or three thousand, I expect."

"How much does that give you for the year?" he asked.

"A little over a hundred grand."

"Have you ever made that much in a single year before?"

"No," I said. I was becoming irritated with his questions.

"Well, there you go," he said. "This week has pushed you to a new high in career earnings. You should feel good about what you've done."

He was right. I was making progress, and I should have been pleased about that. There were certainly a lot of guys who could not say as much.

Although my check was probably larger than I had a right to expect given my mediocre play, I left Texas encouraged about my game. Anthony had helped me learn how to score when I was not playing my best, and it really showed that week.

It is difficult to talk about the subject of scoring without thinking about Corey Pavin. If there is anyone with more ability to score, I do not know who it is. I was looking at his stats for 1995 one day, and they were striking. It was a year in which he won the U.S. Open and finished fourth on the money list, but according to his stats he did not do anything particularly well. He was ranked 159th in driving, 92nd in sand saves, and 100th in greens in regulation. This last statistic is especially surprising, since Bob Rotella has published an analysis of PGA Tour stats in which he found that the category of greens in regulation had the strongest relationship with scoring average. Scoring average, however, was the only category in which Corey stood out; he was ranked eleventh. Corey must know something about the game that has eluded the rest of us.

My stats for '96 were almost a mirror image of Corey's. My scoring average of 71.82 put me 157th on the list, but my rankings for the specific categories were, with one exception, better than this. I was tied for eighth with Phil Mickelson for driving distance, with an average drive of 280.4 yards. Only Tom Watson and Davis Love made eagles at a better rate than mine of one every 120.5 holes. I was ranked 87th in sand saves with an average of 53 percent, and 113th in putting with an average of 1.80 putts per green. I hit 65.1 percent of greens in regulation for a ranking of 119th. Driving accuracy was the only category in which I was ranked lower than scoring average. I hit 63.1 percent of the fairways to earn a rank of 161st. My overall ranking of 106th was not great, but it was a lot better than my position on the money list.

The contrast with Corey's stats was striking. While his scoring average was better than any of his rankings in specific categories, my scoring-average ranking was worse than one would expect based on my stats in the specific categories. I suspect my numbers were better for the second half of the season than they were for the first half, but it was clear I still had a lot to learn about getting the ball in the hole.

The last stop of the year for me was Disney, where I needed at least a fourth-place finish to make the top 125. I was not counting on it, but I did not rule it out, either. I was thinking more about finishing twenty-fifth or better, since that would give me enough money to move into the top 150 on the money list. That would be good enough to get me directly into the final stage of Q-School. I loved the idea of bypassing second stage.

My first round was on Lake Buena Vista, a very tight course with out-of-bounds on most of the holes. I played great, and my 68 could have been much lower with only a lukewarm putter. I played the Magnolia on Friday, and an eagle two on the sixteenth hole helped me to a 67. It put me in good shape at five strokes off the lead, held by Rick Fehr.

Saturday's round was on the Palm, the course where I shot 62 the year before, so I felt good about my chances of making something happen. But I got a bad break. I had a late tee time and the wind came up shortly after noon. It grew stronger as the afternoon progressed, and I grinded hard for my 72. The scores were always low at Disney, so my even-par round meant that I lost ground. The top 150, however, was still in sight. I studied the leader board hard that evening, and it looked as though four under on Sunday might do it.

Everything was going my way on Sunday, and I reached the seventeenth tee at three under. I was confident I could pick up that last stroke on the seventeenth, a medium-length par five. I crushed my drive toward the palm trees that guarded the corner of the dogleg. I was so confident the ball would clear them that I did not even watch it; I bent over to pick up my tee. When I heard

Anthony's "Damn," I knew something had happened that I would not like. The ball caught the last tree and kicked down toward the water. It stopped in the rough, but I had no chance to put it on the green. I got it to the front bunker, but I hit a mediocre shot from there to twelve feet. I did not have quite enough speed on the putt, and it died to the right of the cup. I had to settle for par.

A birdie on the eighteenth could still do it for me, but I hit a so-so second shot and made a routine par, for a three-under-par 69. It left me in a tie for thirty-sixth place, and my check for $5,530 was not enough to crack the top 150. I finished the year 155th on the money list.

The tournament had an odd ending. Taylor Smith and Tiger Woods were tied for the lead, but after the ninth hole, Taylor's playing partner, Lennie Clements, noticed that the grip on Taylor's long putter did not conform to the rules. He informed an official, and the official notified Taylor that he was disqualified. Taylor asked if he could continue to play while he appealed the decision, and he was allowed to do so. When Taylor walked off the eighteenth green tied with Tiger, the crowd was expecting a playoff, but it did not happen. Taylor's appeal was denied, and Tiger won his second tournament of the seven he had entered.

Unbelievable.

Everyone felt bad for Taylor, who had no idea his grip was illegal. But everyone agreed, including Taylor, that Lennie had done the right thing. Like anyone who plays in any tournament, Lennie had an obligation to protect the field.

Something happened earlier in the week that made quite an impression on me. Butch and my dad came down to watch me play, and on Wednesday, while we were doing some work on the range, Omar Uresti's caddy approached Butch. Rusty, Omar's caddy and brother, had met Butch several times before.

Rusty said, "Butch, is there anything you can do to help

Omar? He's in terrible shape." Omar finished second, one shot behind me, at the '95 Q-School, but unlike me, he got off to a great start in '96. By the end of June, he had already earned nearly enough money to retain his card for 1997. But something happened to Omar, and he missed the cut in twelve of his last thirteen tournaments. He still needed around $10,000 to make the top 125, and he was desperate to have a good showing at Disney, since it was his last chance.

Butch said, "I probably could. I see a couple of swing flaws, but I don't think this is the time. He's got to go out and play tomorrow. He can't be making changes now."

"Please," Rusty begged. "If there is anything you can say to him, please do it. You don't know how much Omar is suffering."

"All right, I'll talk to him," Butch agreed.

Rusty summoned Omar, and the first thing Butch asked was, "Omar, how many nights have you lain awake thinking that if only you could win $10,000, everything would be great?"

"Almost every night," Omar answered.

"You know who you remind me of? You remind me of the 15 handicapper who is dying to break 80. One day he shoots 36 on the front nine and he tells himself he only needs to shoot 43 on the back to achieve his lifelong goal. You know what he does? He goes out and shoots 44."

"You're doing the same thing to yourself," Butch continued. "At the beginning of the year when you first came out here, you were all gung ho about having top-ten finishes and maybe even winning a tournament, weren't you?"

Omar nodded.

"And when you noticed that you only needed another $10,000, you started to play to win that $10,000, didn't you?"

Omar nodded again.

"I'll tell you what I want you to do this week," Butch said.

"Every time you catch yourself thinking, 'I only need another $10,000,' I want you to back off and tap yourself on the forehead three times. Don't hit the ball until you can tell yourself that you're playing to win."

I am not sure what Omar thought of Butch's advice. I suspect he wanted Butch to give him "the secret" that golfers at all levels find so elusive. But Omar did acknowledge that what Butch said made sense, and he promised he would give it a try.

After we finished play on Friday, Omar found Butch to tell him what had happened. "I came to the eighteenth hole on Friday, needing a par to make the cut. I hit a poor drive and left myself a three-iron to the green when everyone else was hitting seven-iron. While I was standing over the ball, I caught myself thinking, 'Just get it on the green and you'll make the cut.' So I did what you said. I backed away from the ball and hit myself on the head three times. The gallery must have thought I was nuts. But I put a good swing on the ball and put it to within thirty feet of the pin.

"While I was lining up my putt," Omar continued, "I kept thinking, 'Just lag it up there for a sure par.' I had to back away from the ball three times to hit myself on the head. But when I finally hit the putt, I knocked it into the center of the cup for birdie."

Omar was really excited. He thought Butch was a genius, and I was not about to disagree with him. Omar went on to have a good weekend and earned more than enough to keep his card. I am not sure I have ever seen a more vivid example of how important the mental side of the game is.

Unlike Omar, I was on my way back to the Fall Classic. While the year did not come close to matching my expectations after winning Q-School, I could not help but think I made progress. I earned $40,000 more than I had the year before, but more important, I learned about the game. Like 1995, the two halves of the '96 season were dramatically different. During the first six months, I made only four cuts in the seventeen tournaments I entered, while from July on, I made ten of thirteen cuts. The turnaround in 1995 resulted entirely from my playing better golf. In 1996, I did play better over the last four months, but the improvement resulted largely from my increased ability to score when not playing my best. I owed Anthony a lot for helping me with that. It was a lesson that would serve me well in the years to come.

I had no doubt that 1997 would be better than 1996. All I had to do was get by Q-School.

# CHAPTER 12

# Q-School, 1996

I finished the '96 season a better player than I began the year, so there was no reason to expect that Q-School would give me any trouble. I went into it thinking top-ten finish, and a high priority ranking for 1997.

I was realistic enough to know, however, that Q-School was never a sure thing. One bad round can put you out of it, so even though I felt my game had progressed, I still felt the same overwhelming pressure that everyone experiences at the Fall Classic. I hated it, and I hoped this would be the last time I would ever have to return.

I elected to play second stage at the old reliable, Greenlefe in Haynes City. It was a somewhat difficult choice, because Florence was an option and I had played well on that course too. But in the end, I could not argue with the success I had had at Greenlefe. I qualified there two years running, and since it was such a tough course, it offered me the best chance of qualifying again.

The tournament began on the third Tuesday of November, and I had a plane reservation for Orlando for the preceding Wednesday. That Tuesday night, I came down with a bad case of flu. I saw the doctor on Wednesday morning and changed my reservation for Thursday, since I did not want to fly with a stuffed-up head and ears. I did not feel much better on Thursday or Friday, but I did take a late flight out on Friday.

I met Dicky Pride in Orlando, and we played a practice round on a local course on Saturday. I practiced some on Sunday, and by the time Anthony arrived on Monday, I was feeling quite a bit better—not one hundred percent, but much better.

My first round of the tournament was solid, if unspectacular. My lone birdie was offset with a single bogey, and my 72 put me in good shape. Par at Greenlefe will get you to the next stage every time.

The second and third rounds were similar to the first. I hit the ball solidly, but at the same time, I was struggling. It seemed as if I was playing well enough to have better scores, but it was not happening for me. I shot 74-73 to put me right at the cut line. I had to have a solid fourth round if I wanted to go to the final stage.

Friday, the pressure I felt was as intense as anything I had experienced since the '94 Q-School. In '95, I got off to a fast start and there was never much doubt that I would make it. But now I was faced with the prospect of absolutely having to have a good round. The cut would probably go up by a stroke, so I had to shoot no worse than a 73 to make it. I began with solid pars on the first three holes, but then bogeyed the fourth to go four over for the tournament. I was in trouble.

Beginning with the fifth hole, however, everything seemed to fall into place. Suddenly the game seemed easy again, and I played the last fourteen holes three under par to qualify easily. I was pleased. My back was against the wall, and I handled it.

I had a week off before the finals, and as is traditional, I spent it at my brother's place in Atlanta with Heather and my parents. I found an hour each day to hit balls.

To say the least, I was not happy about playing the finals in California. My record there as a professional golfer, of never having made a cut, left a great deal to be desired. I tried to put that out of my mind, but those thoughts seemed to find a way of sneaking back in.

When I arrived in California and learned about the courses we would be playing, I was not happy about the selection. They were in the Santa Barbara area, but they were fifty miles apart. Not only would the driving be a pain, but the distance between the courses made it possible for the conditions to vary greatly on the same day. It was an odd choice, to say the least.

My first round was at Sandpiper, the secondary course, and I hit the ball extremely well. I had fully recovered from the flu, I had my strength back, and it showed. The greens gave me fits, but I still managed a one under par 71 to put me at around fortieth place.

The second day, I played at LaPurisima, the primary course, and I got a break on the conditions. It rained all day at LaPurisima, but that was better than the strong winds the guys at the Sand-piper had to battle. From tee to green, I played as well as I can play. I hit all eighteen greens in regulation, but again, I putted like a dog. I finished the day with thirty-seven putts and a one over par 73.

I was mystified by the greens. When I had a putt that looked straight in, one time it would veer off to the left, and the next time it would jump to the right. I could not understand why I was having so much trouble seeing the line.

Despite my trouble on the greens, my 73 was good enough to keep me near the top forty. The scores at Sandpiper were high as a result of the wind.

The wind was absolutely fierce for my third round at Sand-piper. On the holes by the ocean, the gusts were 30 to 35 miles per hour. I could not get the ball close to the pin, and my putting was even worse than it had been the first two days. I three-putted four times and finished the day with a three over par 75.

I was out of the top forty, which meant I had some serious work to do. Not only did I have to worry about climbing back up to the top forty, I had to be careful or I would miss the cut for the final two rounds. It looked like it would take three over par to make it, so I had to shoot an even-par round the following day to have a chance.

My poor putting was especially frustrating because it seemed as if my stroke was good. Butch had come out to watch me play, and he could not see anything wrong. He thought it was a con-fidence problem, so he gave me several pep talks, but I wasn't so sure. I just could not see the line.

I struggled on the greens again during the fourth round and came to the eighteenth hole one over par for the day and four over for the tournament. There was a chance that par would get me to the next day, but I wanted a birdie to be sure. A good drive left me a seven-iron to the green. I tried to do too much with the shot and pulled it long and left. It left me no chance for birdie and very little chance for par. There was a hogback between my ball and the pin, and I did not see how I could get the ball over the hump and keep it anywhere close to the pin. My chip looked as if it would die before it reached the crest of the hill, but somehow it made it to the top. I am not sure that it did not stop for an instant, but it trickled down the slope to within a foot of the hole. It was by far my best shot of the week. I made my par, and I had at least a chance at playing the final two rounds.

There were still a number of players on the course when I fin-ished, so it would be a while before I would learn if I made it. I had some lunch, although my appetite seemed to have disappeared, and afterward went out to the putting green to get in a little practice. It seemed like hours before I heard that my score of four over par had made the cut.

I badly needed to make a move during the fifth round, but it never happened. I shot another 73, and again I was a mess on the greens. For the five rounds, I hit fourteen greens in regulation on my worst day, and yet I was five over par. My dad counted fourteen putts of eight feet or less that I missed.

I was working with Butch on the practice green after the fifth round when Larry Watson stopped by. Larry works for Scotty Cameron, the club designer who makes his own line of putters for Titleist. After about five minutes, he said, "Carl, your putter doesn't have enough loft. You're driving the ball into the ground and it's bouncing off line. Let me have it for a minute."

Larry took the putter, put it over his knee, and bent it slightly. "There," he said as he handed the club back to me, "that should be about three more degrees of loft. Try it now."

I could tell the difference with the first putt. The ball held its line and dived into the center of the cup. I practiced six- to ten-footers for another hour, and I made most of them. I could not believe that my putting woes on the West Coast could come down to something as simple as three degrees of loft.

It was more than a little painful to think about the "what ifs." What if Larry had noticed me on the practice green before the tournament began? What if I had made half of those fourteen putts of eight feet or less? But those things didn't happen, and I could not dwell on them. I had to focus on the last round.

Fortieth place was even par, so I figured a 68 would get my card back for 1997. I had played great from tee to green all week, so if I could sink a few putts with my adjusted club, I could do it.

It rained hard Sunday night and the course was unplayable. The final round was postponed until Tuesday, but when it rained again late Monday, the sixth round was canceled and the standings following the fifth round were deemed final. I did not make it. I did not get my card.

For the first few days after returning to Virginia Beach, I was numb. Everyone, including me, goes into Q-School knowing that anything can happen. The best player in the world has off weeks, and if you are not playing solid golf, you will not make it no matter how good you are. But I was playing solid golf. I did play solid golf. And I still did not make it.

Before a week passed, I snapped out of it and began to view the experience in a new light. The Nike Tour was a good place to play, and there were some real advantages to having full playing privileges on the Nike Tour compared to sneaking into the top forty qualifiers for the PGA Tour. If I had played the sixth round and shot 68 to make it into the top forty, it would be 1995 all over again. I would be sitting at home much of the winter, I would never know until the last moment when I would be able to play, and I would be lucky to get into as many as twenty tournaments. As it turned out, I could schedule my entire year in advance, and I could enter any Nike event I wanted to. The planning part turned out to be easy. My intention is to play in every single Nike tournament.

Perhaps the biggest advantage of playing on the Nike Tour is that it gives me a way to get back to the PGA Tour without having to go back to Q-School. The PGA modified the rules for 1997, so the top fifteen money winners on the Nike Tour will earn their card for the PGA Tour in '98. Also, anyone who wins three tournaments on the Nike Tour receives an instant promotion to the PGA Tour.

My goal is to win the first three tournaments of the year.

The Nike Tour will also give me another opportunity to experience the camaraderie that came so easily to the guys on the minitours. My friends who have played there tell me that the atmosphere is more relaxed than on the PGA Tour. Perhaps it is because not as many of the guys travel with their families, but I understand you never have a problem finding a group of guys who want to go out for a few beers and shoot a little pool. The PGA Tour is a much lonelier place.

There is much about the PGA Tour I will miss. I will miss the excitement of playing before large galleries. I will miss competing against the very best golfers in the world. I will miss the friends I have made, people like Scott and Jennifer McCarron. And I am sorry I will not get to travel with Michael Christie, my good friend and former teammate. Michael won three Nike tournaments in 1996, finished second on the money list, and earned his PGA Tour card for 1997.

Many of my friends have offered their support and encouragement after I did not retain my card, and I appreciate it greatly. But I don't view what happened as a setback or a failure. I see it more as a normal, and indeed typical, part of the process of developing as a professional golfer.

My story may be more typical than exciting. Yes, I was a good junior golfer, and my game has developed gradually. Unlike some stars, I did not grow up beating everybody in sight. I did not go to college and win the NCAA championship my freshman year. My best finish was sixtieth during my sophomore year. But my game is continuing to develop, and I have no doubt that I will reach the point where I can compete with anyone.

For every Phil Mickelson, Justin Leonard, and Tiger Woods, there are dozens of guys like me. I think of Mark Brooks, who hovered around 140th on the money list for four years before he could establish himself on tour. He turned pro in 1983 and he won his first major, the PGA, thirteen years later in 1996. Mark Calcavecchia is another good example. He too spent four years near the 150 mark before breaking through to the fifty-eighth spot in 1986. Three years later, he won the British Open. The best example of all is, of course, Tom Lehman. He struggled on the PGA Tour for three years during the middle 1980s, spent the late 1980s traveling the world in search of places to play, and then burst on the scene in 1992, ten years after turning pro. He won the British Open in 1996 and finished strong in the other majors, and many people today are calling him the best player in the world.

I believe my career will parallel those of Brooks, Calcavecchia, and Lehman. I am only into the fourth year of my five-year plan to make it to the Tour, and I have already been there for two years. That experience, reinforced by the year I will have on the Nike Tour to develop my game, will make me more competitive when I return to the Tour in '98. The past two years have had their ups and downs, but they have taught me that I belong out there.

This is still the beginning of the Carl Paulson story.

# *Epilogue*

## *1997*

To increase the odds that I would get 1997 off to a better start than I had the previous two years, Heather and I rented an apartment in Orlando. Even a mild winter in Virginia Beach might allow me to practice ten to twelve days at the most. I wanted to be able both to play and practice regularly, and moving to Florida would assure me of being able to do that.

It worked out well. While playing in a minitour event in early January, I ran into several guys I knew from college golf—guys like Bobby Doolittle from Clemson, Jason Bohn from Alabama, and Robert Dean from Wake Forest. They, too, were hoping to make it to the PGA Tour, and between minitour events we had our own tournaments for the usual five bucks per hole. I hoped the competition would help me stay sharp.

Because I would be driving from tournament to

tournament, I had to find something more suitable than my old Ford Taurus. It was fine for getting me to the airport, but I could not see taking it across country. I found a great deal—an '88 Lincoln with only 40,000 miles on it. I thought it was a steal for $7,500, and it was roomy and heavy enough to make the long drives between tour stops reasonably comfortably.

The Nike Lakeland Classic, held in late January, was the first tournament of the year. It was less than a two-hour drive from Orlando, but it felt good to take the Lincoln on the road to christen the new season. My first day as a full-time Nike player was almost a disaster. I had an early tee time so I left a wake-up call for 5:30 A.M. I woke up on my own and assumed the call would come any minute. I went down the hall to get a soft drink and was surprised to see several of the guys leaving for the course. "What time is it?" I asked, trying to keep the panic out of my voice.

"A few minutes before seven," someone answered.

My tee time was at 7:30 and I was not sure I could make it. I did get to the course in time and ended the first day with a 65 to tie for the lead. I cooled off on Friday, but I finished twelve under par, good enough for a 13th place tie and a check for $3,015.

I missed the cut both in Moreno Valley, California, and Monterrey, Mexico. Next I took my Lincoln to Broussard, Louisiana, for a tournament during the last week in March. I hit the ball well, but a couple of bad holes ruined both rounds and I missed my third cut in a row. In Gaulter, Mississippi, I played solid golf the first two rounds, but a poor third round dropped me well back into the pack, and I finished 49th and earned a check for $540.

I missed the cut in the next two tournaments, but it turned around for me the following week at the Carolina Classic, outside of Raleigh, North Carolina. The conditions were tough. It was windy and the course was firm so it was nearly impossible to get the ball close to the hole. I came to the last hole of the tournament needing only a par for a top ten finish, but I skulled the ball out of a bunker, across the green, and into the water. Eleven guys passed me with that shot.

I was looking forward to the following week, the Dominion Open, held outside Richmond the third week in May. Heather and my family would be there, and I had finished second there the year before. I played okay, but it did not quite come together for me and I finished in a tie for 36th.

At the Knoxville Open, held during the first week in June, golf was not foremost in my mind. Heather learned she was pregnant and I could think of little else. I was excited—and maybe a little scared. I shot a pair of 74s and missed the cut.

I came back strong the following week in Springboro, Ohio. I loved the course, and it was reflected in my scores. My 274 was good for a 13th-place finish and a check for $3,300, which did not do much for my position on the money list. It looked like it would take $100,000 for the year to finish in the top 15 and earn a PGA card. I needed to win.

The next two weeks, first Cleveland, then Hershey, Pennsylvania, did not help. In both tournaments I had one good round and one bad round and missed the cut both times. The season was half over and I had earned only a little over $13,000.

The Laurel Creek Classic, in Moorestown, New Jersey, was held during the second week in July, and it was my favorite course of the year. It was a links-style course, with very few trees and lots of heather-type grasses. I switched to a long putter that week. I had not been putting badly, but I was not making as many of those ten- to twelve-footers, those scoring putts, as I thought I should. It seemed to work. My score of 274 was good for a tie for 5th and my largest check of the year, $9,750. I jumped up a dozen places on the money list.

The Wichita Open was the last week of July, and I had everything working for me. After three rounds, I was thirteen under par and only two shots off the lead. I played solid golf on Sunday, and even though I was four under after fifteen holes, it did not look like it would be enough. It left me three strokes off the lead.

The sixteenth hole is a long par four and I did not hit my drive well. I was left with 215 yards to the pin; not a good position from which to make birdie. I hit my three-iron pure and it was all over the flag. I saw it bounce on the green once and then disappear. It took me a moment to realize it had gone in the hole for eagle. I was a single shot back.

I did not get a birdie on 17 or 18, but the leader, Chris Smith, doubled the 17th to drop a shot behind, but then birdied the 18th to tie for the lead. Ben Bates and Jeff Behaut also finished at nineteen under par so the four of us headed to the first tee for a sudden-death playoff.

We all hit good drives on the first hole. I was last to hit my second shot, and I thought I had a chance to win it right there. Jeff, Chris, and Ben were all on the green, and Ben had the best chance for birdie with a putt of about fifteen feet. With only 120 yards to the pin, I thought I could get it closer than that. It was the first time I had been in such a position, and I was surprised by how calm I felt. Sure, the adrenaline was flowing, but I was thinking clearly and I felt in control. All I wanted to do was carry a knob on the green 110 yards out; I thought the ball would trickle down to the pin from there. I usually hit a sandwedge 100 yards, but I knew I was pumped up, so I chose it rather than the pitching wedge. After I finished my swing, I looked up and saw the ball flying directly at the flag. "Get in the hole," I said to myself. I watched in disbelief as the ball flew over the pin and into a little swale behind the green. I guess I was more pumped up than I thought.

Ben knocked in his birdie putt for the victory. If I couldn't be the winner, I'm glad it was Ben. It was Ben's seventh year on the Nike Tour, and he is one of those talented players who just can't seem to break through. It looked as if this would be his year at last. My check for $17,233 helped me make a big jump on the money list.

The third week of August was the Ozarks Open in Springfield, Missouri. Despite receiving a ticket for fishing without a license, I had a good week. I tied for 10th and earned a check for $3,950. The following week, in Odessa, Texas, I had two good rounds and two mediocre rounds to finish in a tie for 38th, good for a check for $840.

I had two weeks off before the next event outside Denver and I needed the rest. I had been on the road for eight weeks and I was beat. I went back to Orlando and mostly loafed around the pool with Heather. I did not even touch a club for four days. By the end of the second week, I was eager to get back out there. I was playing good golf and I had plenty of time to make it into the top fifteen.

My first three rounds at the Colorado Classic were solid. I was nine-under and in good position for a top five finish. But when I woke up Sunday with a stiff back, I knew the day would be a struggle. I compounded my problems with some poor decisions, and I limped in with a 74 to drop well back into the field. I was pissed at letting such a good opportunity get away.

The next stop was San Jose, and the California blues got me again. Overall, I did not play bad, but I hit a couple of poor shots the first nine and I never recovered. My scores of 73, 71 were not good enough to make the cut.

From San Jose it was on to Boise, Idaho. It turned out to be the best tournament of the year. Many of the Nike events are on a very tight budget and they cannot afford to provide the amenities I had grown to appreciate on the PGA Tour. But Boise obviously had a great many enthusiastic golf fans; they averaged 40,000 people per day. On the Tuesday before the tournament, Brian Kamm, Fred Wadsworth, and I went whitewater rafting. It was the first time I had done that and it was great fun. I played some of my best golf of the year to make it an almost perfect week. After eight holes on Sunday, I was tied for the lead with Iain Steel.

I bogied three of the next five holes when I missed several fairways and could not get it on the green from the deep rough. In the meantime, Iain was making a couple of birdies. I finished strong with birdies on two of the last five holes, but it was not enough to catch Iain. I finished alone in second and earned a check for $31,213. I jumped all the way to 19th on the money list, and with four tournaments remaining, I had a realistic shot at making the top 15.

The following three weeks we traveled to Richland, Washington, Olympia, Washington, and Shreveport, Louisiana. I played solid golf in all three tournaments to earn finishes at 14th, 17th, and 12th. Even though I collected about $8,000 for the three weeks, several guys passed me on the money list and I dropped to 22nd. I had one week left to make my move.

The final event of the season was the Nike Tour Championship held during the third week in October. It was played on a new Robert Trent Jones course in Opelika, Alabama. I had earned about $85,000 for the year so I knew I needed another $12,000 to $15,000 to make it into the top 15. With a purse of $300,000, that meant I needed to finish in the top five to have a realistic shot at it.

After my practice round on Tuesday, I was not hopeful. I was playing well, but the course was very odd. Several times I hit what I thought were perfect drives, but when I arrived at my ball I discovered I had no-shot to the green. Many of the holes had traps in the center of the fairway, or fingers of deep rough near the landing areas. Clearly, luck would play an important role in the outcome.

I hit the ball well all week but could manage no better than a 19th-place finish. It was frustrating. On Friday, I shot 77 and hit the ball just as well as I did on Sunday, when I shot 70. I like tough courses, but I like them tough in a straightforward way. There are no courses more difficult than those that host the U.S. Open, for instance, but there if you hit a good drive, you have a shot at the green. And if you hit a good second shot, you have a putt for birdie. The same could not be said for the Grand National Lake Course.

The $3,375 I earned was important. It was enough for me to retain my 22nd spot on the money list. Those of us who finished from 16th to 25th were eligible to play the Nike Tour full time in 1998, and we were exempt from the first two stages of Q-School.

I felt extremely positive about my chances at Q-School. The finals were being held at Greenelefe, just south of Orlando—the course on which I had first earned my card. I'm not sure there is a course in the country that is better suited for my game. Knowing I had a place to play in '98 relieved a good deal of pressure, so I had to love my chances of a top ten finish and a low-priority number. The six weeks between the Nike Championship and Q-School were a real luxury. It was the longest period of time I had had in years in which I was completely free to set my own schedule. I could sleep late anytime I wanted to, I could lounge around the pool all afternoon, and I could read as many spy novels as I wanted.

By the first week in December, I felt I was playing well enough to make it through the qualifying tournament without much difficulty. I was having a little bit of a problem with the putter—which was a surprise since I had been putting extremely well for about six months. But Butch was coming down and I was confident that we would get everything worked out before the tournament began.

I played my first round on the long West course, the one I

thought was especially well suited for my game. I hit the ball well, but I could not get anything to drop on the greens. A pair of bogies left me two over par for the day.

The round was disappointing and a little frustrating. I played well enough to be two or three under, but my 74 left me well back in the pack. I was not too concerned, however. The tournament format was different this year; there would be no cut after the fourth round, so there was not the usual pressure to get off to a fast start. I was hitting the ball well enough to make a steady climb up the leader board.

I played the shorter South course the second day, and the first twelve holes were a replay of the previous round. I hit the ball solidly but could not manage a single birdie. I finally broke through on the thirty-first hole of the tournament when I two-putted the par five 13th for birdie. Apparently, I could not stand the good fortune because I followed my birdie with a three-putt bogey on 14. On the next two holes, I hit my approach shots stiff for tap-in birdies. I added another birdie on 17 with a nice twelve-footer for a round of 68. My game was back on track. I was feeling good.

My third round was on the South course again and everything fell into place. I had seven birdies against a single bogey for a 66. I climbed all the way to fourth place and I was confident that I would be back on the Tour in '98.

The fourth round got off to a bad start with bogeys on two of the first five holes. I turned it around on 7 and 8 when I made a couple of eight-footers for birdies. Nothing happened for me on the back nine, however, and a couple of weak chip shots resulted in bogeys. I finished with a two over par 74, five under for the tournament. I was not pleased with the round, but it was strong enough to keep me two strokes within the bubble. Two solid rounds would still get me back on the Tour.

Sunday's fifth round was rather uneventful. Again, on the

front nine, I hit the ball well but could not get the putts to drop. A birdie on 12 put me one under for the day, so even though my score could have been better, I felt fine. I was doing what I had to do—play solid, if not spectacular, golf.

The fourteenth hole is a short dogleg right. It offered a good chance for birdie, but I pushed my tee shot into the woods on the right. I hit a good second shot, but the ball caught a lone branch hanging over the edge of the fairway and kicked back in the woods. Double bogey. I managed to get back to even for the day with a birdie on 17, but I knew I had lost some ground. I was still five under par for the tournament, but I fell into a tie for 38th place. I needed a solid final round to get back into the top 35.

I was looking forward to the last round. I knew I had to shoot one-under, certainly no worse than even par to make it, but I could do it. I was not especially nervous as I teed my ball up on the first hole. I had been there before and I was capable of responding to the pressure.

Despite my confidence, I must have been tight. I was not letting it fly and I started the round with a pair of bogies. I played the next six holes well, but on the ninth, I hooked my tee shot deep into the woods. I had no shot, so I played down the left side and it was all I could do to get my third shot into a bunker. A mediocre explosion left me a ten-footer for bogey and I missed it to finish the front nine with a big, fat 40. Unless something spectacular happened, I was dead.

Birdies on 11, 12, and 14 gave me reason to hope. But a poor chip on 15 resulted in a bogey so I knew I needed at least two birdies on the final three holes to have any chance. I hit a good tee shot on the par-three sixteenth, but my twenty-footer slid by the hole. On 17, I lipped out a fifteen-foot chip and had to settle for another par. My only chance was to eagle the par-five eighteenth, but at 575 yards into a slight breeze, I had no chance to reach it in two. I made a routine par and finished the tournament in a tie for 58th place. I would be on the Nike Tour once again in '98.

Yes, I was disappointed that I did not make it back to the Tour, but how bad could I feel? My life is nearly perfect the way it is. I am making a good living playing a game I love, I am married to a wonderful woman, and my first child will be born in early February 1998. I've got it knocked, and except for those brief moments when I see my tee shot hooking into the woods or those four-foot putts spinning out of the cup, I fully realize just how fortunate I am.

While the last two Q-Schools have been frustrating, I have made steady progress with my game and I am a much better golfer now than I was in 1994. I am only a hair away from being where I want to be, and there is no doubt in my mind that I will get there soon.

Keep an eye out for me.